An Outlaw's Diary:
The Commune

AN OUTLAW'S DIARY
THE COMMUNE

by

CÉCILE TORMAY

An Account of the Bolshevik
Revolution in Hungary

ANTELOPE HILL PUBLISHING

An Outlaw's Diary: The Commune by Cécile Tormay first published in 1923, printed in Great Britain, by the Hereford Times ltd., Hereford.

Republished 2020 by Antelope Hill Publishing with the additional subtitle of *An Account of the Bolshevik Revolution in Hungary* to give added clarity to the modern reader and to present the work as a stand-alone novel, independent of the first volume of this work, which deals with the establishment of the First Hungarian Republic in the Chrysanthemum Revolution.

Second printing 2022.

Cover art by Swifty
Formatted by Margaret Bauer.

Antelope Hill Publishing
antelopehillpublishing.com

Paperback ISBN-13: 978-1-956887-28-0
EPUB ISBN-13: 978-1-953730-38-1

CONTENTS

I

THERE followed a moment's silence, the awful silence of the executioner's sword suspended in the air. Humanity in bondage draws its head between its shoulders, and, like the sweat of the agonizing, cold rain, pours down the walls of the houses. Now...

A bestial voice shrieks again in the street: "LONG LIVE THE DICTATORSHIP OF THE PROLETARIAT!"

The neighboring streets repeat the cry. A drawn shutter rattles violently in the dark. Street doors bang as they are hurriedly closed. Running steps clatter past the houses, accompanied by two sounds: "Long live... Death..." The latter is meant for us. Shots ring out at the street corner.

"Death to the bourgeois!" A bullet strikes a lamp and there is a shower of glass on the pavement. A carriage drives past furiously, then stops suddenly amid shouts. A confused noise follows and the shooting dies away in the distance. Other cars follow its track into the maddened, lightless town. What is happening there, beyond it, everywhere, in the barracks, in the boulevards? Sailors are looting the inner city: a handful of Bolsheviks have taken possession of the town. There is no escape!

One thought alone contains an element of relief: we have reached the bottom of the abyss. It is disgraceful and humiliating, but it is better than the constant sliding down and down. Now we can sink no lower.

Presently the streets regained their former quiet, and nothing but the throbbing of our hearts pierced the silence. There is no escape for us. The opened gutters have inundated us. St. Stephen's Hungary has fallen under the rule of Trotsky's agent, Béla Kun, the embezzler. And all round us events are taking place which we have no longer the power to prevent.

I have no idea how long this nightmare lasted. We were silent: everybody was struggling with his own sufferings. The lamp burnt low, and again the clock struck. I caught at its sound, and counted the strokes: nine. Countess Chotek, who had been with us, was there no longer, nor did I see my brother. Time went slowly on. My room appeared to me like the dim background of a painting; figures sat in the picture rigidly, disappeared, and then were there again. The door opened and closed. I saw my journalist friend, Joseph Cavallier, in a chair which had been empty a moment before. He spoke and pressed me to go—mad rumours were circulating in the town, awful events were predicted for the night. Lieut.-Col. Vyx and the other members of the Entente missions had been arrested, and it was intended to disarm the British monitors on the Danube. The Russian Red Army was advancing towards the Carpathians, the Bolsheviks had declared for the integrity of our territory. Béla Kun's Directorate had declared war on the Entente. "You must escape to- night," said my friend; "they are going to arrest you. Come to us."

My mother called me and I opened her door with apprehension. She was sitting up in bed, propped high between the pillows: her face was livid and appeared thinner than ever. She too had heard the cries in the street, was aware of what had happened, and knew what was in store for us. Her haggard, harassed look inspired me with strength to face our fate.

"Why don't you come here? Why can't we talk things over in here?" She did not mean to cause pain, but her words stabbed me. Poor dear mother!

When Joseph Cavallier told her of his proposal she shook her head:

"You live on the other side of the river, don't you? Don't let her go so far." Suddenly she recovered herself and turned to me: "It is raining hard and I heard you coughing so badly all day."

The others had followed us into her room, and all had something to say. My sister-in-law mentioned her brother Zsigmondy who lived nearby: he had offered me shelter in his home. My mother alone was silent. Though she could not say it, it was she who was most anxious for me to go. She looked at me imploringly. That decided me. "It can only be a question of a day or two," I said. "Then, when they have failed to find me here, I can come back."

Did I believe what I said? Did I imagine that things would happen like that? Or did I attempt to deceive myself so that I might bear it the more easily? I noticed a deep shadow that stole suddenly, I knew not whence, over my mother's face. It appeared on the other faces too, as if all of them had aged suddenly. And beyond them, around us, in the houses opposite, all over the town, people aged suddenly in that ghastly hour.

They all went away and left me alone in my room. I knew I ought to hurry, yet I stood idle in front of the open cupboard. How many, I thought, are standing, hesitating like this tonight, how many are hurrying and running aimlessly about, not knowing whither to turn? Will it be the same here as in Russia? Quietly the door opened behind me: my mother had risen and came to me so that we might be together as long as possible.

"I will take just a few things, very few," I kept repeating, as if I wanted to force the hand of fate to make my trial short. "Perhaps I may be able to come home tomorrow"

My mother did not answer. She tied the parcels together for me.

"The housekeeper must not know till tomorrow morning that you have gone..." She looked out into the ante-room to see that no one was about, then opened the door herself and accompanied me down the corridor. The house seemed asleep, the sky was black, and the courtyard underneath was like a dark shaft, in which rain-water had accumulated.

Leaning on my arm my mother walked along with me. In silence both of us struggled to keep control over our emotions. At the front door we stopped. Nothing was audible but the patter of the rain. My mother raised her hand and passed it over my face, caressingly, as though she would feel the outlines that she knew so well.

"Take every care of yourself, my dear, dear one!"

I was already running down the stairs. She was leaning over the balustrade, and I heard her voice behind me, keeping me company as long as possible, calling softly, "Goodnight!"

"Goodnight..." I called back, but my voice failed me in a pain such as I had never felt before.

Beyond the street door there was a rattle of gunfire. I tried to keep cheerful, and kept saying: "Tomorrow I shall come back to her, tomorrow." I groped my way across the dark yard and knocked at the concierge's window. He came out, looking curiously at me in the glare of his lantern: "There is a lot of shooting out there. It would be wiser to stay at home." But I shook my head and the key turned in the lock; the door opened stealthily, and closed carefully behind me, as though unwilling to betray me.

Next instant I stood alone in the rain. I shuddered: my retreat was cut off. Home, everything that was good, everything that protected me, was behind that door, beyond my reach.

Motor horns, human shouts, rang here and there in the distance, whilst the rain poured in streams in the broken gutters. The road seemed absolutely empty. Suddenly I heard steps on the other side of the street. They had not approached from the distance but had started quite nearby; someone must therefore have stepped from out of the shadow of the house opposite. Had he been waiting there spying on me? The steps became hurried, passed me, crossed the street. A dark shape hugged the wall under the recess of a door. No bell was rung. I stopped for an instant:

the incertitude of the past few weeks reappeared. The knowledge of being watched, pursued, the torture of being deprived of my freedom, made me catch my breath. The threat had followed me so long, appearing and disappearing in turn, menacing me from under every porch, from every dark corner. Should I fly from it? Should I turn down a by-street?

Suddenly I felt tired and ill: my pulses were leaden and my brain seemed weighed down with heavy stones. For an instant I contemplated giving in. I seemed to be of so little significance compared with the enormity of universal misfortune. The crash of general collapse had drowned the small moans of individual fates.

The shadow suddenly emerged from under the porch and barred my way. We stared at each other. Then a well-known voice said, "Is it you?" It was my brother Béla, who had been watching for me so that he might accompany me.

Only a few lamps were alight on the boulevard, and our heels crushed the fragments of glass from the broken ones. Empty cartridge cases shone in the puddles.

Machine-guns stood in the middle of the street. Some men passed, carrying a red flag; then a lorry, bristling with bayonets, rumbled heavily by, full of armed sailors. One of these shouldered his rifle and aimed at us. He did not shoot, and when for an instant he appeared in the light of a lamp before the darkness swallowed him again, I could see the bestial grin which contorted his face. The lorry disappeared, but we could hear his voice shouting something in Russian. There are many of these here today. "A bourgeois, to hell with him!" The cry of Moscow fills Budapest.

Frightened forms ran across the openings of the streets on the other side, and the air was filled with wild movements and lurching fear. At last I rang the bell of the front door which was to shelter me, and my brother wished me Godspeed and turned back. It was some moments before the door opened, and a woman came along, dragging her feet. She looked at me suspiciously and seemed frightened. Where was I going?

I murmured something, crammed some money into her hand, and brushed past her. Here too the courtyard was absolutely dark. I hesitated in front of the door of one of the flats: something urged me to go on, something else drew me back. At last I knocked, and a friendly face appeared. The table was still laid under the welcoming light of a swinging lamp: how peaceful was the sight of that quiet little home after the howling, dirty, soaking street! Michael Zsigmondy and his wife welcomed me, but whether or not they had expected me I cannot say; at all events they seemed to consider it quite a natural thing that I should have come.

"What is the time?"

"Past eleven."

There was a knock at the door... We looked at each other. A tall, dark young man entered. "Count Francis Hunyadi," announced Zsigmondy, relieved. He did not mention my name, and they carefully avoided addressing me. The newcomer spoke:

"Nobody knows what is happening. It is said that the Communists want to hand the town over to the rabble to plunder."

I thought of my mother, who was surely thinking of me too. Behind her I saw more faintly other faces: brothers, sisters, friends, acquaintances. I began to tremble for all those I loved.

Zsigmondy went to the telephone, but the exchange gave the invariable answer: "Only official communications are permissible." Then that stopped too. The telephone exchanges have passed into the hands of the Communists. The rain stopped; the streets livened up, and now and then the howls of the excited rabble came up to us: "Long live the Dictatorship of the Proletariat!"

The children were taken into another room, and my bed was made up in the night nursery. Bright pictures of fairy tales were on the walls, lead-soldiers and toy horses on the floor. However long I may live I shall never again feel as old as I felt in that nursery.

* * *

March 22nd.

THE day was already breaking when weariness overcame me and lulled me into something resembling sleep. It must have lasted a short time only, then an almost physical pain about my heart woke me. I felt like a person who has lost someone very dear to him and on awakening is reminded of his bereavement not by memory but by grief. I shrunk from complete awakening. Not yet, not for just one more minute! But it was in vain I tried to hide from consciousness, swiftly I remembered everything. Hungary was no longer. She had been betrayed, sold. *Finis Hungarice.*

I found myself moaning inarticulately. My heart was wounded and bleeding, and the blood that was flowing was 'the blood of all those who were Hungarian. I pressed my clenched fists to my eyes, pressed them so hard that my eyeballs hurt and red flashes passed before them. Then I opened them quickly and the grey dawn stared at me with dimmed eyes. Their day had come!

The street seemed dead, but it was only resting from the night's revels.

It must have been an hour later when steps interrupted the silence—a hunchbacked little monster was coming down the street with a sheaf of posters over his arm and a bucket in his hand. Now and then he stopped, smeared his paste over a wall, and when he went on red posters marked each of his stopping place.

"Long live the Dictatorship of the Proletariat!"

The town must be given no chance to regain its breath, to recover consciousness. When it wakes its whole body will be covered with the red eruption. It will be everywhere. It will cover the barracks, the royal palace, the very churches.

I turned away from the window: it was useless looking out: everywhere it was the same thing. A morning paper was lying on the table. Yesterday's compositors strike was over. Socialist compositors had set the papers of the Communists and the red was pervading the black print: "Unite, Proletarians of the World!" This was followed by Károlyi's proclamation:

> To the Hungarian people! The government has resigned. Those who till now have governed by the will of the people and with the support of the Proletarians have come to the conclusion that circumstances require a new orientation. Orderly production can only be secured by handing over the power to the Proletarians. Besides the danger of anarchy in the productive activities of the country there is the danger of foreign politics. The Peace Conference in Paris has secretly decided that nearly the whole of Hungary is to be occupied by armed forces. The mission of the Entente has declared that the lines of demarcation will be considered in future as political frontiers. The obvious reason for a further occupation of the country is that Hungary is to be made the battle ground of the war against the Russian Soviet troops, now fighting on the Roumanian frontier. The territories robbed from us are intended as the reward of those Czech and Roumanian armies which are to be used to defeat the forces of the Russian Soviet. I, the Provisional President of the Hungarian Popular Republic, am obliged by this decision of the Paris Conference to appeal to the proletariat of the world for justice and help; consequently I resign and hand over the powers of government to the Proletariat of Hungary.—Michael Károlyi

I was filled with disgust. He admits that it was he who has handed it over! I felt with horror that this proclamation was nothing but the base documentary evidence of the sale of a betrayed nation.

"I alone can save Hungary!" It was with these words that Michael Károlyi started his lies on the 31st of October, 1918. "I hand the powers of government to the Proletariat of Hungary," he declares on the 21st of

March, 1919, when lies fail him. In the interval he has squandered and sold Hungary. The mask has fallen, and behind it appears boldly the rabble which he calls the Proletariat of Hungary. Practically all its leaders appear in the list of the "Revolutionary Government Council." Just as in Károlyi's Government it is headed by a deceptive Christian clown; Alexander Garbai is the President. The others are all foreigners. All the People's Commissaries are Jews, there is now and then a Christian among the assistant commissaries, then again Jews and still more Jews. Jews are to administer the capital, Jews are at the head of the police. A Jew is to be governor of the Austro-Hungarian Bank.

This list gives one furiously to think. The puppets of the October show have been swept from the stage by the events of last night. The demoniacal organizers, the raving wire-pullers and prompters have taken their place, and for the first time in the long history of Hungary, Hungarians are excluded from every inch of ground, whether in the hills and the vales of the Carpathians; or on the boundless plains. The country has been divided up among Czechs, Roumanians, Serbians and Jews.

The newspaper continues to address "Everybody." The Revolutionary Council proclaims haughtily that, it has taken over the government and that it is going to build up its workers', peasants' and soldiers' councils. Hungary becomes a Soviet Republic. The Revolutionary Council will start without delay a series of fundamental changes. It decrees the socialization of big estates, wholesale businesses, banks and means of communication. The land reform will not take the shape of dividing up the land into small holdings but of organizing it into socialistic productive co-operative societies. The death penalty will be imposed on the bandits of the Counter-revolution as well as on the brigands who indulge in looting. It will organize a powerful proletarian army. It declares its intellectual and sentimental community with Soviet Russia. It offers an armed alliance to the Russian Proletariat. It sends brotherly greetings to the working masses of England, France, Italy and America, appealing to them not to tolerate any longer the looting expeditions of their capitalistic Governments against the Soviet Republic of Hungary. It offers an armed alliance to the workers and peasants of Bohemia, Roumania, Serbia and Croatia. It appeals to German Austria and Germany to ally themselves with Moscow... "Long live the Dictatorship of the Proletariat! Long live the Hungarian Soviet Republic!"

I thought of the stories related by returning prisoners of war, the vague news of the Russian Revolution, the distant outlines of its nefarious actors and its beginnings at Petrograd. Russia's awful fate filled me with anguish and apprehension.

This was the first ordinance of the Revolutionary Council:

MARTIAL LAW: Anybody resisting the orders of the Soviet Government or inciting to rebellion against it will be executed. Revolutionary tribunals will sit and try the criminals. Budapest, March 21st, 1919.

I jumped up: I felt I should choke unless I did something. "That soldier down there is still walking up and down," said Mrs. Zsigmondy quietly.

"It is lucky that the house has entrances on two streets. I shall go out by the other."

A sharp wind, cleared by rain, was blowing on the boulevard. The carriages seemed to have disappeared, and only motor-cars were rushing about, armed sailors standing on their steps and long-haired Jews, smoking big cigars, sitting inside. The shops were closed, and red posters flamed from their lowered shutters.

"Long live the Soviet Republic allied to Russia!"

The wind blew the torn down posters of the Károlyi Government over the unswept pavements. Now and then hurrying pedestrians passed with bent heads, their eyes expressing stunned bewilderment. They could not understand what had happened.

A chemist's shop was open: that was the only concession. My head was on fire and my chest torn with coughing. I went in. Many people were waiting for their prescriptions. Two people whispered to each other: "The resignation of the Government was simply a sham to frighten the Entente into re-establishing the old lines of demarcation." "Goodness no, my dear sir, there has been too much of Károlyi's cowardly pacifism. The Bolsheviks want to reconquer the whole of Hungary." A lean young man standing by began to gesticulate wildly: "If that is so, every Hungarian ought to stand by them." The other nodded: "We shall soon go home to Pressburg.[1]"

I was staggered. So they are still credulous, they still believe! I went on sadly. When I reached the offices of the National Federation of Hungarian Women I was taken aback. There was nobody waiting there, the ante-room was empty.

What a great thing we had been attempting, we women! To stop a cart running down a slope! We wanted to spread light and confidence and strength into the homes and people of Hungary. Was it to be all in vain, our sufferings, our labour?

---

[1] Bratislava

As I opened the door into the inner office there was a sudden silence within, and the secretary rose from his table. Familiar faces turn d to me, but they looked at me in silence, as if a question were on their lips, as if they expected something.

Faithful, brave women! In this moment I felt that after all everything was not lost. What we had sown could not be trampled down, the flames we had lit could not be extinguished.

A young girl looked in and nodded. "Soldiers are gathering in front of the house..."

We began to hurry. One gathered the list of names, another threw our appeals into a basket: "There is a corner of my house where they won't look for them, I shall hide them there." Another tied some documents together: "My husband will hide them somewhere in the National Museum."

"I will take these to a decorator who has hidden many other dangerous documents," said the secretary.

I wrote a farewell letter to my collaborators at the long table on which I had done so much work. "We won't dissolve and we won't cease to exist. Let everyone continue our work as best she can till we meet again. And if there is any trouble and anyone is persecuted, say that I am the cause of all."

A girl leant against a cupboard and covered her eyes, while two others dragged a heavy basket through the door: it contained our office outfit. Suppressed sobs were audible near the wall underneath the high crucifix. We shook hands, no one said a word, and they let me go alone. But when I turned back from the door, I saw they were all looking after me.

The guardians of the house were some quiet, gentle nuns. I knocked at their door and the Mother Superior opened it as if she expected me.

"I thank you for your hospitality and pray your forgiveness if our presence brings you misfortune."

"Nothing happens but what God wills," answered the nun, with a resigned expression on her gentle face bordered with white veiling.

Meanwhile the soldiers had retired from the vicinity of the house, so I, as usual, bent my way towards home. Only when I reached the beginning of my street did I realize what I was doing. It was too late to turn back. Something attracted me painfully, as though my heart were attached to an invisible thread which was being drawn rapidly towards the further end of the street. There it was that I used to turn in other times when I felt weary. If only I could go there, just for the time necessary to open the door, look in, and nod. And the thread pulled me harder and harder, with ever increasing tension. I crossed the street. Just one more step to be nearer.

Just one more! As I leant forward I put my hand to the wall of a strange house. For an instant I perceived our entrance and saw the windows shining above. I looked at each of them separately. The fifth was that of a room of many memorable evenings, my mother's window. I bowed to it, as if in greeting. Someone quite near to me bowed at the same time. What was that? It was only my shadow that followed my movements on the sunlit wall. Had anybody observed me? How ridiculous I must have seemed! With hastened steps, very fast, I returned to those who had given me shelter.

Hours followed which have escaped my memory. News from the impenetrable tangle filtered through in the afternoon. The town has become more and more strange and incomprehensible: it has put its neck into the halter while talking of reconquering the country. Reliable news is now obtainable of Károlyi's resignation, and the proceedings of the ministers' Council have been divulged by journalists. Before the meeting Károlyi had a long secret talk with Kunfi; thence Kunfi proceeded directly to the prison, where he made formal compact with Béla Kun and the Communists in the name of the Social Democratic Party. The agreement was drawn up in writing. Meanwhile, in the old House of Parliament, Pogány-Schwarz proclaimed the Dictatorship of the Proletariat. After that everything went quickly: barracks, arsenals and munition depots had already been given up to the Communists. Now the post office and the telegraph have come into their power.

Kunfi obtained from Károlyi an order for the release of Béla Kun and his fellow prisoners; he then drove to fetch them and they left their prison, as Hungary's all-powerful masters, to occupy the sleeping capital.

Meanwhile Károlyi was sitting with his Countess and the former Prime Minister Berinkey in a room of the Prime-Ministerial Palace. The town was getting restless in the dark night. Wrapped in a blanket, Károlyi shivered and asked what was happening out there. When he was told that his proclamation had already been read in the Workers' Council he asked sleepily, "What proclamation?"

"Why, your resignation!"

"Impossible! I scarcely remember what it contained, I was so hurried to sign it. Its publication must be prevented."

An official told him that he was too late. "It is already being printed by the papers and will appear in the morning." Károlyi stammered that he had no intention of withdrawing it, he only wanted to alter some passages. But the Communists had taken good care that by then it should have already been telephoned to Vienna. The wires carried the news of Károlyi's resignation and his disgrace, and the document, as edited by

Kéri-Krammer, is preserved for the edification of a horrified posterity.

This is not a tale, not a figment of imagination devised to make people's flesh creep. In the night of the 21st of March Károlyi stood with his narrow head bent to one side, his hollow chest heaving, in the room formerly occupied by Stephen Tisza, and before the cock crowed thrice...

This morning someone met Károlyi and his wife walking on the embankment of the Danube. A big red carnation was glowing in his buttonhole, and his wife wore a bright red hat in the shape of a Phrygian cap and a red collar on her coat. Both looked happy and were laughing. "I am so pleased," Countess Károlyi said to a friend, "Hungary has never been so happy as it is now." At the Prime Minister's house, when taking leave, Károlyi expressed himself in the same sense, declaring:

> It must not be forgotten, that, though it may ruin a few individuals and now and then inflict hard-ships on certain people, it has to be borne in the interest of the community. Let us pour oil on the wheels of the new Government and let us do all in our power to make it a success, because that is the interest of the Hungarian people.

They speak like that. Adorned ostentatiously with red flowers and a red hat—wearing the hangman's colors—these two human beings walk about after having achieved their work. One of their confidants, a Communist comrade, said of them: "Károlyi and his wife wanted a revolution that he might become the President of the Republic. Now they want Bolshevism that in the reaction which they hope will follow in its suit they may rule as autocrats." And the confidant grinned as he spoke. Is this the solution of their enigma? I don't know. Those who say so have stirred the witches' cauldron with them.

Suddenly I saw Béla Kun. I saw him as he had appeared to me on New Year's Eve at the barracks when he went to incite the soldiers. Károlyi let him, Pogány helped him. Now they sit all together. And Számuelly is with them, so are Kunfi, Landler and Böhm. They have not yet recovered from the first shock: their good fortune has surpassed their wildest expectations. Even in their dreams they had never hoped for so much.

At Limanova and at Doberedo the Hungarians showed themselves obstinate heroes; who would have thought that they would so easily bend their heads under the yoke?

The all-powerful Peoples' Commissaries are already moving. The people are crowding in front of the editorial offices of 'The Red Newspaper,' where Számuelly's belongings are being packed on a carriage. Béla Kun too is leaving the two rooms which he had hired with Russian money under the name of Dr. Sebestyén. Whither are they going? Into the royal castle? Into the Prime Minister's palace, or elsewhere? They have the widest possible choice: everything is theirs.

There was a knock at my door. One friend after another came in bringing news. Béla Kun has sent Communist agitators all over the country. They drive through the villages in motor-cars, beflagged in red, and shout: "The Dictatorship of the Proletariat has been proclaimed! Kill the gentle-folk!" A new order has been issued: it is forbidden to wear arms; even revolvers have to be delivered to the authorities. Only the 'reliable people,' Red soldiers, factory guards and workmen's levies, are allowed weapons. The shops remain closed: their goods are declared common property. The newspapers are to be communized or prohibited. The buildings of the conservative *Budapesti Hirlap* have been occupied by the editorial staff of 'The Red Newspaper.' Armed men occupy the tables, and on the front of the building the Red flag floats.

A message reached me from Elisabeth Kállay: she and her family have gone into the country and she asked me to come to them. But I shook my head; tomorrow I return to my mother.

Many have left town. Those who could went by train, others fled by carriage, on foot, by whatever means they could manage. All traces of them disappear—they simply exist no longer. One political party after another pronounces its extinction. The general officers and high officials have disappeared from the scene. Nobody attempts to raise a dam against the deluge, though yesterday a sluice-gate might have stopped it.

October 31st has returned like a haunting spectre and we live the evil day again. Then the trap was baited with the device: 'Independent Hungary,' now it is: 'Territorial Integrity.' The whole thing is like the semi-conscious feeling during a nightmare that one has dreamt the same horrors before.

Where are those who used to be always ready to give advice to the King in Schönbrunn and the halls of the Vienna Burg? Why do they not advise our unfortunate nation now? And where are now those who during the war were ready to order thousands 'over the top' into the jaws of death whenever a single trench was in danger? Where is my whole haughty race which used to go so proudly, singing a merry tune, to face death on foreign fields? Why does it stand now, with glaring eyes, inactive, on our fields at home? Since Károlyi's treason, four and a half months have passed. And this new danger finds us again without a leader, without organization. Running shapes are in flight. Shadows are disappearing in the distance, shadows which once were thought the great realities of Hungary. And those who stay with us, in offices, in poor officers' quarters, are but hungry, ragged, grey little shadows with bended heads.

Wherever the red hand of Bolshevism has grasped the rod of power it has always raised a spirit of resistance. The streets of Moscow, Petrograd, Helsingfors, Berlin and Altona have run with the hot human blood of revolt—Budapest alone has submitted in dizzy apathy. Is the hideous enchantment more powerful here than elsewhere? Here, where in the time of Károlyi's revolution there were no more than two hundred and sixty thousand organized workers and even yesterday no more than five thousand Communists? What has happened? Austrian bugles have called on Hungarian troops for too many charges during the war. Those who might have saved us today are dead.

I felt a desperate longing for action: to do something even if one had to die in the effort, to do something which would break the charm and free the energies benumbed by its humiliating spell! I clenched my fists and shook my head in frenzy; it cannot remain like this. Tomorrow – tomorrow I shall go home. And wearily I shut my tired eyes. The hours dragged on so slowly that they never seemed to come to an end. Night was falling. The lamp was lit in the next room. The street door was locked;... What was that? The slamming of it resounded as if a lid had been banged violently on a giant box. And we are all sitting in the box and waiting helplessly for our fate to be decided out there. As long as the house doors were open the houses along the street seemed to hold each other by the hand, and if one had got into trouble the slightest movement would have been enough to warn the others. That is so no longer. When the doors are shut the houses release each other's hands and each is left to itself with its own misfortune.

Out there in the dark threatening streets the stolen motors are racing to and fro without a stop, carrying treacherous plans, hostile orders, all over the town. And behind the doors no one is safe until these plans and orders have decided his fate.

It was just before midnight when the bell rang in the ante-room. Its sound choked the breath in our throats. Zsigmondy went out to open the door. It was all right: only my brother Béla had sent me a message not to go out tomorrow till he had spoken to me.

Then we retired for a restless sleep. A lamp was burning on the table of the night nursery; my bed was made, but I sat for a long time on its edge, waiting like a patient in the surgeon's waiting room. There was a smell of printer's ink somewhere: if only one could read in these times, I thought. There was a newspaper on the table. No, not that. I turned from it in disgust. I wanted to escape the present.

How often have I found consolation in books during sad hours! But is there a book that could lull the present sorrows to rest? I remembered having read *Faust* during a great storm at sea till the night had passed, and during an evil night of the war my mother and I had read *Toldi* till the morning came. I wondered if today the armed knight could carry me off with him as he rides to Buda to fight a last fight for Hungary's honor, to kiss faithfully great King Louis's hand? I shook my head. Was there nothing? *Hamlet*, with visionary raving eyes, came and went, but did not arrest me. *Niels Lyne* and *The Idiot*, and rusty, armored *Don Quixote*.

A patrol passed under the window. A soldier pulled his bayonet over a corrugated shutter as if sharpening it for some future victim. The others laughed, then they went on. Silence followed, the silence of a huge wicked town that gapes.

How long will it last? Why can I not think of anything else? If I were at home now I would count my books to pass the time. One, two, three... I imagined myself faking an old volume from the shelf. Kant's *Critique of Pure Reason*. What good is that? At the other end of my bookcase there is another book in a parchment binding as smooth and cool as ivory: the Iliad. I thought of it—I had bought it in Siena, a long time ago. Bright, great heroes, Homeric songs, would mean nothing to me now. And Dante. No, I do not want him. His *Inferno* knows nought of the tortures we endure.

The horn of a solitary motor resounded through the night, and volleys were fired in the direction of the barracks. Quietly, so as to make no noise, I began to walk up and down in the nursery. There were books lying about among the toys; picture-books, colored animals, big, funny alphabets. I looked at several; and thus a much used, shabby story book came into my hand.

I sat back on the edge of the bed, the book open. It brought to me the memory of holidays, old Sundays, mild childish illnesses... Someone is reassuring me, kisses me, hushes me and reads in a subdued voice at my bedside, strokes the hair from my forehead... The pages turn quickly. And where neither Goethe nor Arany nor Dante nor Kant could succeed in carrying away my thoughts this revolutionary night, the eternal fairy-tale, that consoler of children, of sick and of suffering, triumphed.

II

ONE gets the impression that things have been like this for ever so long, though it all started only the day before yesterday. Good Friday was just two days ago. Today is Sunday—but not Easter. The resurrection has failed and the grave-diggers sit grinning on the tomb.

In some churches the bells were ringing, in others the people had gone to Mass, my brother's message kept me at home. Again there was a newspaper lying on the table. In huge black letters Béla Kun's proclamation to the proletariats of the world was glaring at me: "To Everybody!" It was revolutionary incendiarism, inciting hatred. In their old-fashioned way the church bells appealed above the roofs for love and goodwill. Meanwhile the wireless had spread broadcast the news of Hungary's shame and misfortune. And from Moscow there came the triumphant answer. It is published in *The People's Voice*:

This afternoon at five o'clock the Hungarian Soviet Republic got into wireless communication with the Russian Soviet. The Hungarian Soviet called Comrade Lenin to the apparatus. Twenty minutes later: Moscow answered: "Lenin speaking. Request Comrade Béla Kun should come to wireless station." But Béla Kun was at the meeting of the People's Commissaries, so another comrade answered from the wireless station: "Last night the Hungarian Proletariat seized all powers, established the Dictatorship of the Proletariat, and greets you as the leader of the International Proletariat. The Social Democratic Party has adopted the Communist point of view and the two parties have united. We call ourselves the Hungarian Socialist Party. We ask for instructions in this matter. Béla Kun is Commissary for Foreign Affairs. The Hungarian Soviet offers the Russian Soviet a defensive and offensive alliance. Fully armed, we turn against all the enemies of the Proletariat and ask for information concerning the military situation."

At nine in the evening Moscow called again:

> Lenin speaking... Hearty greetings to the Hungarian Soviet's Proletarian Government, in particular to Comrade Béla Kun. I have just communicated your message to the Congress of the Communist Party of Bolshevik Russia. Enormous enthusiasm... we will send a report on the military situation as soon as possible... A permanent wireless connection between Budapest and Moscow is absolutely necessary.
>
> With Communist greetings,
> Lenin.

'Lenin speaking'... How terrible these two words sound; how terrible the deathly silence that follows them! 'Lenin speaking'... So he is there now, with his bald head bent sideways, his enigmatic smile frozen on his broad mouth, his Kalmuk eyes open wide and his nostrils expanded as though he smelt blood. 'Lenin speaking'... And Trotsky is there too, his bestial, cruel face peering over us; his mouth broadens and the red beard on his chin shakes. All the other Russian Jewish tyrants are there too, and they wave their bloody hands. They may give their orders; their lieutenants will obey, and we shall live or die according to their good pleasure and instructions.

My brother Béla came into the room and I learned from him that I could not go home any more. In hasty excited sentences he told me that yesterday evening when he had gone to see our mother the glaring lamps of a big car had suddenly lit up the dark street. It stopped in front of the next house, though this has no entrance from our street. Three men dismounted from the car and kept our street door under observation.

"Mother's housekeeper has been talking to them this afternoon, probably to inform them that you have left. She had scarcely returned when the car pulled up before our door and the men asked for you. They wanted to come up to our flat. They insisted, affirming that they came from the police, and had to see you personally. The concierge told them that you had left town and banged the door in their faces. The car, however, remained where it was and kept the house under observation. The men only left at dawn, hoping to see you return."

While he told me all this I had a feeling as though an ugly hand were groping for me in the dark, trying to get hold of me, but missing me, passing beside me. It was the hand of Lenin.

My brother said, following up his own thoughts: "You cannot remain with the Zsigmondys. It is impossible for you to go home. They informed the concierge that they would come and fetch you today."

My mother's face appeared before me, a haunted expression in her blue eyes. It would be terrible for her to see me arrested. What was I to do? I had sent a message to Count Stephen Bethlen this morning, but he had already left home. Everybody for whom I send has disappeared. The threads are broken. How shall I start? Left to themselves, what can women do at a time like this?

I had not noticed that the Secretary of the Women's Union had entered. He told me that in a few days it would be impossible to travel without a permit and advised me to leave town while it was still possible. The Kállays had been prevented by the crowds at the station from leaving by train today, but would start tomorrow, and invited me to go with them.

I hesitated; but, after all, it was only a question of a few days. So as soon as I was alone I wrote to my mother and told her I should leave next day, though I did not yet know my destination, and asked her to spend the evening with me.

Hours have never passed so slowly. When it was quite dark I escaped from the house. A cold wind blew through the empty streets. The tired town had once more resigned itself to its fate and now suffered in silence; the posters alone spoke; huge sheets covered the walls. The same words everywhere: Proletariat... Dictatorship... Proletariat... The broken street lamps had not been repaired, and the pavement was covered with refuse: for days the streets have not been swept.

The staircase was in darkness. A single lamp was burning in my sister's sitting-room. And there, in the dim light, I saw my mother again. I was shocked by her appearance: she seemed to have become shorter since we had parted and her face was much thinner. Did she fret for me? Was I the cause of this change? Never in my life did I feel so moved in her presence as then.

And yet she seemed quite calm, and on one occasion she even laughed, with her own hearty laughter. We talked of all sorts of things, except the fact that I should no longer be with them on the morrow. The children seemed quite happy, chattering among themselves in a corner. The hours passed so happily for me that now and then I had the illusion that the old times had returned for a moment before disappearing forever.

One or the other would say: "At most it can last a week or two." Or again: "Colonel Vyx has been locked up and an English officer has been assaulted in the street. Insults of this kind will surely not be taken lying down by the Great Powers. It is impossible that the Entente should suffer the establishment of Bolshevism in Hungary. She knew how to send ultimatums demanding lines of demarcation, so that the Roumanians and her other friends could loot at leisure, now she is sure to display more energy when her own interests are at stake."

"Let us put no hope in anybody but ourselves," said my brother-in-law. "It was the Entente who brought us to this."

One of my nephews said: "That is the reason why so many people are rather pleased that the Communists display hostility to the Entente. Who knows, perhaps our territorial integrity..."

"Don't expect any good from these people," I interrupted. "Among the apostles of Communism there may be some idealists, but those who apply it practically are all scoundrels. It is impossible, man cannot withstand nature."

Suddenly someone asked if I had decided where I was going to. Should I accept the Kállays' invitation, or should I attempt to get across the river Ipoly to Pressburg and thence into foreign territory?

"Do the Kállays realize what this invitation means in these days? "

"You must not accept it otherwise," my mother said.

"Wherever you go, you must mislead those who are after you," said my brother-in-law." Write a letter and have it posted in another part of the country."

My mother rose: "It is time to go."

My heart stopped beating. But she held her head high and there were no tears in her eyes. Only when leading her down the stairs did I feel that she leaned more heavily on me than she used to. Who will lead her when I am gone? My nephew, Alexander Eperjessy, took her home. I asked him to occupy my room and stay with my mother, otherwise I should not be able to tear myself away.

"Don't worry about me," mother said; "and don't you come back till you can do so openly and without danger."

I have been with her almost daily as long as I can remember, yet it was only this evening that I really learned to appreciate her. She had never asked for anything and yet was always ready to give. She never spoke of herself and listened to everybody. She had no words of endearment, she kissed vaguely and her arms were rarely caressing. She was never demonstrative, the seat of her affections was her heart and not her lips. And while we were walking side by side through the dark night on our short, sad road, I felt that if this heart were one day to stop, then mine would throb but haltingly ever after. We had passed the house which had given me shelter.

I thought my mother had not noticed it, being accustomed to go on towards home. But suddenly she stopped, and, as was her wont on rare occasions, she drew my head to her quickly and gave me a kiss which went half into the air.

"Now, my dear, God bless you!"

I tried to find her hand but failed. She had already left me and I could no longer see her in the dark. I could only hear her step in the empty street. That quaint, dear step, which sounded as if she dragged one of her feet a little. Then that ceased too. Silence, empty silence, dominated the night. Silently I wept, and the world disappeared in my tears.

*   *   *

March 24th.

DAWN. The dawn rose with a dull greyness over the ill-fated city, as though the light had risen from the mire. Morning was in sole possession of the dirty unswept streets. I leant far out of the window, and in the distance I noticed two soldiers staggering painfully along. One of the achievements of the Dictatorship of the Proletariat: prohibition of alcohol!

As I turned back I caught sight of my travelling bag. My mother had packed it yesterday and had smuggled it out of the house without the spying servant observing them. I sat down by it and waited. After a time the, house awoke and the time passed more quickly. I do not remember all that followed: Zsigmondy changed my money, and I noticed how little I had—one thousand six hundred crowns. I counted it over again, but that did not make it more. My mother had wanted to give me some, but it had all come so unexpectedly that we had only very little money in the house, and she would need that little.

I should have liked to put back the clock, but there was the cab waiting in the street and they were carrying my bag down the stairs. As I waved my hand from the corridor Mrs. Zsigmondy leant out of the door which had opened to me so hospitably and smiled through her tears.

When I was in the carriage it suddenly occurred to me that perhaps I ought not to have accepted Zsigmondy's offer to come with me to the station: he might get into trouble; but he insisted so simply and heartily that I could say no more.

From behind the clouds a pale sun lit up the gloomy town. All the shops were closed, and the tiny red flags adorning the buildings fluttered in an icy wind. Careworn faces passed rapidly before the window of the rattling cab. A black crowd had gathered on the pavement in front of a pork-butcher's shop, the signboard of which advertised luscious hams and appetizing sausages, looking now like the impossibilities of a prehistoric age. But the shop window was absolutely empty. Further on a baker's shop displayed a wooden sign on which were painted beautiful loaves and rolls. This, too, gave the impression of a diagram in a museum, showing things of the past; it made one feel suddenly hungry. Posters everywhere, innumerable red posters. But there were no goods in the shops, and disappointed women slunk along the walls.

"The Red Newspaper!" howled a tiny urchin. "The Young Proletarian!" And he waved the papers in the air. Few passersby bought any, but went on with their beads drawn between their shoulders as if they expected blows. Is this the town of the glorious revolution, this sad mass of dirty, frightened buildings standing amidst piles of dustbins filled to the brim? Is this the rapturous achievement for the sake of which Hungary had to perish—a town where the factories have stopped, the shops are closed and all work has ceased? A town where all and everybody have but one of two thoughts: either "We have lost everything," or "Now everything is ours!"

The appearance of the principal railway station was like a nightmare. Its walls were covered with obscene drawings and dirty scribblings; it had not been swept, and sawdust had been strewn over the mud. Machine-guns were standing in the ankle-deep dirt, greasy pieces of paper were flying about, unnameable filth covered the flagstones and oozed beneath the people's feet. A rough, impatient crowd pushed and jostled, and the air was pervaded by an insufferable stench.

While Zsigmondy took my ticket I looked at the people. Many of them kept their eyes to the ground as if they wanted to hide—these were in flight. Some swore obscenely. A sailor was examining luggage at the entrance, and rewarded himself for his trouble by continually putting things from them into his pocket. At a distance I saw Elisabeth Kállay. She saw me too, but we did not take any notice of each other. Suddenly I found my sister Mary standing by my side. She was very pale and only her eyes greeted me. The Secretary of the Women's Union came towards me: "The trip won't last long and I shall bring you news!"

I passed the newspaper stall. Nothing but 'Red Newspapers,' 'The People's Voice,' 'The Young Proletarian,' and the little red and blue volumes of 'The Workmen's Library.' In the crowd I managed to embrace my sister. Then, "God bless you, Zsigmondy!"

Now I was on the platform. I had to walk a good distance before I shrank into the corner of my compartment. The train was a long time in starting, and human shapes were hurrying down the corridor. A fat man tore the door open and looked inside as if searching for somebody. Then I, too, looked on the ground like those anxious to hide. Suddenly the columns before the window slowly began to move. Then the shape of goods sheds passed slowly by. The wheels rattled over the points. Then the compartment became lighter: we had reached the open track. And as the train gathered speed I knew that I had left the town, with its People's Commissaries, its police, its prisons, behind me. I was free!

For a moment I realized this, then again my consciousness became dimmed and a pleasant fatigue overcame me. From the window I watched the telegraph wires rise, then came a post and jerked them down, then they rose again till the next post came. I turned to look my fellow travelers. Every seat was occupied. In one sat an officer whose insignia of rank had been torn from his collar, leaving the marks of three stars. His field-gray cavalry cap was ornamented with a red rosette. As soon as Budapest was left behind us he took his cap off and threw the rosette out of the window. An old lady looked on in alarm and drew away from him: her husband wore the 'red man' ostentatiously in his buttonhole. Both seemed scared. Opposite sat a well-dressed man, who buried his face deeply in a book, using it as a screen. I looked at it: *The Workmen's Library*. On the title-page was the drawing of a book from the pages of which sprang a, naked, unkempt workman, holding a burning lamp in his hand. This lamp, I suppose, represented the light spread by the contents of the book. I strained my eyes to catch the title: it ran "*The Principles of Communism*, by Frederick Engels. Translated by Ernest Garami.*"

Why read it now? I thought. Why did he not read it long ago? Why have not all those who suffer today read it long ago? It was there, always, in their midst. Its principles were set out in a thousand publications, in a thousand minds. These little books have been doing their work for a long time, and their wrappers were pink only because for the time being they did not dare to demonstrate outwardly that they were red.

"The slave is sold once for all. The proletarian has to sell himself every day, every hour... The slave frees himself if he abolishes the institution of slavery. The proletarian can only free himself by completely destroying private property. This cannot be achieved by any other means than by a revolution." And in the Socialist revolution there is an end to the family, the country, and religion.

I stared at the stranger. Why did he want to read about these things now? They have been proclaimed aloud for tens of years. But what had been done in Hungary to counteract them? Has anybody been at work among the people contradicting them? Has anyone founded a popular library to proclaim the tenets of Christ, the significance of country and family, the primary conditions of human society, with similar persistence among the people? The Communists worked hard. They fixed their goal and with every action: every word, every letter, strove to achieve domination. Meanwhile, Magyardom let the decades pass passively, inactively, and now that the earth has given way under its feet it has lost its head.

The alarmed fellow-traveler went on reading his book, hastily turning page after page. I should have liked to tell him that it was no good hurrying now—he was too late. Just then a man stopped in the entrance of our compartment, a violin in his grimy black hand. His low forehead was surrounded by curling oriental black hair, his eyes were bloodshot, and one of his nostrils was missing, as though it had been gnawed away by some animal. He pressed his fiddle under his bristly blue chin, a smile began to spread over his horrible syphilitic face, and with a slow rhythm the bow passed over the chords. His body swayed to and fro with the tune, and each movement seemed to raise a filthy stench in the compartment. The tune and the musician became one, and above the rattling of the train sounded the strains of the 'Internationale.'

"I'll play it again if anybody wants to learn it," he said, as he finished, and looked round with a sly, aggressive look. But nobody answered. Only the man with the 'red man' in his buttonhole jumped up nervously and waved a twenty-crown bank-note in his hand. The filthy black hands seized it eagerly and disappeared. Then we heard the fiddle whining in the next compartment: the Jew-Gipsy was teaching the new tune to the people.

"If anybody wants to learn it..."

Aszód!... The train stopped. I had often heard that after Budapest Aszód had been the place where the Communists had met with the greatest measure of success. I looked out of the window. Over the Reformatory a huge red flag was flying, and a similar flag was hoisted over the station. A crowd gathered in front of one of the carriages, and some people who were late came tearing along and took their hats off. A fat little man with Semitic features and a red rosette descended from a reserved compartment. He might have been a broker, but now he was addressed as "Comrade on a Political Mission." He was received by a deputation and people cringed before him. I noticed that the crowd was composed of two types only: the impudent adventurer and the frightened coward, but presently others joined them. Someone said they were agitators from Budapest and had come with armed soldiers. Propaganda and terror—the two means of government of the Communists. The fiddler was one of them: he, too, was an agitator.

I passed through the festive crowd unobserved, they being too busy to pay any heed to the travelers. Far out beyond the platform a dilapidated little local train was smoking. Mrs. Kállay and her two daughters were heading for it, so I followed them. At last we dared to get into the same compartment. We even exchanged a few words, and the further we got from the Red town the freer we felt.

Elisabeth Kállay whispered to me that she was hiding her diadem in her dress, and Lenke furtively produced an old revolver from under her coat. We could not help laughing. Other passengers also seemed to have their secrets, for many of them were abnormally corpulent and sat uncomfortably on their seats. Everybody was saving whatever he could, and nowadays only that which one can carry on one's person can be said to belong to one.

The air blowing in through the window was pure and sharp, and beyond the line were lush meadows, deep, swampy fields, budding trees, white cottages, roads, carts and peasants. Here everything seemed to be going on as usual, as if nothing had happened. The mud of the country roads was cleaner than that on the asphalt of the town.

We had left the flat country of the disgraced capital and presently the hillocks of Nográd came to meet us under the evening sky, the bare, red-brown woods and white villages on the banks of the Galga forming the landscape. A landau was waiting for us behind the station. The coachman took off his hat respectfully and spoke to us just as in the old days. How strange it seemed! Springless carts rattled down the road and the elderly men in them doffed their hats: had not they yet been told that they were in duty bound to hate those who had always protected them? A church bell pealed somewhere on the top of a hill, and the light of a bright fire streamed out of the door of a house. A woman stood within its beams and made the sign of the Cross. She did not yet know that the new power had declared war on God.

Now the road goes up a hill, the wheels crunch on fine gravel, a gate opens between the trees, and a sudden light flares up in the night. We have reached the Kállays' turreted castle.

In a few minutes we are all sitting together in a well heated room. A wide garden surrounds the house, the night surrounds the garden. And the world is far away, somewhere beyond.

*   *   *

Berczel. *March 27th, 1919.*

DAYS have passed since my arrival, yet I do not think that I shall ever forget the first morning when I awoke here. I seemed to be floating in a pure ocean of absolute silence. Then, quite suddenly and unexpectedly, a small voice fell from above into the ocean of silence. After the threatening hum of the revolution in the city, the wild howling, the panting hatred and the ominous nightly tramplings, there was such beauty in this voice that I remember being enraptured in the semi-consciousness of waking.

A small bird was sitting on a twig before my window. Instead of the abyss of human infernos, of narrow streets and worn dark walls, my eyes lighted on a twig and a bird, and I wept out of sheer gratitude that such things still existed. I should have liked to gather in my hands every tiny particle of the sound so that I might send it to those who remained prisoners among the stones of that accursed city.

How different is life here! It is like a fairy-tale related to soothe children at bedtime... It is a quiet village. On the hillock can be seen the bell tower and the shingled roof of the church. Below, at its foot, are small cottages and small farmyards. People go to bed early in the evening: only now and then is a window lit up. The cow bells ring, a dog barks somewhere. And horror does not creep through the night, worry does not sit on the threshold of the morn, threatening the dread shadow of events to come. Today is like yesterday and tomorrow bears no different aspect. Sometimes I fear that conscience has died of exhaustion within me. A clouded glass screen has risen between me and the world. Even the village seems to be beyond the screen and there is nothing on this side of it but a castle, a wide park, and narrow, useless little paths on which the past treads undisturbed. These are set with white seats which have not been provided for fatigue. Beds of flowers which only exist in order to be beautiful, dark violets, without a purpose but just to flower.

A white lace hat appears and disappears in the cool sunshine: the widow of Benjamin Kállay passes under my window. Her husband, the most brilliant Finance Minister of Francis Joseph's reign, the inspiring spirit of the Monarchy's Eastern policy, the governor of Bosnia and Herzegovina, had been a scholar and a historian. The old lady had been the uncrowned queen of the small southern provinces and one of the most beautiful women of the receptions at the Vienna Burg. Now she discusses with the bailiff the spring sowings, though when the harvest comes they may no longer be hers. For that matter, are the house and gardens still her own? Everything is uncertain. She also worries about a son and a daughter. Elisabeth Kállay had been the one Hungarian maid of honor of Queen Zita, accordingly the Communists eye her with distrust. Frederick Kállay is an aide-de-camp to the Archduke Joseph and had left Budapest with him. She has had no news since then. "Good God, what are we coming to?"

When she says this her two daughters rise in revolt: they will have no despondency. I like to hear them speak: they voice the fine, strong vitality of my race:

"And you, why are you always staring into the air?" Elisabeth has put her hand on my shoulder. "Instead of moping like this you had better go and commit your thoughts and sorrows to paper."

"I have taken a good many notes. When I left I asked my young nephew to keep them for me. But what's the good of going on with them?"

Elisabeth Kállay, however, urged me on: "Go on writing your diary; it will come in useful someday."

Thus one evening, when I was left to myself, I took up my pen and looked back on the past days and gathered fading memories. It is a practice, however, that makes things both easier and harder. This diary affords the relief of self-confession, but it also tortures me by compelling me to live the past over again. And who shall say if I shall ever reach the end?

I looked up from my writing: Lenke Kállay appeared at my window, holding her head high. She brought news, good news. Elisabeth said: "Let no one dare to speak of evil tidings."

Stephen Bethlen is in Vienna and has petitioned the Powers through the French High Commissioner, M. Alizé, for help against Bolshevism. The Entente is certain to intervene and will send troops to checkmate the Proletarian Dictators. Thirty thousand French soldiers have embarked at Marseilles, with General Pétain in command.

"It won't continue like this much longer, we shall get on our legs again presently."

Did they say it, or did I? We have said it for a thousand years and when the men grew tired of saying it the women said it. They said it during the Tartar invasion, after the defeat at Mohács. Today we say it again, though everything has collapsed, though we have been robbed of our all and are the most unfortunate people on earth.

Yet we still trust and have faith. Why? Nobody knows. Yet how often have I felt in me that faith which is stronger than our fate, and how often have I noticed it flaming up in others? What is it? The mysterious desire for existence? Or is it more than that, is it the subconscious knowledge of our vitality?

It is like the belief in the miraculous deer—an old legend which is ever present in the Hungarian mind in time of trouble. It tells how among the endless swamps of Maeotis, at the beginning of time, a white deer with shining antlers appeared to two brothers who were lost in the morass. The divine deer lured them on and guided them over invisible tracks. And to this day, whenever we fall in the morass the miraculous animal appears, gleaming white and leaping lightly across the bog, and guiding us along invisible tracks towards the future.

Things can't remain like this: we shall get on our legs again presently. The Miraculous Deer is leading us.

* * *

March 28th.

THE folding doors of the big drawing-room on the first floor open quietly, and in the room beyond books with gilt backings are set among flowers. The fire is already burning brightly in the porcelain stove in the dining-room, whilst above the red-shaded lamp the ceiling appears heavy and dark. Between the windows stands a chest that once belonged to Imre Thököly: the walls are ornamented with Oriental dishes and old Chinese plates... The footman stands stiff in his black dress coat: his white shirt gleams, and his hands holding the dish are gloved in white. Little silver buttons glitter on the page's jacket.

My thoughts fly homeward: in the villages there is still a sense of home, which has long since departed from the towns. I thought of the past winter, the closed shops, the scanty tables. If only I could give that sense of home to somebody... And again I feel the glass screen raised between myself and reality.

Mrs. Benjamin Kállay, dressed in white silk, presides over the table. Her head is held up a trifle haughtily; her sharp profile is crowned with snow-white hair, and her full chin disappears in lace. Somehow she reminds me of a portrait of Louis XV. Presently she nods and rises; her gait is solemn and slow; the wings of the door open before her and we follow her into the drawing-room.

Outside, drums are being beaten in the village, and now and then a scrap of the crier's announcement reaches our ears.

"The revolutionary council Revolutionary tribunals... the president and two members prosecuting commissary... clerk of the court... No restrictions whatever... any hour of the day... in the open... death sentence... carried out without delay."

I had a curious impression that the words seemed to have little connection with what was said: 'Lenin speaking' Nobody actually said that, yet I seemed to hear those two words as a sort of refrain.

The drumming went on:

"False reports... revolutionary tribunal executed... The Revolutionary Council is abolished... In the Soviet republic all rank, title and nobility are abolished"

At this moment the footman brought the coffee on a silver tray: "Is it your Excellency's pleasure that coffee be served here?"

How incongruous it all seemed! The huge room, the unreal continuation of the old aristocratic life. Is it real, or is it a mirage? The snow-white lady, her head erect, among her lace, sitting in an arm-chair. Her two daughters, one leaning gracefully over her embroidery, the other turning the leaves of a book. The huge Venetian glass chandelier, which once shone over Maria Theresa, spreads a gentle light. On the wall, between two pastels representing children, the Empire clock of gilded wood ticks slowly, and its ticking sounds as if ripe corn were being rubbed together. Slowly life is passing before our eyes, a grain of life with every moment that departs beyond recall. The mirage is still there. Nothing is altered. But outside, the filthy tide is rising, spreads and rolls onwards from the Red town, covers the fields, touches the villages, laps at the walls of the cottages. It comes nearer and nearer; and the wind which it raises drives before it phantoms which rush by and in their flight glare in through the windows. Elsewhere it is different. The glitter of the peasant's scythe menaces the castle. The despoiled landlords have to flee or become the bailiffs of Béla Kun's 'Co-operatives of Production' on their own estates. Our fate is coming without doubt. But still, here in the great drawing-room, life has not yet altered. These people round me are just waiting for whatever is to come, and whether death or reprieve be their destiny, they are faithful to the blood which is in them.

III

COMMUNISTS from Aszód have arrived in the village. The glass screen between myself and reality has suddenly cracked. The agitators dragged a table in front of the town hall, climbed on it and addressed the crowd. When we asked the coachman what had happened, he looked down and gave an embarrassed, evasive answer:

"They are going to stay till tomorrow..."

These Communists boasted that the workmen of the aeroplane works at Aszód had got the town in their power and that the directorate had had the lord of Iklad, Count Ráday, and his wife, arrested.

The news has only just reached us. When the Rádays heard of the proclamation of the Dictatorship of the Proletariat they wanted to go to Budapest with the manager of the aeroplane works. But the Communists of Aszód were quicker than they. They closed the barriers, and the Lord Lieutenant of the county and his wife, who had nursed the wounded in the hospital of Aszód during the war, were escorted back by armed Red soldiers, some of whom she had herself nursed back to life. They locked the Countess up in the Reformatory, the Count and the manager they put up against the wall. A firing squad was drawn up: a lieutenant enquired if all was ready. At the last moment they let them go. It was all done for amusement, to give them a good fright. One often bears of such things nowadays; the novelty and strangeness of it are wearing off.

Countess Ráday did not know that her husband was still alive until he returned to her.

But this villainy was relieved by a generous action. When the people of Iklad heard what had been done to their landlord and benefactor, they rose and armed themselves with scythes, and went to his rescue, but before they reached Aszód the prisoners had been sent to Budapest. For a long time this band of armed peasants threatened the Reformatory. Unfortunately not every village is like Iklad and not all landlords like

Count Ráday.

Other news reached us too, uncertainly and stealthily, from castles and towns. Then the first newspapers came from the capital: the great day they had prepared and announced had at last dawned, and we shrank from its contact. With what a voice was it proclaimed! Our language had never yet been prostituted in this way, their alien press uses our tongue to torture us. It spits on our past with grinning contempt and drags in the mire everything that might still promise a better future. The triumph of the revolution howls from its pages. Vulgar brutalities, foaming, abject hatred, are enclosed in the wrappings of world-saving theories.

The only paper of the Counter-revolution has been suppressed: the conservative *Budapesti Hirlap* has been strangled and the subscribers sent 'The Red Newspaper.' The newspapers which have been allowed to continue their existence approve, fawn, incite and lend their old reputation to facilitate the conquest of the groping, tottering countryside. Unsuspecting people absorb the poison from the papers to which they have been accustomed. Ideas become confused; even the honest lose their bearings. The papers propagate their news as ordered by the head of the Bolshevist press-directorate—a Jew.

If ever the time comes to call to account this soul-killing, defeatist, alien press, which reveled over the revolution, over Károlyi, the capitulation, the Republic, the foreign occupation, and now lauds Béla Kun and Bolshevism; should ever that time come, I can imagine the defense: '... the terror... brutal force...' But why do the papers carry on? Why do they not stop publication? The press-dictator elucidates this point when he declares proudly, "the Free Union of Journalists played an important role in the preparation and realization of the political revolution in October and the social upheaval of today." These mouthpieces of Hungarian public opinion have for the last few decades been exclusively Jews.

Though I shudder with disgust, yet I cannot resist the temptation of taking the newspaper into my hand, and I read 'The People's Voice' of March 25th:

> The work has begun... The courage to demolish, the relentlessness of destruction and the unfaltering determination to rebuild, these are the spiritual instruments by which the Proletarian State must be established and its socialism must be realized.

What can be their physical instruments when destruction is only a spiritual aid? I read on:

Lenin predicts victory in the near future!... The Russian Red army is victorious on the Galician frontier, and the enemy is in flight. The victory surpasses all hopes... The position of the Imperialist Government in England is shaken. Hungarian events have caused the downfall of Clemenceau... Serbian imperialism is on the verge of complete collapse. The southern counties have accepted the principle of the Dictatorship of the Proletariat. There are signs of disruption in Serbia. The Proletariat is preparing for the final battle.

The papers lie in a heap, and I pick them up at random:

The Revolutionary Government has decided to raise a Red army. It has been decided to change the names of the barracks from that of imperialist kings and militarist generals. In future they will bear the names of Lenin, Marx, Liebknecht, Rosa Luxemburg...

A Red army instead of the national army. Instead of Francis Joseph and Maria-Theresa barracks we shall have Lenin and Rosa Luxemburg barracks.

Austria has recognized the Hungarian Soviet Republic and has accredited the envoys of Béla Kun... Two new Soviet Republics: On the 28th a Soviet Republic was proclaimed in Wiener-Neustadt. In Chotin the Bessarabian Soviet Republic has been proclaimed. At the elections for the Workers' Councils in Brunswick the Communists have gained a victory.

My nerves began to give way: though it might be all untrue, I could stand it no longer. I fled, out of the room, out of the house, out of the garden... In the village the drum was beating. "The Revolutionary Government has decreed..." I turned back. Is it impossible to get away from it for a moment! I locked the garden door behind me so that I should hear it no longer. A white dog was playing on the lawn and its mistress followed; she was carrying a Viennese newspaper.

"At the request of Clemenceau allied troops under General Mangin are to be sent against Béla Kun's Soviet Republic. Balfour protests. The British–"

"We are the prisoners of the Entente and what happens inside the prison depends upon the gaolers."

Suddenly the window-panes rattled with the vibration of a distant, dull boom.

"Guns!" we both exclaimed simultaneously. "From the direction of the

Ipoly river. Far away... At last!..." Then we suddenly looked at each other in amazement; what we felt seemed so incredible. It is to our enemies that we must look for liberation, to France, to the country of Franchet d'Espérey, Colonel Vyx, and to our little neighbors who for months have been robbing and tearing our country. What has happened to us?

Humanity has sometimes forgotten for centuries the plans and the power of the Jews. The fate of Egypt, the conquest of Canaan, the dissolution of Rome, the religious strife in Byzantium, the decline of Spain... these and many other things. And far away are the great persecutions of the Jews, which were always the consequence of too much audacity, too great activity, on the part of the chosen people. These persecutions, the fruits of exasperation, were never of long duration, and after them Jewry quickly sank back into obscurity, whence it threw sand into the eyes of the peoples that they might be blind for a generation and forget.

In the years before the war the suspicions of the Hungarian nation, so often aroused before, had been lulled to sleep. We saw how the Jews, corning from the East, took possession of the land after acquiring the liquor shops of the villages. From the little draper's shop in the town they laid grasping hands on our whole economic life. We saw them during the war withdrawing into safety and acquiring millions while our own folk gained crutches. We heard that the Zionist Congress of Paris carried the following resolution: "Jewry must try to get possession of Budapest first, then Hungary, so as to have a base for the establishment of its world-rule." And many of us read in 1917, during the war, the declaration of their leading spirit in Hungary, published in *Világ*, the mouthpiece of Freemasonry: "We reserve our institutions, our means and our men for a superhuman effort later on." Now the *later on* has arrived, has emerged from obscurity. Twenty-four Jewish People's Commissaries lead the rest and pronounce judgment of life and death upon Hungary.

The sound of an enemy gun is heard in the distance, and suffering humanity breathes freer and thinks of liberation; perhaps it will come nearer and shoot down the walls of our prison... But no: happier nations would never be able to understand that that was needed.

*   *   *

March 30th-31st.

ITEMS of news arrive daily, but there is no sequence. Only a few days ago it was announced that 'the British Foreign Secretary protests. London will not permit it... Thirty thousand French troops have embarked in Marseilles...' Now the talk is of General Mangin's Anglo-French armies: he is on the way and has taken the field against the Bolsheviks.

I put out my candle and sat alone in the dark. A vision of spectres rose about me, shaking their heads, apathetic spectres of suppressed doubts which extinguished all hope. What if nobody comes to our help, if the nations allow us to perish miserably while they stand round and watch us being eaten up by the worms which arise from our own decay? Surely we cannot descend utterly into the depths unless the victorious Great Powers permit it? Why do they not prevent it, if they do not want Bolshevism? With Károlyi forever cringing, Colonel Vyx, the head of the Entente's Military Mission has stopped at nothing. Taking advantage of his position he has trodden for months on our self-respect. He has treated the Eastern bulwark of Europe, a highly cultured people with a lineage as ancient as his own nation's, like the French officers treat the savages in their own colonies. Why did this egotistical little Jew of Alsatian origin, possessed of plenipotentiary powers, withdraw all the French troops from Budapest on the eve of the proclamation of the Dictatorship? Why did he permit the Posts and Telegraphs, over which he had absolute censorial sway, to serve Béla Kun in the preparation of his revolution?

Someday these questions will be answered. The message signed by Colonel Vyx, published in the papers of the 26th, although the provinces only got the news today, throws some light upon one point. The Military Mission of the Entente unexpectedly *appeals* "in the name of conciliation and justice" to the Revolutionary Government "to give without delay every possible publicity to the following communication." It refers to the document in which Károlyi announces his resignation:

> In his proclamation to the Hungarian people the President of the Republic said that the Mission of the Entente had stated that it would in the future consider the lines demarcation as political frontiers. I formally declare that this is an erroneous interpretation of the words used... It has never been intended to suggest such 'political frontiers.'

So it appears that once again Michael Károlyi has deceived the nation. But is it not curious that Colonel Vyx's mission has delayed this explanation until now? Why did it not take action at once, when Károlyi endeavored to justify his resignation by the alleged finality of frontiers fixed in the Entente's note? Why did it allow him to use nationalist arguments in order to throw Hungary into the arms of Bolshevism? And why did Colonel Vyx permit Béla Kun to creep in under the same nationalist flag which had covered Károlyi's exit?

Who consented to play the game of these two abject creatures in the fateful hour when the stakes were a country's fate? The tardy explanation of the Entente Mission inevitably creates the impression that Colonel Vyx played into their hands, or, at the least, that he showed considerable partisanship in their favor.

The exposure of Károlyi's deception concerning the fixing of frontiers shows the falsity of Béla Kun's battle-cry: "For territorial integrity! " Now that he wields both armed forces and finances, he sings another tune. He has declared to a correspondent of the Viennese *Neue Freie Presse*: "In Soviet Hungary we do not insist on territorial integrity... We do not recognize any economic frontiers." These are the men who have Hungary's fate at their mercy! The very thought makes one's blood boil. Is all our ancient pride of race, all our glorious history, to be thus trampled underfoot by Jews? Why does the Entente delay? Why does it give Bolshevism time to recruit an army for its own support?

The Red Soldier, a new daily paper, has just appeared in Budapest. Propaganda is active: Pogány recruits, Számuelly directs. What a nightmare it is! The cradle of the Red army is draped with low-class comedy. Its advertisements take the shape of newspaper paragraphs and vicious posters. From a world of brothels, of cheap upholstery, of merry-go-rounds, of foul-mouthed agitators speaking from red stands, is the Red army recruited.

It is proposed to hold Red soldiers' gala performances at the theatres, and the newspapers are devoting unending columns to rapturous approval of the idea. "The temple of the Muses stands in festive attire!" Yes—and to the sounds of the Internationale the crowd rushes the free seats. In every theatre a different leader will address the audience: the Galician Neros will mount the stage and play their parts. "There is no such thing as one's own country! Long live the country of all the Proletarians! An army is the tool of nationalist society. Death to militarism! Long live the Red army!"

Someone knocks at my window: it is Elisabeth Kállay in a fur coat standing in the twilight. Yes, by all means let us go. The evening has become heavy and unbearable indoors. Let us get some fresh air.

We walked along the river Galga, and frost from the hills came on the breath of the icy wind. Coming home we crossed the courtyard. There was a light in the stable and a pink-cheeked, fair little girl was sitting on the threshold. Indoors a woman was sitting on a stool beside & cow and one could hear the milk squirting regularly, sharply, into the pail. The coachman doffed his hat and remained bareheaded, a farmer who was leaning against the wall stood up and saluted us. I could not help thinking of the war-cry of 'The Red Newspaper': "Class war must be carried into the villages! "

They were talking of the agitators in Aszód.

"Let them bark," said the farmer placidly; "first we'll see what those people in Budapest are up to."

I could not distinguish his face but it seemed to me that it was not an individual but the whole Hungarian peasantry, suspicious, cautious, who had spoken. The Hungarian peasant speaks little and is not over-fond of work. Now he leans on his plough and watches gravely who shall be the owner of the soil.

"Michael Károlyi has promised it to us. It is true he did not redeem his pledge, and what he gave of his own was, as it turned out later, no longer his property."

"The Communists have promised even more," said Elizabeth Kállay in the cautious way which the times had taught us.

"They only promise the townsfolk that everything is to be theirs," said the farmer; "here they say that the land, too, is common property."

"Well, well," said the coachman, "it is not easy to understand these new-fangled laws."

"That is why we first listened to the Communists," continued the farmer reflectively. "We wanted to see what was going to happen to the land. But later on..." He remained silent for a time, as if debating with himself if he ought to speak out or not. So the coachman continued: "When they started to talk about the law abolishing religion, we did not like it."

"That's so," agreed the farmer; "nor did we like it when they made a law that, if I may be excused mentioning such things, if people lived together for a year in free love, that should make them a lawfully wedded couple." There was silence for a time. The men, ashamed to talk to us of these matters, seemed to whisper among themselves.

"But what roused the women into white heat," the farmer laughed, "was the decision that even a married man could marry like this over and over again, as his old marriage was automatically dissolved by any subsequent union."

The former gravity had disappeared.

"After that the Communists were in a hurry, I can tell you, to get on their carts. They would not dare to come back here at any price."

The woman had finished the milking some while ago and was standing in the stable door beside the child. Now she spoke from her dark corner: "They said they would make picture-shows of the churches, and that there would be no more illegitimate children, nor any inheritance, and that the State would take over our children."

At these words the little girl clung crying to her mother's skirts. "Mummie dear," she implored, "you won't let the horrid State take me away from you..." The woman shook her head. The coachman laughed and said: "I don't know, if you are really naughty..."

The child howled, so her mother picked her up in her arms and in that one tender movement negatived all Communist ordinances. She disappeared, carrying the weeping child and seeming to become one with it. I followed them with my eyes: beyond them, set in a sea of darkness, were the soft outlines of the sleeping village: the roofs of the cottages alone were visible under the starry sky. And Lenin is to come here too!

Bled white, the villages sleep and offer no resistance. But in their very dreams the villagers cling to the soil; and the soil is their country, and their country is Great Hungary.

My heart went out to the villages. The village, the Hungarian village, is selfish like a child, indifferent like a sign-post, and as strong as wind and weather. Its sins are the wild revels derived from its vineyards; the desire for fecundity in men, women and soil alike. Its blessings are sowing and reaping.

There is here a ray of hope. Will the Hungarian village be our salvation?

* * *

April 1st-2nd.

EVEN a few days seems a long time when one is counting the hours. And now the second week has gone and there is no sign of our distress coming to an end.

Bolshevism is destroying with the impudence of ignorance and building with the inexperience of barbarism. Lenin decreed that the old order should be ruthlessly destroyed and the new order constructed without delay. The Bolsheviks of Budapest hasten to obey. With such insatiable zeal do they set to work that their topsy-turvy legislation is but a disclosure and a legalization of their previous arbitrary actions.

The papers give practically no other news. They aim blows at human ethical conceptions and at Hungarian life. They provide a defense for evil-doers and for brigands.

The Jewish Commissary for Justice has proscribed the administration of justice, for he has suspended the sittings of the law-courts!

Never before have I realized to what an extent we are at these people's mercy. Károlyi set the criminals free; the criminals let crime loose to supply their needs. Immorality and lawlessness require the freedom of crime for their sway. To produce unlimited means for its rule Bolshevism abolishes the private property of others, distributes it among its own adherents, and uses it to pay its servants.

Anxiety is now perpetually with me: I feel like a person going late at night through a dark abandoned street who hears moaning from behind a closed window. It is impossible to enter: no policeman can be found. What is happening? Dark speculations haunt one's mind as long as night endures.

Class hatred has established spies and watchers in all the houses of Budapest: the secret agents of the new power are to be found in every house; they watch, blackmail, and report. On their good-will depends the distribution of food-tickets within the house, and those whom they suspect are deprived of bread. Their sanction is required to obtain permits if one requires wood, soap, or boot-laces, and Proletarians alone receive the permits. There is a meatless week in Budapest. The countryside is refusing to send supplies, and food is running short. Yet they proclaim boisterously that Plenty is the outcome of social production! It is the business of the 'confidential man' in every house to see that the Proletarian should not notice the wolf at the door. But it is the intellectual workers who are on short rations: the middle classes are to be deprived of food tickets. Everything is for the Proletarian. Such privileges have never before been known, but it is not love for the Proletarian that inspires these privileges; it is the hatred for the Hungarian Christian citizens, the delight in their sufferings, that are the principles upon which the new rulers govern.

Under the guise of philanthropy Galician Jews and Proletarian rabble are planted among the hated bourgeoisie. The kitchen is common property and the middle-class occupier is obliged to put his furniture at the disposal of the intruders. Home is home no longer. Even in the restricted area assigned to them the bourgeoisie is to have no peace. The Jewish Dictator of the capital has decreed: "Baths for the Proletarian children!" It sounds a very human provision, but is really only a pretense for new provocation. A tendentious poster has appeared, announcing that the bourgeoisie women who "from their silken couches used to step into their perfumed baths" shall make room for dear little Proletarian children, who till now were deprived of the luxury of cleanliness. The order runs:

> ...We also requisition the bath-rooms of private dwellings once a week, on Saturdays, for the whole day, for the gratuitous bathing of the children sent by schools and nursery schools with their certificates. The owners of the bath-rooms have to provide gratuitously the necessary fuel, lighting, towels and soap.—Moritz Preuss.

And the class they call bourgeois can buy neither fuel nor soap! They want the bourgeoisie to perish, perhaps they revel in the idea that they may thus introduce vermin and infection into clean homes. Abroad they create the impression of being philanthropists, and at home they amuse the rabble. For days the houses of Budapest have been terrified by the rumour that Tibor Számuelly intends to allow the mob three hours' plunder.

My own home was continually in my mind. I could see my mother sitting alone among her household gods. I could see her walking through the rooms, touching now one thing, now another, things that remind her of my grandmother, of my great-grandmother, of old times, things that are part of her life... She cannot write to me, nor can I write to her. I long to go to her for a day, or only for an hour...

As I said this Elisabeth Kállay looked at me:

"Do you know how many of us are already in prison? Do you want to go there too?"

It seemed to me that my mother's face was leaning over me and that she repeated: "Don't worry about me, and don't come home till..."

A carriage drove through the gate, came slowly up the drive and stopped in front of the house. A carriage in the village! The hospitable generation which lived before us saw nothing terrifying in that. But now I asked myself: "Have they come to requisition? Are they agitators, Socialist delegates, or detectives? Are they on my track?"

My heart beat fast, and a plan occurred to me. I resolved that if they came for me I would escape by the other side of the house, where there is a little door under the walnut staircase, and that thence I should make for the vineyards, and over the hillock on to the main road. I was quite astonished to find how exactly I remembered every ditch, every lane, as if from the very start I had observed the country with a view to a possible escape.

Then came a sound of movement and of laughter, starting under the porch and spreading all over the house. The newcomer was a friend, Baroness Apor, lady-in-waiting to the Archduchess Augusta. She brought us newspapers and news. A Vienna paper gave a long account of how Count Louis Salm had boxed the ears of Michael Károlyi in the street— the latter was in Vienna on behalf of the Revolutionary Cabinet. As he was emerging from the door of a house of doubtful reputation Count Salm ran up to him: "Take that for the Italian front, that for Hungary..." and as the blows fell each was similarly explained. A crowd gathered round them and a cab was passing. Károlyi made desperate signs for it to stop. Then Count Salm exclaimed: "Look at him, this is Michael Károlyi who has betrayed Hungary!" The cabman swore a big oath, lashed out with his whip at Károlyi, turned his horse and drove on, while the blows were still falling hard. I wish it had been a Hungarian who had given them!

Baroness Apor told us that Archduke Joseph's palace had been occupied by the Red commander. The furniture had been carried off and 'communized' by the comrades. The Archduke and the Archduchess had been compelled to flee on the evening of the 21st. They escaped on foot in pouring rain, to the accompaniment of a good deal of shooting in the town, and hid with some faithful friends until next evening. Then they managed to escape in a ramshackle old coach through the excise barriers of Buda and made off for the hills. The Archduke travelled south with two aide-de-camps; the Archduchess went to Alcsuth after having given all her jewels to her husband for travelling expenses. He will attempt to get into communication with the French commander in the hope of raising the nation.

New hope!... The room seemed to brighten up and life ceased to seem a burden. Perhaps after a week, or a few days... No, neither after a few days, nor hereafter—because when it came to crossing the frontier into occupied territory the Archduke turned back: he could not bring himself to leave that last bit of our country which is the only hope of our resurrection.

Meanwhile his son had been arrested and had been taken on a springless cart to Kanizsa, his guards telling him all the way that Számuelly was waiting there to settle his business. They asked him if he wanted a 'black coat' for his journey, and pointed to trees: "This one would do nicely, or do you prefer that one?" Now he is imprisoned in Budapest.

So is the former Prime Minister, Alexander Wekerle, and Bishop Count Mikes, and Count George Károlyi who hates the Communists. Countess Raphael Zichy stayed at home, refusing to leave. Is she repeating her famous saying: "There is no terror, there is only cowardice!"

"Under pretense of looking for arms," Baroness Apor told us, "armed Red soldiers invade houses at night. The safe deposits have been broken open and pilfered by the Government. It is impossible to withdraw money from the banks. All jewelry worth more than two thousand crowns becomes 'public property.' Mine has been taken too. A friend of mine preferred to throw her pearls into the Danube. Anybody who still possesses anything is hiding it if he can. There is a perfect exodus to the hills of Buda. At first people only buried little jewel-cases. Then came the rumor of a new order. The larders were going to be ransacked. Off to the hills went the barrels of lard, the boxes of sugar and tea, the household linen."

One of us broke in:

"Yes, but what do people say, how long will this last?"

"Nobody knows. People are in despair. News is contradicted as soon as published. Károlyi negotiates with the Missions of the Entente in the name of the Bolshevik Government. The Italians, they say, are sympathetic. It is even said that they are disposed to recognize the Soviet Republic. The Italian delegate, Prince Borghese, is a great friend of Béla Kun and the beautiful Jewesses of the Commune. It is also rumored that a Boer general called Smuts is to be sent here to force the Bolshevik crowd to resign." Baroness Apor glared rigidly before her as if she saw something terrible. "Számuelly is getting more and more to the fore," she continued after a short pause. "The Government threatens in his name whenever it wants to cause alarm. The others are busy drawing up the new Constitution. They speak and issue orders as if things were to remain like this forever."

None of us said anything. Our thoughts were so similar that speech was superfluous.

* * *

April 4th.

SOMETIMES nobody visits us for days; but it happens occasionally that people come to see us. As soon as I hear their steps on the gravel I run and hide in my room. The other day while I was sitting there Countess Dessewffy was saying in the drawing-room that the police were after me, but that she knew I had made good my escape to Switzerland. It seemed quite amusing. With the exception of one friend nobody knows that I am here or who I am. This is Baron Jeszenszky, whose property is nearby, at Kövesd. He often goes to Budapest. Then we wait impatiently for the news he brings back. Anything that gives hope finds credence with us. Baron Jeszenszky waves his hand in despair: "Mark my words, this will never come to an end."

The more we contradict him the more pessimistic he becomes. If, however, we agree, he gets angry and becomes hopeful. "What lack of faith!"

I feel similarly inclined, and so does everybody else, for we express our doubt only in the hope of being contradicted; we try hard to raise some hope in ourselves and are angry when it is thrown over.

We went early to bed and I read Sir Thomas More. The book opened where the conquering Utopys reaches his island where he is going to found the realm of universal happiness:

> ... But Kyng Utopys, who.so name, as conqueror, the Iland beareth (for before his tyme it was called Abraxa) which also brought the rude and wild people to that excellent perfection in al good fassions, humanitye and civile gentilnes, wherein they nowe goe beyond al the people of the world: even at his firste arrivinge and enteringe upon the lande, forthwith obteynyge the victory... (sic)

Sir Thomas More, the forefather of Socialism, imagined it like that. He wanted to found his land of universal happiness on a gentle, civilized people. Will there ever be people like that on this earth? Until there is, Socialism will remain the island of Utopia.

* * *

April 5th.

THE men of the village Directorate came up to the castle today. There was some formality about their visit, and they wore their black Sunday hats. Mrs. Benjamin Kállay received them herself. The bad man of the village spoke the loudest among them, and whenever this occurred the others cast their eyes down and nudged their neighbors: "Come, speak up, now!" I thought of the little peacock-blue Sévres vases up in the drawing-room; the Persian dishes and the old hand-painted fans in the glass-case. How were they going to describe them in their inventory? One of them declared that no more wine must be brought up from the cellar, for prohibition had been enforced. Nothing in the house must be removed, for it all belongs henceforth to the State. The others nodded as they looked around. "The people from the towns are going to come soon." And so they left without making an inventory.

The day has not yet come, but what of the morrow? Incertitude is increasing daily. Everything becomes transitory. In one's plans one does not even dare to make arrangements for the following day. Generally one makes no plans at all. Days and hours become independent units, without continuity or cohesion among them.

The Sunday hats of the Directorate were flocking back to the garden gate. One of them lingered behind, then seized the opportunity of turning back. He stood there before us, an old man, humble, hat in hand, with sad eyes:

"Dear little lady," he stuttered shamefacedly, "might I ask your Excellency for a little wine? Nobody will know. I want it for an invalid. A young woman who is dying." A bottle was given to him and he hid it furtively under his coat.

The Soviet Government threatens with its summary jurisdiction anyone found drinking wine. Not even the sick are allowed any. But drunken soldiers stagger unmolested in the gutter. The People's Commissaries have champagne orgies in their special trains and throw the empty bottles from the windows. They have drinking bouts in the Soviet House of Budapest, the former Hotel Hungaria, which they have requisitioned. The occupants were expelled without notice and within a few hours the Commissaries, some with their wives, others with their mistresses, occupied the place.

Everything I see, everything I hear, carries my thoughts to the guilty town, bids them seek among its million people, for the sake of one! Today I received the first message from home. Charles Kiss, our faithful friend, has escaped from among the accursed walls and brought me a letter from my mother. She is well; she has already left for our cottage among the hills of Buda. She was in want of nothing, nobody interfered with her. They have not been looking for me. Thus Kiss brought me nothing but good news.

While I listened to him I was filled with joy: "Then there is no longer any reason why I should not go home!" At this his face changed suddenly. No, not yet, better wait a little longer... And as he argued the point I suspected his former statements more and more. So they had only been designed to re-assure me!

Hans Freitag, Councilor at the German Legation, had come to see my mother and had warned her that I ought to escape if I were still there. Now the removal of my mother to the hills had a different meaning to me: my mother had to choose between her flat in town and her cottage in the hills. Need for choice came suddenly and she had moved the previous day. But I learnt that the flat was now occupied by very decent people; the Red soldiers who brought them behaved quite nicely. They had put altogether three families and a school into the flat; they were Jews and Proletarians but it was all right, no harm had been done, everything had gone smoothly. Only a little furniture and a few pictures were left behind in the flat.

Slowly I began to visualize the whole thing. Red soldiers... That meant she had been expelled by force. All sorts of insignificant trifles swept through my head. The tiny treasures of the old show-case... The snuff-box which had a tinkling little tune hidden within it... The yellow porcelain dame with her crinoline and her unnaturally slender waist... Where have they gone to, those friends of my childhood? And the ash-tray which used to stand near the clock? Has it gone? And the water- colors? And my mother's work-basket, her patience cards? The crucifix from Ravenna on my bookcase? Who has removed it? My manuscripts, my books, my pictures?

The Jewish Commissary of Education had decreed that books left in houses became the property of the Soviet Republic. All collections of books have to be reported. Valuable pictures become common property.

Charles Kiss re-assured me: "Everything is still there," but I could believe his kind-hearted statements no longer. A torturing picture haunted me incessantly: I saw a home pulled to pieces, strange people in our rooms and the front door, through which my lonely mother had to leave, wide open. The subject had been changed a long while ago, but I had not noticed it. I realized it only when I heard someone say: "It will last longer than we had expected."

I shuddered as a hopeless silence ensued. The ticking of the clock above fell on our ears. One by one the minutes dropped into eternity seeming to make time unbearable. Yet from the silence of despair victorious hope dared to raise its head.

"The People's Commissaries seem to be already quarrelling among themselves," said Charles Kiss. "They are even said to have come to blows. Számuelly wanted to put the Red army into his own hands."

"Yes, they may quarrel over a question of power, but when it comes to oppressing us they hold together."

"Yet it ended with the downfall of Pogány. The adherents of Számuelly informed the Soldiers' Council that he intended to abolish the system of 'confidential men' which had been so successful in poisoning the mind of the remnant of our army. Now the Social-Communists require a well-disciplined, serviceable army.

"Marxism only sticks to its principles, ends and catch-words as long as they serve as weapons to attack society. The 'confidential men' would not stand the plan. It happened yesterday. In the afternoon they drew up the

International Red Regiment, which is ready for any mischief. Accompanied by an infuriated mob of dissatisfied workmen and hungry good-for-nothings they went up to the Royal Castle. They invaded St. George's Square, clamoring for Pogány. The 'confidential men' of the regiment broke into the Commissariat of War. From the balconies they urged their men on. The system of 'confidential men' to which Pogány owed his shameful power, by means of which he had removed Ministers of War and terrorized the whole nation into submission, now became the instrument of his own downfall."

The dogs barked somewhere in the grounds. This alone broke the silence. Then Charles Kiss went on:

"In a few minutes the news spread over the town. Many heard the howling of the demonstrators who were cursing Pogány. People were already saying that he had been hanged and that Béla Kun had been hanged at his side. Later on it turned out that the news was false. All that had happened was that the Cabinet had increased the number of its members and had made certain changes. There are now more Jewish People's Commissaries than ever. Pogány and Számuelly have become Commissaries for Education. Béla Kun controls the War Office. Then people found a new ray of hope. We put all our confidence in General Smuts."

"So the news was true after all?"

"We expected a lot of him," Kiss went on. "Budapest was confident that a British general, one of the Delegates of the Paris Peace Conference, would not come to an agreement with Béla Kun and his company. The town was full of hope. Everybody had some good news. Számuelly's declaration was attributed to the general's coming."

"What sort of declaration?"

He took a newspaper out of his pocket and spread it over the table. There it was, in huge type, in a conspicuous place. It was characteristic of the world we lived in that it was considered within the province of the Minister of Education to make such a declaration.

"For several days unscrupulous elements have been spreading the news that I intend giving permission for general plundering. This is a base calumny and a disgraceful lie. I appeal to the Comrades to give me an opportunity to face the scoundrels who spread this news and to make an example of them. I ask them to help me to put those who spread this news before a Revolutionary Tribunal and have summary justice meted out to them. Tibor Számuelly, Assistant. People's Commissary for Education."

"When it became known," Kiss went on, "that General Smuts, though he had ordered rooms in an hotel, had not even entered the town but had summoned Béla Kun to the railway station, there was no limit to our illusions. But it did not last. This morning the Communists informed us triumphantly of their success; the Entente had entered into negotiations with the Governments of Moscow and Budapest."

My mind reverted to Brest-Litovsk. We did not know it at the time, but it was there that we lost the war. Now even the victors may lose it in Budapest and Moscow.

"General Smuts came here," Kiss added sadly, "not to threaten but to negotiate. The journalist friends of the People's Commissaries told us that General Smuts had offered the Government a favorable line of demarcation. If Béla Kun will consent to come to some arrangement, the Powers are prepared to compel the Roumanians to retire eastwards and to form a neutral zone occupied by British, French and Italian troops. The journalists also say that the General will recommend in Paris that the interested States should hold a conference which would finally fix their respective frontiers. He promised to use his influence to persuade the Powers to invite Béla Kun's Government to Paris. He will have the blockade raised and provide fats and other articles of which we are in need. All he required in compensation was the cessation of all attempts to spread the idea of a world-revolution. The success made Béla Kun dizzy. He would be satisfied with nothing. The attempt of the Entente to compromise with him has strengthened his position incredibly, and now he is proclaiming to the world that the Great Powers are afraid of him. He wants no increase of territory, he wants free trade and free propaganda in the neighboring States."

Last autumn, the great collapsing Monarchy appealed to Wilson and asked for his intervention. Through Mr. Lansing, his Secretary of State, he sent the following answer: "We will not negotiate with you." And with cruel irony he referred the peace-begging Power to its little neighbors. Then he did not deign to speak to us, but he has no hesitation in bargaining with Béla Kun. Are they really afraid of him? Or do they think that he will surrender Hungarian nationality in exchange for the freedom of Bolshevism? Is the national ideal of Hungary more dangerous in the eyes of the Entente than the national ideal of the Jews? The British General has gone. His steps die away in the distance. He has knocked at our window and we could not move and appeal to him. The villains have tied our hands and gagged us and we strain at our bonds in helpless agony.

IV

THE woman for whom we were asked for wine yesterday was buried today. The coffin was placed on the ground in the clean-swept little farmyard, and her mother arranged the corpse as though she were putting it to bed. Suddenly she knelt down beside the coffin and with her trembling, rugged old hand stroked the rough boards and cried aloud: "Good God, why hast thou taken her from me, why could not I die in her place?..."

Thus do mothers address grim death. What will they say when the attempt is made to take their living children from them? Her lament became louder and louder and dominated the ceremony. The Cantor said farewell to the deceased in verses, singing them to an old-fashioned melody which he repeated over and over again. This melody contained the memory of ancient bards and the sorrows of wandering troubadours; the verses mentioned by name all the mourning relations, each of whom, as his name was pronounced, sobbed loudly, as though expressing his personal grief in the general mourning. When the husband was named he pressed his face into his doffed hat and his shoulders shook with sobs. The others had their turn, but the old woman alone lamented from the beginning to the end.

Everybody wept over his own sorrow, in the coffin alone there were no tears. The tree in the yard stretched over it, and as the branches swayed in the wind the dim sunlight threw their shadow over the coffin. The shadow revealed that there were fresh buds on the branches, signs of nature's resurrection, and I realized that spring was coming.

"*In Paradisum...*" The priest blessed the coffin, blessed it as he blesses an infant at a christening, the couples at a wedding, with the same large movement which has served since the time of Christ for the blessing on this earth of new life, of love and of death.

In Budapest the Red Power has decreed that from this day Christ's churches are to be closed and kinematographs established in them. The Christian priesthood is threatened with the halter. The teaching orders are expelled and the nuns driven from the bedside of the sick and the cradles of the orphans. The dresses of their Orders are torn from them. Their buildings become Communist meeting-places and the scenes of secret orgies.

Theoretical Socialism has declared that religion is the private affair of the individual. Now that it has got past the stage of theory and has entered that of bloodthirsty reality religion has ceased to be a private affair, for not even the soul must possess private property. Private property has been abolished and common property has been substituted. Religion is no longer a private affair, it is public business. And public business in Hungary is now controlled in the name of the Dictatorship of the Proletariat by twenty-six Jewish People's Commissaries, who this day crucify the Word with the same panting hatred with which they crucified Him two thousand years ago. And the people stand now as before, unimpressed, at the foot of the Cross, again not understanding what is being crucified above its head with laughter, contempt and hatred.

It is easier to drive cattle on than human beings; this the Communists realize. By taking from the people its religion they take everything from them but the couch, the platter and the cup; they deprive them at a stroke of morals, philosophy and beauty.

The people knelt round the coffin and prayed, because someone was there to tell them to pray; they turned to their inner selves, above the cup and the platter, because there was someone who told them that there was a God above.

Then the funeral procession wended its way out of the little farmyard. Four men lifted the coffin, one of them the dead woman's husband. His head leant against the boards as though leaning on her shoulder. The weeping crowd followed them up the hillside. The bell tolled in the steeple above the roofs. And the bell was still ringing for the dead when, the funeral over, the mood of the people had changed. The girls, gay in their finery, displayed their charms. Two farmers bargained over the purchase of a cow. A young man pinched the arm of a grinning maid...

*   *   *

April 7th.

NEWS reached us today. After driving the King from Schönbrunn, Vienna has driven him from Eckartsau too. An escort of British officers protected him and his family. Henceforth he is to live in Prangins. Thus the little mountainous region whence long ago Rudolph, Count of Habsburg, set out towards the Imperial Crown, bearing in his hand his great destiny, has now, after eight hunched years, received his heir, holding nothing in his hand but the past. But there is as much force in an historical past as in an historical future.

The event provokes a few sardonic lines, set among the brief news items of the Red papers. The French mob shouted insults at its King when he was taken to the Temple. Today the rabble shouts too. But the Hungarian nation has nothing in common with the rabble. The same crowd which knocked down one night the statue of Francis Joseph in Budapest and smashed the effigies of kings on the millenary memorial, is now vomiting insults shamelessly in the columns of its newspapers. But it is the foreign hand, the foreign voice, that acts and speaks.

The double-headed eagle which swooped down on so many thrones of Europe, has returned with broken wings to the mountains. Its shadow passed like a cloud over the fields of lost battles.

A short notice is all that the foreigners' press has to give to the King of Hungary. Those who fawned before him in endless columns so long as they could use him against the country, now have no more to give to him when he in turn can give no longer. Cowardice knows no mean between cringing and slinging mud. As for the Hungarians, whatever they may think, in presence of the misfortune of a man and a King, they bow respectfully and in silence.

King Charles IV expiates not only his own mistakes, but those of his predecessors for four centuries. The descendant pays with the loss of his country, because the ancestors would never make Hungary their home. The dynasty allowed its advisers systematically to weaken Hungary. And this camarilla, to keep the people of the Great Plain in check, has let loose upon it every possible nationality, ending with the immigrant gabardined fathers of Béla Kun and Számuelly. But it was not alone upon us, it was upon them too. The Hapsburgs never understood that our strength was their strength and our weakness their weakness. Their whole country was made up of peoples which were attracted by their kindred beyond the borders. The peoples of the Monarchy were all looking outward. The petted Austrians looked towards Germany, the Poles towards Warsaw, their favorites, the Czechs, towards the Slav giant, the Roumanians towards young Roumania, the Southern Slavs towards Serbia, the Italians towards Italy, the Jews towards the Jewish Internationale. The Hungarians alone had no such kin. We did not look longingly anywhere, nobody tempted us beyond the frontiers. And yet the rulers preferred all the other peoples to us, and loaded them with goods, treasures and power. And now the peoples have gone, taking with them our land, our goods, our treasures. This is the harvest of four hundred years policy of *divide et impera*; the peoples are divided, but the Habsburgs rule no longer over them. Between the torn pieces the crown has fallen to the ground.

*   *   *

April 8th.

THERE were elections yesterday in what is left of Hungary. Now that Socialism is in power it shows how it carries out the principles of universal suffrage and secret ballot, which for decades were the catchwords with which it endeavored to seduce the electorate. The time has come when no obstacle to Marxism exists, all ways and means are at its disposal. In the village since early morning men and women have been flocking to the communal hall. In the Soviet Republic, Proletarians alone have a vote, but those who do not avail themselves of their right are deprived of their food tickets and are liable to be summoned before the Revolutionary Tribunal. Priests have no votes. Hungarian gentry cultivating their own land have no votes, nor have crippled heroes nor invalided officers. Lawyers are not Proletarians. But any Russian or foreign Jew can vote if he is a Proletarian. And the Jews who, before the social upheaval, claimed that they belonged to cultured classes, have now turned Proletarians. Even the sons of bank directors. At the town-hall door stood a man who handed out the printed list of the official candidates.

The voters looked at the list. One or two read it and swore.

"Let's cross this one out and write our cousin's name instead" the women advised. The returning officers shouted: "Let no one dare to cross out the names of candidates or substitute others in their place!"

"Well, Mr. Comrade," a labourer asked, "then what am I to do with this bit of paper?"

"You just go and vote with it, comrade," was the answer, and the ticket was taken out of his hand.

"Devil take it!" exclaimed the men, passing lists over the table. And in this spirit the proud and triumphant Proletariat elected its council.

In the neighboring villages and even in Budapest it was done in the same way. Comrade Landler's emissaries had prepared the lists of candidates in advance. Preliminary meetings and the assembling of crowds were prohibited. Even the privileged class of Budapest working men only saw the printed list of the candidates when the voters entered the booth.

Somebody who had visited Budapest told us who were the candidates of the People's Commissaries. In one single constituency there were twenty-two comrades whose name was Weiss—a typically Jewish name. Under the supervision of Red soldiers everything went off smoothly. In one single ward only was there any disturbance. There the terrorists had not dared to forbid gatherings; consequently the electors put their heads together, made up a list of their own, and defeated the official candidates. This little incident was quickly settled by the Commissary for the Interior: he simply annulled the election and the official list was declared duly elected. Socialism has shown how it applies its own principles when it achieves power. The advocates of the unrestricted freedom of the press tolerate nothing but the official newspapers. The champions of free assembly will not tolerate the gathering of a few people in the street. Those who incessantly clamored for a reduction of working hours have introduced forced labour. The frenzied enemies of militarism shout at their recruiting meetings: "Join the Red army!" The foul-mouthed demagogues of secret universal suffrage impose on the people their official candidates.

The foreign intruders have put the roof on the edifice of which Hungarian laborers had been the masons and bricklayers. Does Hungarian labour see at last for what ends its trade-unions have been used? Those who attained power through the trade-unions are now attempting to destroy them. By a single decree the Jewish tyrants of the Soviet Republic have abolished the unions. The Commissaries of Hungary boldly declare in their official newspaper, 'The People's Voice':

> Part of their task has been achieved by the power displayed in the great battle of class-war. They caused the upheaval of the Proletarian Revolution. Class-war is marching on victoriously and has left trade-unionism behind it. It has become superfluous. The humanitarian task of trade-union organizations must come under State control.

* * *

April 9th.

CATASTROPHES get more and more frequent, evil spreads and takes root. Early in the morning of the 7th a Soviet Republic was proclaimed in Münich. Will Bolshevism stop there or will it involve unfortunate Red Austria? If our premonitions are realized, the horrible rule which attempts the subjugation of the world will extend from the Eastern border of Asia to the banks of the Rhine.

Bestial tyranny spreads like a deluge over the earth, and the bloodless victims of the war are dragged helplessly into the vortex. It has already swept away towns, countries, even continents in its uncurbed stream. It has surged up from under the earth through the gratings of gutters, through the doors of dark dwellings, down the marble staircases of banks, over the columns of the newspapers. The groping, mystical Slav, the high-spirited yet conservative Hungarian, the meditative clumsy Teuton, what a contrast of races! Yet the realization of the Soviet system has been accompanied in every case by wonderfully similar symptoms. The awful conception shows no trace whatever of the racial characteristics of the three peoples, yet it has been carried through on the same plan and by people of the same psychology in Moscow, Budapest and München.

When Russia collapsed Kerensky was ready, and Trotsky's spirit was watching behind Lenin's shadow. When Hungary was fainting and reeling from loss of blood, there, behind Károlyi, were Kunfi, Jászi and Pogány on the look-out, and they were followed by Béla Kun and his band. And when Bavaria began to totter, Kurt Eisner was waiting to organize the first act. As with us and with Russia, the second act followed and there stood Max Levian (Lewy), the Moscow Jew, to proclaim the repetition of the Proletarian Republic and the replica of Hungarian and Russian Bolshevism.

While I was tracing the connection of the bloody events, my mind turned to certain incidents of the past. Early spring was looking through my window and gentle winds fanned my face. But I thought of a dense, sticky fog. It was from the fog that a man's howl rose: "Long live the Revolution! To death with Tisza!" There it was again, howling from the staircase of the House of Parliament: "Let us see no more soldiers!" What demoniacal power, hidden by the fog, prompted these cries? What power cast its spell to lure a haughty, brave nation into shame, cowardice and perdition? Months have passed since I first asked this question, and the obvious answer revolted my conscience, which required time to be convinced. But Calvary has taught me the lesson. Now I seek no longer, I know. It is not by accident that the scourge and the executioner, the law and the law-giver, the judge and the sentence, of the Turanian Hungarians, the Teutonic Bavarians and the Slav Russians were one and the same. The racial differences of the three peoples are too great to render that mysterious resemblance possible. It is clear that it must originate from the soul of another people which lives among them, but not with them, and has triumphed over all three. The demon of the Revolution is not an individual, not a party, but a race among the races. The Jews are the last people of the Ancient East who survived among the newer peoples of shorter history. As the carriers of biblical tradition they have been assured a certain tolerance and they look for the accomplishment of certain ancient curses. Despised in some places, they were feared in others, but everywhere they remained forever foreigners.

The Jew comes uninvited and declines to go when dismissed. He spreads and yet holds together. He penetrates the bodies of the nations. He invisibly organizes his own nation among alien peoples. He creates laws beyond the law. He denies the conception of 'patrie' but has a 'patrie' of his own which wanders and settles with him. He scoffs at other people's conception of God and yet builds churches of his own everywhere. He laments the fallen walls of Jerusalem and drags the ruins invisibly with him. He complains of his isolation but builds secret ways as arteries of the boundless city which has by now spread practically throughout the world. His connections and communications reach everywhere. Otherwise how can it be possible that his finances and his press should, wherever they may be centered, strive for the same goal all over the world? How is it that his racial interests are identical in a Ruthenian village and in the heart of New York? He praises one individual, and the praise rings over the globe. He condemns another, and that man's ruin begins wherever he be. Orders are given in mysterious secrecy. What the Jew finds ridiculous in other people, he keeps fanatically alive in himself. He teaches anarchy and rebellion only to the gentiles, he himself obeys blindly the directions of his invisible leaders.

Mirabeau was led towards the Revolution by Moses Mendelssohn and the influence of beautiful Jewesses. They were there, in Paris, behind every revolution, and they appear in history among the leading spirits of the Commune of 1871. But they are only visible during the hours of incitement and success; they are not to be found among the martyrs and the sufferers. When the returning powers of order proceeded to take revenge on the Commune, Marx and Leo Frankel had fled.

It was during the days of the Turkish Revolution that a Jew said proudly to my father: "We made that: the Young Turks are Jews." I remember at the time of the Portuguese Revolution, Marquis Vasconcellos, the Portuguese Minister in Rome, telling me: "The Revolution of Lisbon is instigated by Jews and Freemasons." And today, when the greater half of Europe is in the throes of revolution, the Jews lead everywhere in accordance with their concerted plans. Plans like these cannot be conceived in a few months or a few years. How, then, is it possible that people have not noticed it? How could such a worldwide conspiracy be concealed when so many people were involved? The easy-going and blind, the bribed, wicked or stupid agents of the nation did not know what the game was. The organizers in the background belonged to the only human race which has survived antiquity and has remembered how to guard a secret. That is the reason why not a single traitor was found among them.

* * *

April 10th.

BARON Jeszenszky paid us a visit.

"You would not recognize Budapest any longer. There are queues in front of all the restaurants. Many people take up their seat on the curb early in the morning, so as to make sure of a dinner. They have to take tickets beforehand if they want to get a meal, just as one used to book one's seat for the theatre. The meals too are like stage meals, for they consist of tiny portions of bad food which have to be gulped down in a hurry because the following number is waiting impatiently. A porridge of millet, greens and stewed cabbage, that is the menu. That is the food for which people wait for hours and pay exorbitant sums. They enter hungry and leave hungry. They stagger, sick with hunger. Everybody is emaciated."

Only the new privileged classes, the families of People's Commissaries, the millionaires of the Revolution and the bodyguard of the Cabinet, the 'Terror Boys,' live well. I thought of the Batthyány palace. A band of terrorists occupied it in the first days of the Commune, and they have remained there ever since. The grand drawing-room, where I used to see masses of azaleas between the magnificent old furniture, is theirs, with everything that artistic and beauty-loving generations have collected. I wonder who listens now to the ticking of the old clock which once belonged to Michael Apafi, Prince of Transylvania? What hands finger the ivory Christ of Countess Louis Batthyány? Dreadful tales are told of the palace. It is said that those who are dragged there by the terrorists are never seen again.

Baron Jeszenszky then spoke of other things.

"Palaces are treated worse than other places. The finer the mansion the dirtier the people who are installed in it. Cooking ranges are put into the drawing-rooms, their chimneys rest against the brocade-covered walls. Libraries are transformed into sculleries."

Somebody mentioned the National Club.

"The whole place is unspeakably filthy," Jeszenszky said. "The silver, the whole equipment, the library, have all been confiscated. The office which disposes of the property of the Church has been established there. An unfrocked priest of the Piarist Order sits there organizing the despoiling of the Church and the confiscation of the property of the various creeds. The provincial Soviets receive their orders to attack convents and the palaces of bishops from this place."

Evening was darkening the windows. The clock struck. For a while we stayed with Jeszenszky, then we walked towards the village.

"Let us look at that house which is for sale," said Elisabeth Kállay, as we turned off the main road.

We crossed a small farmyard. The house was surrounded by mud, and it took some time before the good wife could be found. She asked us to wait as the master was out, and brought us chairs. A young man strolled out from the stable, doffed his hat, and sat down on the stairs. Now and then he looked stealthily at us, then went on smoking his pipe in silence.

Lenke Kállay spoke to him.

"One knows little that is good and little that is bad about this new order," he said cautiously. "There are some who like it and some who don't. It may be true that the Government intends to give every farmer three hundred acres and make them free of taxes." Then he cast his eyes down and began to stir the mud with the point of his boot. "You see, they will confiscate nothing but big fortunes, and that for justice's sake."

The sound of a cart was heard approaching from the main road. Elisabeth Kállay turned in that direction.

"I have heard that carts and horses are being requisitioned for the Red army."

The attitude of the man changed suddenly. He raised his head threateningly and his voice was full of rage: "Just let them try. I will knock down the first who touches mine!"

* * *

April 11th-13th.

PALM Sunday. Spring has come. Easter is approaching through awakening nature, and yet this Palm Sunday is very different from all those I can remember. The days of persecution, forgotten for thousands of years, are rising from their grave and haunting us. Life is like the ravings of a fever-stricken brain; the Christian faith is persecuted in Hungary today. Our churches are in danger. Kunfi, the People's Commissary for Education, the Jew who has so often changed his religion, has decreed that the priests must read from the pulpit every Sunday for three weeks only that which they are directed to read.

The apathetic village has cast off its apathy: as if rising in defense of its property it becomes demonstrative. In the be-ribboned costumes of the country, girls in white shirts, with long waists and short skirts, women in shawls, are going up the hillside. Behind them comes the throng of men. The procession has a determined obstinate look about it. Besides its faith, beyond its prayers, there is in the soul of this people the old Hungarian spirit of rebellion. There are many of them; the whole village, even the invalids, have turned up. The banners of the church are swaying slowly, higher and higher up the hill. A cross, carried aloft, shows against the sky. The little sun-kissed square in front of the church swarms with men in black and women in all colors of the rainbow. Bells ring and the smell of incense pervades the cold air of the church. Palm leaves are consecrated by the priest at the altar.

I hid behind the Kállays in the dim light of the oratory. The crowd surged at the end of the aisle, furrowed faces, seamed with toil. In front of them little girls, starched little figures rendered artificially ugly, their tightly plaited hair standing up on the sides of their heads, like little horns ornamented with ribbons. The boys stood on the other side. Those who stood bare-footed on the cold flags raised their feet alternately to warm them against their legs. A tall boy nudged his small brother. The little one looked back, but prayed on without laughing. Even the children seemed more serious than usual. I have never seen a more serious crowd.

The poor village organ struggled pantingly with the Gregorian chants. Under the motionless church banners the human voices rose, some high, some low, a little out of tune and clumsy. Yet the ancient liturgical song, the thousand-year-old mournful song of Palm Sunday was very touching.

"... And they betrayed the Son of Man to be crucified..."

These words, so often heard, fell like blows on my heart, and had now a new meaning for me. I felt that this Palm Sunday was not a commemoration of the past, but a statement of the dark happenings of the present. Christ was undergoing a fresh Passion on this earth. The ancient plaintive tune of the Passion continued in the church.

"Then did they spit in His face, and buffeted Him; and others smote Him with the palms of their hands, saying Prophesy unto us, thou Christ, who is he that smote Thee?"

As if all the church were thinking the same, a shudder went through the crowd: *the same people had smitten Him two thousand years ago.*

"... And when He was accused, He answered nothing..."

It seemed an awful duty to repeat the cry of the Jews from the Gospels: "Let Him be crucified!" And the words followed by which the people of Jerusalem accepted the responsibility for the sentence:

"His blood be on us and on our children!"

There was a moment's silence, as if the people were following the burden carried by their voices. And then, as from afar, the song resumed:

"... And led him away to crucify Him..."

The organ, like a decrepit old shepherd, gathered the flock together. The voices rose in unison and clamored in such despair as has probably never been heard in this our land:

"My God, my God, why hast Thou forsaken Me?"

The people chanted it with pale faces, with broken hearts, and in that moment every one of them was Christ and Christ's words were their own.

The sounds had died away, and yet a feeling as of a wound remained. The church door opened and through the doorway the bright sunshine floated in. And the centuries-old hymn of Hungarian Catholicism rang out in a last appeal. It spread, rose, and mingled with spring, and its eastern rhythm and western faith clamored to the endless blue sky.

*   *   *

April 14th.

NOWADAYS I often feel like one who has lost his way in an unknown country on a dark night. He dares not move: he stands in the dark and waits for the sun to rise. But sunrise never seems to come, his terror becomes insufferable, and his mind becomes unhinged.

The whole of Hungary is in darkness today. Those who were once together are separated. Each isolated district hears its tribulation in solitude. What is happening in Transylvania, in Upper Hungary, down in the South, beyond the Danube, or in Budapest itself? In the dark one hears nothing but the awful crash of collapse, one is ignorant what has fallen down and where the cataclysm happened. Then all of a sudden news comes in secret whispers. The whole country is falling. In Transylvania and in the South the Roumanians and Serbians rule with the scourge in their hands. In Upper Hungary the Czechs labour to fill the prisons. They persecute and punish everything Hungarian. But for that, life must be more tolerable there than in the Red area, because there people have the hope of resurrection. The events here, if they are to continue, can only end in death. In Budapest and in all that remains of Hungary the miscreants are erecting gallows. At first they promised integrity, bread, peace and freedom. Now they are sneering at our territorial integrity. They give us starvation instead of bread, a Red army instead of peace. Here and there the disillusioned, betrayed victims raise their voices. Deception, as a means of government, can never be anything but transitory, and can only be followed by the honest truth—or by terrorism. What will become of us? How often have we asked that question?

I gazed out upon Nature's calendar. When I left home it was still winter; it snowed now and then and the bare branches showed up black against the bleak sky. Then one day the sickle of the moon appeared, like the windblown flame of a torch, above the hillock, and green clouds covered the bushes. The green clouds have turned into young leaves and beyond the hillock above the steeple night raises a round red disk in the sky. Many days have passed. Enough days for the moon to grow to its full size.

*   *   *

The Night of April 14th-15th.

THE embers have died in the stove. I watched them for a long time: now they are collapsing, and it is cold. There has never been a cold like this, yet I sit here and write, though there is no reason for it. But after all, I do not write for others, I do not write to keep a record of my thoughts, I write only to relieve my feelings.

Charles Kiss came this evening, running the gauntlet of the police in order to bring me news.

It may be an afterthought, but it seems to me that I knew he was coming. I believe I felt something impending, something I had feared for days, something unavoidable. In the evening the others had discussed the coming Easter festivities. I did not join in the conversation; I kept out of it whenever I could, and perhaps it was this that gave me a lonely feeling. There is such a thing as presentiment.

I am not allowed to stay here.

Today everybody who is Hungarian is outlawed and homeless on every inch of Hungarian soil. To their bloodhounds our 'rulers' throw the lives of those who dare to fight against them. I have fought against them and my life has been proscribed.

They have selected for the deed a certain Mikulics, a one-eyed

56

terrorist, nicknamed 'the Cyclops' by the others. I never heard of him before, but it appears that he is the plenipotentiary chief of the Air Service. Számuelly said of him that he was so cruel that even he could not stand up against him. This man has been commissioned to settle with me. He himself said: "I must do away with her." And henceforth my life will depend upon my ability to avoid him. There is another one also who is after me, and he too is quite unknown to me. He is the head of the newly established Secret Service, and is a bosom friend of Számuelly. He is called Otto Korvin, though his real name is Klein. He is a hunchbacked little Jew who used to be a bank clerk.

The idea of it fills me with terror. A hand seems to be feeling for me, slowly, steadily, trying to grasp me. I have had that feeling ever since Charles Kiss told me about it. Faithful friend! How concerned he was, and how pale he looked; he could only talk in whispers. When his carriage stopped under the porch, Lenke Kállay shouted to him:

"Do you bring good news?"

"I'll tell you when we are alone." And when no one else was within earshot he told us the news he brought. I remember clearly that I nodded and wondered at the same time why I did so. My mother has been examined... Eight armed soldiers surrounded our cottage. Meanwhile detectives examined everybody in the house separately. It lasted two hours. They were threatening and declared that it was useless to try to deceive them, they were on my track and knew full well where I was.

My mother showed the letter I had written to her and declared it had reached her from the other side of the Danube. That was all she knew about me. She seemed cool and composed all the time and she looked so haughtily at them that suddenly they ceased calling her comrade. They even took their hats off and talked to her bareheaded. After they had left, my sister Mary found my mother in her room lying on the sofa. She was in a state of collapse and cried bitterly. On her table lay the warrant for my arrest.

"I cannot bear the sight of it," she said. "Put it somewhere where I cannot see it."

No tears came to my eyes, and yet I was sobbing inwardly and unseen. I saw by their faces that they thought I was quite collected.

My brothers and sisters were questioned too, principally Vera, who had worked so much with me in the interests of the Counter-revolution, and Géza. They were called to the police station. Charles Kiss also was arrested. He came before a Jewish monster called Juhász, the head of the investigation department of the political police. The other officials were just like him. The office was all dirt, confusion and Jews.

"They filled me with disgust and when I found myself unguarded I escaped." He laughed like a naughty boy who had played a prank. And I laughed too, though my heart was breaking. Then suddenly I thought, what if they were to arrest my mother in my place? Or take some other hostage?... The room reeled round me at the thought.

"I must go home and give myself up," I stammered.

All of them began to argue at this. It would be sheer madness, they said; nobody would suffer for me.

"I shall bring disaster on this house too..." I tried to find words to express my regret. Meanwhile the others were planning my escape. I only realized this when I heard that my family wanted me to fly the country.

"Through Balassagyarmat..." I heard Elisabeth approve the plan. Aladár Huszár was sure to help me across the river Ipoly.

It was Lenke Kállay who pointed out that it was essential that the servants should not know whither I went. I was to travel to Aszód as if I were going to Budapest, turn back there and go to Balassagyarmat. I shuddered with disgust: the station of Aszód with its red flags, the fat political delegate, the fiddler, the Internationale, came to my mind. I remembered a seat on the platform and reflected that I should have to sit there from seven in the morning till five in the afternoon. The people would be able to look at me without my being able to hide my face.

As soon as I was alone these details assailed me with redoubled force. I leant my forehead against the windowpane, which felt smooth and cold, and soothed me as a cool hand might have done. I looked at my watch. It had stopped: I had forgotten to wind it up. A carriage rattled by under the window; it was taking Charles Kiss to the station. Tomorrow at the same time it would carry me, and I shall be alone. I had refused to go with him, my fate must not be shared by others: anyone arrested in my company would be dragged down with me to the same disaster. Let him go, if possible, in peace; let him make his escape, my gratitude will go with him. No one has over shown me greater kindness than he.

V

MY last day in Berczel. It seems to me as if a mischievous hand had passed over the pleasant picture and had effaced it. Here and there a tinge remained. This morning the sun was shining on the lawn in front of my window and in its golden rays the dog scampered eagerly. Afternoon wore quickly on, and the sun shone no longer. The ears of corn rustled together in the gilt clock on the wall. How many grains are there still in store for me?

Young George Kállay went for Baron Jeszenszky, whose advice was certain to be worth having. When he was told what had happened he grasped the situation at once. He wrote me a letter of recommendation to the dismissed magistrate of Aszód and took charge of my papers.

"I shall put them up the chimney. They may not find them there."

Beyond the garden on the crest of the hillocks the train from Aszód was passing along like a tiny, smoking toy. This train had been haunting me the whole day. Now it was gone. For this one day I need not fear the arrival of the bloodhounds. And if they should come tomorrow they will find the place empty.

"A carriage from the station should be here by now," said Lenke. So they had been thinking of the same thing. The horn of a motor car resounded on the main road. Mrs. Kállay looked up from her embroidery: "I had a bad dream last night. I dreamt that a big motor stopped in front of the house and that detectives stepped out of it."

The car had passed the garden gate, but the shock it had given us remained. Now I could think of one thing only; the slow passage of time and the wish that it would pass faster. If only I were gone from here and knew that the people who had befriended me were no longer incurring danger on my behalf! I made a miserable attempt to say something to that effect: "Thank you, and please forgive me." Henriette Apor gave me her box of matches: there were only a few left in it, yet it was a precious gift, for there had been no matches in the house for a long time.

I never thought a human being could be so alone in the world. Now everybody must be for himself only. I had premonitions of death, and thought of those I had seen, whose deaths I had witnessed. I began to understand their feelings at the approaching struggle in which none could render them aid. It had been of no use to hold their hands, to adjust their pillows, to sit up with them. And now there was nobody even to hold my hand, to sit up with me.

The rain began to fall in scattered drops, as though a sad spirit had wept upon the windowpanes. On that fateful night of March it had rained thus when I left my home and the streets resounded with the shout: "Long live the Dictatorship of the Proletariat!" These had been the words that brought calamity upon us. Here with the rain the feeling of outlawry and isolation seized me, and I faced a dark vindictive world. I shut my eyes, wishing I could escape from myself.

I may have slumbered restlessly, tossing about, for a few minutes; then I jumped up as if I had been shaken and began to dress with needless speed by the light of the candle. It was dark outside when the door of my room opened quietly. Elisabeth Kállay was standing there. She came to bid me farewell, and the action steadied me. We shook hands: "God bless you!"

When the big gate of the castle opened before me, the piercing cold cut me like a knife, and I shrank back. Night stood in front of me like a damp black wall, through which I must pass. For an instant I felt as if someone were dogging my footsteps. The gate slammed with a bang behind me and made me feel as if all gates had closed on me and as if I were excluded from everything; a homeless, countryless, beggarly wanderer on earth.

I penetrated deeper and deeper into the damp blackness, making my way through the garden towards the stables where the carriage was waiting for me... The wheels splashed in the mud, rain poured, my shoulders and my skirt round my knees were soaked. Dawn was breaking when we reached the main road.

From the way-side station a dark, cold little train carried me through the frosty morning. I may have fallen asleep for awhile, but I remember the last violent jerk: Aszód! It was just the same: putrid filth covered the platform. There, on the side of a wagon, was the inscription written in human excrement: "Death to the bourgeois!" The station was if possible even dirtier than before. Not-withstanding the early hour, a sad and sleepy deputation with red flags was waiting there. One of them said at the exit that there was going to be a recruiting meeting, a comrade from Budapest was going to make a speech, his special train was already signaled. This made me hurry. The parcel of food given me before I started was pulled from under my arm, but it did not matter. My valise was already in the cloakroom and I hurried off towards the town. A red flag was floating on the Reformatory like a piece of raw flesh. There were flags everywhere, and strange big posters covered the walls. The lines on them appeared to represent mad knots of tangled intestines. When I looked more closely, my eyes made out the outlines of horrible soldiers, pregnant giant women, skulls, blood-stained workmen, bare to the waist, glaring at me. "Join the Red army!" "Alcohol is dead!" "To arms, Proletarians!"

I was so tired that everything frightened me. The bare trees on the sidewalk stood in a row as if waiting for victims to be hanged on them. The dais which stood covered with red under the grey sky in the middle of the marketplace looked like a scaffold and the houses seemed to watch it wickedly, disdainfully. The streets were covered with mud: the repulsive mess spread all over the place and the houses alone seemed to keep it within its bed. If one of them had been removed, it seemed that the mud would have overflowed the whole country.

People lived in these surroundings, dragged themselves resignedly along in the black mire, surrounded by the monstrous posters. Nobody rebelled, they just let themselves sink and drown. This resignation stretched beyond the town, and the whole country surrendered to its fate.

A Jew dressed like a townsman except for his cap passed in a carriage, stopped, and beckoned. Two men of the working class ran up to him. He pointed towards the market and gave orders. The men listened respectfully. Then the man in the cap looked at me, and as his gaze fell on me, I felt the blood rush to my head, for he turned back as if he knew me. It seemed to me that I too recognized this weak face, these thick, soft lips, these shapeless ears. Perhaps it has bowed before me over the counter of some Budapest bank, this puffy face which now looked slimy and dark as if it had been shaped out of the mud. But it passed from my sight.

A number of Red soldiers were loafing in front of a low house. They wore flat caps ornamented with red ribbons, and red-bordered blouses after the Russian pattern. This group impressed me strangely and filled me with anxiety: they were not Hungarian soldiers, they were enemies. They were the armed servants of a foreign power, the sole relics of our disbanded army! The Red army! Hungarian national guards, Hungarian hussars, were you disbanded to become like these? This was the first time I had seen the Red guards of the Soviet.

Behind the soldiers the walls were posted with orders and regulations.

A door was wide open and machine guns could be seen pointing from the disordered yard within. A few steps further a woman was standing on the pavement talking through an open window. She kept glancing anxiously behind her and I heard her sigh. Nowadays only those who look round in fear and sigh can be trusted, so I went up to her.

"Can you tell me where M. Sárkány, the magistrate, lives?"

"That door there." The woman looked frightened and went away quickly. I entered a small house.

"No, Comrade Sárkány is not in, he has left town."

The earth seemed to give way under me. What was I to do? Could they let me in, I asked. I had come from far and was tired. But it was no good. Then I said I had a message, and at this I was allowed to enter. It was still early in the day. I had a long time to wait. Then Mme. Sárkány came in. While she read Baron Jeszenszky's letter, she became more and more excited.

"Then... I see... That is the reason the Reds have been looking this morning for a lady and a gentleman."

I thought of Charles Kiss. Was it possible they were looking for us?

"You cannot stay here," said Mme. Sárkány. "The house is watched. Bokányi has come from Budapest and is going to give an address in the marketplace. There are journalists with him. They are going to be quartered here and they are sure to recognize you." She turned very pale. "No, you cannot stay here. The best thing you can do is to take the next train and travel on to Hatvan."

The instinct of self-preservation rebelled in me so that I was astonished at the heat, with which I replied: "That would be to run straight into the prison gate. Why does everybody send me nearer Budapest, when the train is the most likely place where I could be recognized?"

"Here you are not in safety for a minute."

"If I could get a carriage..." Then a sudden idea came to me. "I could go to Iklad, to Countess Ráday..."

Mme. Sárkány nodded and left the room at once. How long she was away I could not tell, I only know that she came back once more and told me to get ready as there would be a carriage for me presently. I was very cold, and asked for a cup of tea. Then I hesitated before making my next request. Could I have a few matches? In great haste she gave me some. "Be quick... Be quick!"

The door was torn open and an old lady stood on the threshold. Her face was grey and she clasped her head between her hands.

"It is too late. The Reds have taken the carriage!"

I went out all the same. Three soldiers stood near a cart and I pressed money into the hand of one of them. He looked at it stealthily so that the others should not see. I implored them to let me have the cart. I did not want to go far, not half an hour, and I would send it back....

While they were debating the matter I suddenly jumped into the cart and the driver whipped up his horses. "To the station, for my luggage!"

The soldiers shouted insults after us but the noise of the wheels drowned their words. The cart was covered with liquid manure. There was a hole in one of the bottom boards and through it I could watch the road running past. I shuddered; once more I had to cross this awful town.

At the station I snatched my valise. "Be quick! Drive on!" Then suddenly I caught sight of the mud-faced man with the cap. The coachman looked back at me and seemed to understand my trouble; he gave the horses their heads and the rickety little cart flew over the sea of mud. The puffy face looked after me, but we turned off into a side street and the low houses and closed shops were quickly left behind. Astonished faces peeped out of the windows: I must have looked rather quaint in my town dress on a manure cart! Motor-cars passed from the opposite direction, probably carrying agitators from Budapest. Nowadays one only sees Jews in motor-cars. Instinctively I covered my face with my handkerchief. The road passed under the walls of a fine old castle: its outlines appeared for an instant against the grey sky from among the trees of the park. It was the only spot of beauty in the sea of mud.

"The one who lived there committed suicide," the driver said, pointing with his whip towards the castle. The board put across the cart which served me as a seat was jumping to and fro. I caught hold of the edges of the cart and leant forward.

"Who lived there?"

"It used to be a boarding school. Little ladies were taught in it."

I asked for more details.

"Well, you see," he said, weighing his words, "when the new order of things came, a comrade was sent down here. He was no older than fifteen and he was a Jew, the beggar was. He used to declaim to the school children in the marketplace..."

I asked him to go on.

"I am ashamed to speak of these things," the man grumbled, "but, with your leave, that son of a bitch used to explain aloud there in the marketplace how children were produced. He also said that one need not obey one's parents. He also said that it did not matter if girls went wrong, it was only the priests who pretended that it was a sin. No more need to worry about bastards, the State would look after them." He pushed his hat back on his head and expectorated violently. "Damn his eyes! No more

God, no more honor! Here in the boarding school he said the same thing as in the marketplace. He encouraged the little misses to make love freely with the boys. He had pictures to show them how it was done. The headmistress just wept and wrung her hands. At last she did for herself."

The cart rattled. Something seemed to shake within me too. I looked down and saw the road through the hole in the bottom: the earth receded rapidly under the cart. When I looked up at last the town was no longer in sight. I had left the execution ground.

Rain now began to fall anew, but I did not heed it, for a fresh breeze was blowing over the fields, and those whom I met, peasants on carts or on foot, were different from those in town. A village came in view, a. house, a garden full of flowers. The cart entered the yard of Iklad, and a girl came running towards me from the corridor:

"They are not at home! Since they have been taken to Aszód they have not been allowed to come home."

I was very cold and very tired: "Might I stay here a little—till the train for Balassagyarmat comes?"

"Please don't!" exclaimed the frightened girl. "We are expecting the Communists every minute. They are coming to requisition things."

"Of course, it does not matter..." And I thought of the heavy clang with which the gate of Berczel had closed behind me. All gates were closed as this one now.

"Let us go," I said to the coachman.

By this time the girl had recovered her senses. "You might go to the house of the railway guard, and wait for the train there. Uncle Nagy, the guard, is a kind man, he'll let you." And she added something about bringing me some dinner when the Communists were gone.

Under centenarian trees, on the other side of the road, the guard's house was hidden beside the roadway. A fowl-house, a little stack of wood, a garden with quaint little flower-beds... A tall elderly man, dressed in the blouse of the railway guards, came towards me. He touched his cap and asked me what I wanted. The office was closed, the train would not arrive till five... So he was going to send me away too... I felt again how tired I was, wet to the bone, and ravenously hungry. I spoke slowly, so as to gain time and to be able to stay for a little longer under a roof, out of the rain, and also to nurse my hopes a little. But the man did not send me away. He shrugged his shoulders:

"Of course you are welcome to stay here if you like. But you won't find it over comfortable."

I laughed from sheer joy, laughed aloud. I could stay, and it was my host who apologized! Tears came to my eyes: comfort? He did not realize what royal comfort he offered me. A corner where I would withdraw out of sight, a nook whence I should not be driven, a seat which is not drenched with rain and on which I might rest.

His wife came in too, a kindly little woman, aged before her time. She invited me into the room and wiped a chair with her apron, then began splitting wood in the kitchen. When the fire had burnt up she opened the door so as to let in the warmth.

Warmth! As it slowly thawed me it also thawed my heart. At first my mind remained inactive; I was just happy. Then I began slowly to take notice of the things around me. Under the low roof, above the piled-up bed, a text was hanging in a gaudy frame. I read it over and over again during my long wait, and yet I cannot remember it. Oleographs and family portraits hung on the walls, the women sitting in stiff poses, the men with long, waxed moustaches. A fretwork basket stood on the chest of drawers. Everything shone in a reddish, warm light. A red piece of cloth served as a curtain over the window. And as I sat on my hard chair the guard's hut seemed slowly to become strangely familiar to me, as did the room with its cheap ornaments, as if I had been there before. But then the house stood in another landscape, far away, on the Carso, amidst bleak rock, on a wild mountain. Then I was young, and writing my first novel: *Stonecrop*. That other house, to which I had given the youth of my creative power, stood between two tunnels. And it dawned upon me that perhaps there was no such thing as hazard, that even little guards' houses return to you the love you have once bestowed upon them.

Something caught my eye, I had not noticed it before—a calendar hung on the whitewashed wall and I read in the dim, reddish light: April 16, 1919. That recalled me to reality. Carriages passed on the road coming from the direction of Aszód—stolen carriages, and in them sat suspicious-looking people, Jews in fur coats, and they all drove into the courtyard of the castle. I watched them from behind the red curtains. They entered the house noisily: was it not all theirs? And the windows of the castle stared in rigid astonishment out into the garden, as if they wondered what was happening behind them.

Hours passed by. In the castle yard the Communists were packing up, taking whatever they fancied. I sat quietly in my room and looked out through the window. Sometimes a noise made me draw back, then I returned to my post of observation. It may have been about noon when a hand-driven trolley car arrived from Aszód. Voices issued commands in the small office and steps were heard all over the house. I held my breath in alarm. At last they went, and silence ensued. Dinner was ready in the kitchen: there was a smell of boiled potatoes. I was very hungry, and the good woman offered me some, but there were so few on the little earthenware dish. "No, thank you, it is too early."

Later on the girl sent a message from the castle that the Communists had eaten or carried away everything eatable from the kitchen and the larder. She could send me no food, but would I write my name down so that she might inform the Countess when she came home? I remembered the *alias* Elisabeth Kállay had selected for me to hide my identity when I came to Balassagyarmat: 'Elisabeth Földváry'... I repeated it to myself several times. It seemed funny that henceforth this should be the name by which I should be known. The guard's wife tore the date from the calendar and told me I could write it down on that, but I did not do so, and she took no notice. She came and went, working in the house like an ant, tidied up her kitchen, then took the red curtain from the window and began to wash the window panes.

The rain had stopped and a cold wind whistled and howled, driving the clouds before it. In the house the signal bells hummed all the while. The guard came in, rolling a grimy little signal flag in his hands, and spoke to his wife about the Communists. If this went on much longer they would carry off everything from the castle. He spoke to me too, and told me that when the people from Aszód had arrested Count Ráday he had been compelled to wash the Jews' cars in the street. "But he gave it them! He turned up the sleeves of his shirt and ordered the scoundrels to watch him, saying 'now you shall learn how to do this job properly!" The guard laughed to himself: the story pleased him immensely: "But then the men of Iklad got out their scythes, and the next two villages joined them. They were going to fetch the Count and the Countess with six horses, because each village insisted on supplying at least two horses for his carriage..." Suddenly the guard went out. I saw his cap in front of the window and he held the signal flag in his hand. With a great clatter a clumsy goods train passed over the rails. Soldiers with red ribbons were escorting it and shouted at him as they passed. A chalked inscription ornamented the black wagons: 'Long live Béla Kun! Long live the Red army!'

"The vagabonds, they are conveying arms! And as for the Directory of Aszód, they are a lot of cruel Jew boys. The people live in terror of them. Even at night the inhabitants have no rest. During the war the Czech deserters were kept in cotton wool at the aeroplane factory. Now they are the greatest Communist heroes. They steal more than all the others together." Then he scowled. "But things will be different soon! It is no good giving us a lot of their worthless bank-notes. They won't take us in. We railwaymen will have something to say in the matter!"

The telephone rang in the office: Aszód on the line, my train was signaled. My lassitude vanished suddenly, but as I stepped out of the little house I felt as if a veil had been torn from my face, and the exposure seemed physically painful.

Slowly, hissing and panting, the train approached. People were sitting on top of the wagons, people hung from the steps, and even the buffers had their riders. I tried to get up but was pushed back. I ran along the train but not a door would open, for inside the people were pressed against them. I ran on and on, saying to myself 'anywhere, anyhow will do.' I struggled with another door-handle. The train started. What on earth shall I do if I lose it? The guard came to my rescue at last, but boxes and trunks blocked the door. Someone pushed me forward, someone else pulled. My bag hit me in the back. And then I could move no more and the train carried me away.

I had got into an old condemned carriage and an icy wind blew unhindered through its unglazed windows. People were crowding against one another on the narrow floor—women, soldiers, an officer, a dirty fat man. Wedged between them, I stood on one leg, the only foothold I could secure, indeed I was practically suspended by the pressure of their fetid bodies. But as things were, I thought myself lucky. I had to take my ticket on the train, and when the conductor forced his way to our compartment he asked me for my trade-union permit. So now they were going to make me get off again, I thought. I pretended to look for it in my bag, but the officer who was crushed up against me spoke to the conductor and shewed him some paper: "make the ticket out for two." The conductor did so and the officer pocketed tickets for himself and for me. I paid him the fare; he too was going to Balassagyarmat.

Suddenly I found myself standing on both feet, and thus I noticed that the crowd had diminished. At every small station someone got off and there were no new passengers. Now one could look through the window into the corridor of the carriage preceding ours. A young man in a fur coat sat there smoking; he wore a soft hat and his face was flushed with the cold. For a time I looked at him indifferently; then suddenly I began to feel uneasy. I didn't want to see him, yet I felt my eyes attracted by him. My apprehensions steadily increased: I was angry with myself, it was all imagination! But if this man should be searching for me?...

We reached the station which serves Berczel: I had left it twelve hours earlier, in the morning. How tired I had become since then! The door of the next carriage opened suddenly and the man in the fur coat jumped on to the platform and strode towards the stationmaster's office. He was searching for me! I was as convinced of it as if somebody had told me. He was going to Berczel and he would not find me there! I felt incredibly happy. He had but to turn his head... Good-night, comrade! Good luck! All sorts of mocking words came to my mind and I felt like making faces at him.

Passengers elbowed their way past me and several got out. The door remained open and the cold streaming in brought me to my senses. I turned my back to the door and looked at the path wending its way across the green squares of fields and meadows. Suddenly I felt as if something had struck me on the chest: the man in the short fur coat was standing in the door looking at me! He was resting his chin in his hand and held his head a little on one side as if he were trying to remember something. Every drop of blood left my face. Without thinking instinctively, in self-defense, I turned to the opposite window. But I could not see the landscape, everything was blurred before my eyes.

How long did it last? I only know that I felt as if something had vanished behind me. The minutes seemed to gather into masses and fall into hollow space. I felt I was falling with them. Good God, how long is this to last? Let him clutch me by the shoulders, if he likes, let him arrest me, but let something happen, let the suspense come to an end! Then I began to take heart: after all, what does it matter now? At least let the scoundrels see that I am not afraid. I pulled myself up, as high as I could, and forced a smile to my lips.

The train started and the shock banged the door to. Was it possible? For an instant I felt the reckless delight of salvation sweep through me: I breathed freely: I scolded and cheered myself mentally. Poor fool, how could you have such delusions! Then the whole carriage reeled before my eyes: the man in the short fur coat was sitting on a box next to me! He was sitting there with his knees drawn up like a mischievous imp.

In spite of myself my jaw began to tremble: I was afraid with a fear I had never known before, and notwithstanding the cold the sweat rolled down my face. But still I managed to keep myself erect and presently forced myself once more to smile. All sorts of possibilities coursed madly through my head. If I were arrested nobody would know of my fate, and the one-eyed monster into whose hands I was to be delivered could dispose of me without difficulty. My mother did not know that I was travelling, the Kállays whom I had left, the Huszárs to whom I was going, would each be ignorant that I was not safely with the other. One could invoke the Entente Mission on behalf of prisoners at Budapest, but if I were trapped now, nobody would seek me until too late....

The man was still sitting on the box. He rolled a cigarette, blew out the smoke and now and then looked up at me. I shall never forget his eyes. Some travelers got into the train at the next station and the corridor again became crowded. Two men who wore red buttons in their coat lapels waxed enthusiastic over the revolution: "That we should have lived to see it!" One could guess that they were speaking from fear. The man on the box nodded. How contemptible were these people who were Hungarians and had sold themselves to the foreigners; the whole thing was degrading and dirty; my pride revolted at it. To be arrested by this scum; miserably, without an attempt to escape; to wait for fate like one paralyzed, unable to move! My passivity suddenly weighed on me like a great shame. I grasped my bag and forced my way through the crowd into the next compartment. There too the passengers stood jammed between the seats. Next to me was wedged a man whose face I remembered vaguely. He had a thin, fair moustache and wandering eyes, and kept making notes in a book, tearing out the pages and going on writing. However, I soon gave up watching him, for I noticed that the man in the short fur coat who was sitting in the corridor got up every now and then and looked into the compartment as if he were watching me. I waited for an opportune moment, and when he sat down on his box and was out of sight of me, I snatched up my bag and went further along the train. I had no plan, I only wanted to go on, get away, do something. It might succeed. I might escape at the next station. I might jump off the train.

As I was moving away from the fair-haired scribbling man, he suddenly pushed something between the handle of my bag and my hand. Then I remembered how curiously he had looked at me and had then written in his book and torn the page out. I thought I felt a scrap of paper in my palm, but I went on quickly from carriage to carriage, each more crowded than the other, between human bodies, boxes, trunks, baskets. I was pushed about, handled roughly, and sworn at. Whenever anybody looked at me I felt as if my face were being skinned. Why did they all look at me so familiarly as if they had seen me before? Why had I not got a face like everybody else? I pushed on. Suddenly I could go no further, I had come to the end of the train, to the last carriage. There was an empty place near a broken window; all the sparks of the engine were blown into it by the wind, so nobody wanted it. I withdrew into that corner and covered my face with a handkerchief; it protected me and hid me. Nobody paid any attention to me, so I opened the little paper in my hand. A sentence was written on it in irregular halting lines. I remember every word:

"A warrant against you, with your portrait, is circulating here. Escape. If caught they will do for you."

Was it death, or was it just fear I felt then? I carefully tore the paper into little bits and threw them out of the window. Everything was in a haze; there were people in the compartment, I could hear voices, but everything seemed remote... I was alone with myself. About an hour may have passed, perhaps more: I liked to think that time was flying, I liked my little corner, although the wind blew through it and cut my face like a knife. My limbs ached on the hard seat and I was ravenously hungry: since last night I had had nothing but a cup of tea. Suddenly everything became dark, and soot-laden smoke filled the compartment. Before I grasped what it was the chance had passed. A tunnel... If I had thought of it earlier I might have... Nonsense, I should have broken my neck.

The train stopped: we were on the open track. There was a deep ditch along the embankment—I might get off here. The passengers crowded to the windows and someone shouted from outside: "It's not likely that the train will be allowed to enter Balassagyarmat. The Czechs are shelling the station." I made myself as small as possible in my corner. It was nonsense, all nonsense... Then there was another station. Red soldiers everywhere. I saw the man in the short fur coat again; he was running about the station, then stopped and stared towards the place where we had pulled up in the open. He shook his head and seemed to be swearing. Was he looking for me? At all events he jumped back into the train.

Night was now falling and we had to wait a long time in the station, for the engine-driver had gone to an inn for his supper. A passenger said that they had sent for him but that he had replied: "Let them get up steam themselves."

It was night before we started again, and rain began to fall. Slowly light began to stream towards us through the clammy darkness, and people in the compartment got ready to get out. A voice said "Balassagyarmat." I stood near the door, opened it suddenly, threw out my bag and jumped. The other doors opened a good deal later, when I was already running through the exit towards the town. Nobody asked me for my ticket, or took any notice of me. I reached a paling, overshadowed by a huge walnut tree, leant against it, and waited till everybody had passed, people and carriages. For an instant I caught sight of the man in the short fur coat going towards the town. Then the lights of the station went out, and I was alone in the dark at the foot of the tree.

It was over! And yet the terror remained. I still felt that strange will searching for me in the dark, saw the hand industriously groping for me, missing me over and over again. It had not yet found me, but perhaps later on... Instinctively I ducked in my hiding-place. The hand missed me. It had missed me till now, but every time it seemed to get nearer its goal. The watching motor car in front of the doorless house in Stonemason Street; the Red soldiers in Aszód; the man with the dark puffy face and the one in the short fur coat... Every time the hand had been nearer. One lucky movement and it would have got me. It had been so yesterday, it might be so tomorrow, but at any rate it had missed me today and I was still free.

I looked round and my eyes became accustomed to the dark. Where was I to go? A broad street overshadowed by trees led from the station to the town. Should I follow that? I retained a confused memory of the instructions Elisabeth Kállay had given me. Soldiers came towards me, then a few people, at last a little boy. I resolved to confide in the latter. "Will you help me to carry my bag?"

The boy caught hold of it but it was too heavy for him, so we carried it together. After all, that had not been my object. What I really wanted was to find the house of Aladár Huszár. The boy was not quite sure of it, but he led bravely on through the rain. We left gardens and small villas behind us and came in sight of a church by dripping trees and a soaking sandy road. A woman was standing in one of the doorways: She put us right: "The end of the town, the last house but one." New anxieties now took hold of me: up till the present I had only worried about finding my way, and now that I had found it, it occurred to me that they might have left the town. Aladár Huszár had the reputation of being a counter-revolutionary and was suspected by the new power. His wife was the president of the county branch of the Federation of Hungarian Women, and she had been attacked by the local Socialist-Communist papers.

The boy passed through an iron gate and we went up a few steps till we came to a door with glass panes. I was very nervous. I was going to ask for shelter from people who themselves were threatened. I felt painfully ashamed of myself.

"There is the bell!" the boy said. Yet I still hesitated.

Only those who have stood on a stranger's threshold, doubting the quality of their welcome, can appreciate my feelings.

The boy deposited the bag, asked for his money and ran away.

The ringing of the bell broke the silence of the house, and the sudden sound frightened me. I imagined the uneasiness caused to those within. In these times even a knock in broad daylight is enough to cause alarm.

Rapid steps approached from the further end of the long corridor and a frightened maid asked me what I wanted. "Will you say that Elisabeth Földváry has arrived?" Doors opened; there was a ray of light, and in its beam a fine setter ran barking towards me, followed by Aladár Huszár. I had only once seen him before, but I recognized him at once; his fair head and his broad shoulders showed up clearly against the lamp light. For an instant he looked at me searchingly: "Elisabeth Földváry?..."

By now we were alone, and I whispered my real name to him. He jerked his head in surprise. "We were told yesterday that you had escaped to Switzerland."

"Help me to get across the Ipoly!"

"There's no hurry, we will discuss it; now come inside quickly." He picked up my bag and we went into the house as if we were old friends. We crossed the small hall and entered a room in which the light was reflected from the glass doors of high bookcases, and comfortable furniture stood on oriental carpets. I was met by a remarkably beautiful young woman. Her forehead was like marble and her eyebrows met over her big blue eyes shaded by dark eyelashes. Her face was cold and her features seemed nearly rigid. I felt anxious: What was she going to say? She seemed neither astonished nor nervous, though she had lately been told I had escaped abroad, and she behaved as if it had been the most natural thing in the world for a stranger wanted by the police to drop in on them in the middle of the night. She gave her orders quietly, calmly: "We will make up a bed here in the library; we have no other room. Red officers are quartered on the first floor. They wanted to plant Communists in our two spare rooms, so we put our old coachman there."

I leant wearily against a book-case: the room was going round. Then they gave me hot food, and I could detect in the sympathetic expression of Huszár that hunger, sleepless nights, cold and suffering had left their marks upon my face. My dress was hanging on me and my hands trembled. The children, two little girls and a boy, came in. They were told I was a relation of theirs. In a few minutes I watched them being put to bed.

Outside, the rain was falling and the world was full of Red soldiers, detectives, hatred, misery, dirt, fear, humiliation. In here the little children were praying in their long white nightgowns and over their bed a tiny red, white, and green flag was dangling like an emblem of faith. The electric lights went out: it was eleven o'clock. The house became quiet. We stayed up for a time round a single candle. Words were unnecessary between us. We all felt equally the terrible misfortune of our country: the sufferings of each of us were due to the same cause.

"Many good friends have fled this way," said Aladár Huszár.

"Will you help me over, too?"

He shook his head. "The river is in flood and the bridges are guarded. It cannot be managed yet. You must stay here; it is only a question of days. Colonial troops have been seen nearby and my men tell me that there are some at one of the bridges. Today we heard that British troops had arrived. They say there are thirty thousand of them. The French are in Arad. They may come here this very night. Wait for the downfall of the

Soviet."

I was tired, dead tired, but in spite of my exhaustion his words refreshed me as though they heralded the coming of dawn. It seemed strange not to be sent away. They did not want me to go. I should be allowed to rest a little. I felt extreme gratitude but could find no words in which to express it.

VI

BALASSAGYARMAT, *April 17th.*

I THOUGHT my excitements had come to an end, but ill-fortune has looked me in the face again. It has just glanced at me, but has not seized me yet. And now, how long shall I be here? Shall I be driven away, or will this be the scene of my capture?

I can no longer see the end of my road. I never seem to know when I shall be able to put a full-stop at the end of my sentence. It makes no difference. If my diary must remain a fragment, fragments can bear witness. Every clod plays its part in a land-slide, and there is some fragment of the great tragedy in every particle that composes it.

When I woke this morning it took me a long time to realize where I was. The daylight was reflected from the glass doors of a bookcase, and I heard the sound of a reed-flute. The primitive melodies of the cow-herd mingled with the trampling of the cattle. But where was I? Something gripped my heart and forced the truth from it. A fugitive, an outlaw! I looked out of the window: cows were coming down the little street on the outskirts of the town. Everything was different from my surroundings of yesterday. The house opposite was indifferently, ignorantly looking at its reflection in the puddles. Somewhere in that direction the railway station must lie, and the road to it crosses the square in front of the town-hall. I had a good idea what this square must be like. A big market with arcades, an old fountain, the old town-hall with its tower... Yes, it must be like that.

"Good morning!" The children's clear voices called me from the next room. Breakfast was ready on a glass- covered verandah, opening on to the back garden. The old flower-bed under the sprouting ornamental trees had been replaced by vegetables, but shrubs remained, and beyond the fence were trees, shingled roofs, little gardens. Aspen trees, willows and graceful, slender poplars were reflected from a soft, brilliant mirror—the Ipoly in flood. On the other side of the river were the vineyards where the Czechs were encamped. For two months their guns have been trained on

74

the town.

I mentioned my notes; Huszár gave me some paper and a pencil. Then the front doorbell rang. Who could it be! It was unusual to have visitors at that hour. Gregory, the faithful old coachman, put his head in.

"Two armed Reds are here!" he exclaimed.

I clasped my hands in terror. Mrs. Huszár turned white to the lips:

"What are we to do if they are after you? The town is full of detectives." She went out and when she came back she was laughing. "I was never so frightened in my life. They asked me: 'Does Comrade Huszár live here?' Then one of them made an awful face and added: 'We have been informed that there is a—er—library in the house.' I really thought they had found you. And all they had discovered was our library!"

It was a good library; I spent a long time among its volumes, and found them representative of Hungarian history and of the development of Socialism. I determined to study.

"You'd better write a book," said Mrs. Huszár. "When we have got over these times, let people know what we have gone through."

*   *   *

April 18th.

GOOD Friday. At the feet of Christ's cross, under the black sky, on the Red land, Hungary has been crucified among the nations.

We hoped that an attack on the town would be delivered this night by the Czechs. It sounds sheer mad- ness, and yet it was so. It was different last year, when Károlyi had opened our frontiers and our predatory neighbors could walk in undisturbed on our unconscious, shackled towns. Balassagyarmat was the only one that rose to arms and drove out the intruders.

Hideous change! We are waiting for the Czechs! And this day all those who are Hungarians in the republic of the Jewish tyrants are waiting in suspense.

*   *   *

April 19th.

THE night has passed. At dawn only a few stray rifle bullets whistled over and into the Ipoly, disturbing the surface of the water for a moment, but the river soon resumed its smoothness and everything is now as it was yesterday. There is no change, and our deliverers still hesitate. But within our shamefully constricted frontiers the outlines of the picture become clear, and the undermining of society goes on with devilish speed. The newspapers which reached us this day publish an incredible order—the sixty-second within three weeks.

> The Revolutionary Cabinet considers it its duty to revise the procedure of such criminal proceedings as have been instituted before the proclamation of the Soviet, so as to save from punishment those Proletarians who were called before the tribunals by the old order in the interest of capitalism alone, and, on the other hand, to punish severely, those who have sinned against the working Proletarians.

This order is without precedent in the history of human law. It destroys at a blow the progress of centuries. It endows the privileged and only recognized class, the Proletarians, with the monopoly of crime.

Even in the administration of justice, Bolshevism stands on the basis of class hatred and serves the class war. If the Proletarian has robbed a member of the middle-classes, he cannot be punished; if he has murdered a bourgeois, he cannot be condemned, because his actions were simply acts of self-defense against the tyranny of capitalism.

And after abolishing crime as such, it proceeds to the destruction of its traces. All records are burnt in stacks, and the files of criminal proceedings which might involve those in power today are made away with. Béla Kun embezzled the funds of a workmen's benevolent society. The papers of the prosecution have been burnt and the leader of the Soviet has purged his honor in the ashes.

Once the Roman Empire of the West, Byzantium, Friul, Saxony, all paid tribute to the old Hungary. The profiles of conquered Emperors, of Caesars and of Princes, minted in gold, flowed into the Danubian province of Hungary, and later on the harvests of peace sent their surplus into the treasury of the land, the fruits of valor and of work.

Today the ruling power burgles safes. Protected by its ordinances, it steals jewels, gold and precious stones, proclaiming, "No compensation is due for property delivered to the State." Everything that can be exchanged for foreign gold is confiscated. Even stamp collections which are worth more than two thousand crowns are taken, the happiness of little schoolboys, the hobby of collectors.

The head of the Directorium of Balassagyarmat returned yesterday from Budapest. Huszár heard him relating proudly in the street that he had spoken with Béla Kun himself. The position of the Soviet Republic has been considerably strengthened abroad and at home, and the economic conditions are excellent. Béla Kun has declared that he has such a reserve in jewels, pearls, medals and art treasures that there was no bourgeois Government in the world that could compete with him. Negotiations are on foot for the disposal, in Holland, of these treasures. Huszár's next statement filled me with shame and anger. Béla Kun was bargaining with foreign antiquaries for the sale of the Holy Hungarian Crown!

It is said they offered him 170,000 crowns for it. The stones are second-rate, the gold is thin, there is just the historical value left. 170,000 crowns for the past glories of the Kings of Hungary! That is their value today.

The Cabinet is still expectant: will anybody bid any more? And if one day there is a higher bidder, Béla Kun and Számuelly, Comrade Landler and the others, will open the iron-bound chest in the Coronation Chapel, lean over it, finger it, and the Jews will take Europe's oldest royal crown to the auction room. Will they have time to do it? I thought of what the president of the Balassagyarmat Directorate had said. They all talk as if they were to last forever. Meanwhile, the other bank of the Ipoly, the hill with the vineyards, keeps silent.

If things were to remain like this for long! The idea tortures me incessantly and forces me to think of my unhappy position. My hosts are hospitable, kind, touchingly so, but have I the right to accept their generosity? Aladár Huszár has given up his office, he declines to serve the Soviet. His wife's jewels have been seized, they have no food coupons. What is consumed today cannot be replaced tomorrow. Every gift means a privation for them. And what if I should be found and arrested in their house? There are ten years of penal servitude in store for those who shelter me. I must do something. If there is no change presently I shall have to go. Have the waters of the Ipoly receded during the night? Perhaps the Czechs are not guarding the banks any longer? Perhaps the bridge is open?

"Let us wait," said Mrs. Huszár. "We confidently expect an attack tonight, and that would save you."

"Let us go and have a look. Maybe..."

We walked slowly along the bank of the river. The air was clear and fresh and the wind rippled the flooded waters. A woman came along the road with a hamper over her arm and greeted us.

"Do you come from the other bank?"

The woman nodded: "We have a little field over there. But in future, from today, the Czechs have refused to let me pass. They shoot at anyone who approaches the bridge. They are preparing something."

As she passed on we looked at each other and then towards the bridge. That road then existed no longer. The barbed wire in the middle marks the frontier. Reds and Czechs stand on either bridgehead. The tree which had fallen across the river near the gardens, the living bridge over which fugitives had quite recently crawled across, is now under water in midstream. The Ipoly is like a sea.

The silver stream is flowing over the green velvet of the inundated fields and meadows. The willows on the banks draw a veil over the silver. Against the lovely blue background of the distant hills, the poplars look like rows of furled flags. All nature seems in ecstasy. Birds sing in the dazzling sunshine.

A cart rattled behind us full of soldiers, carrying bread for distribution among the guards in the villages. It passed us quickly and disappeared at the turning of the road, but the smell of bread remained in the air.

It is the Saturday before Easter. The churches are watched by the mercenaries of the new power and I must avoid their eyes. Only the banks of the river and the main road are free to me. And yet I am in church. Under the long cupola of the branches, the mild winds of spring sound like an organ, recalling to me the eternal mysteries of the Resurrection.

*　　*　　*

April 20th.

EVENTS cast their shadows before them, and as they arrive they enter the shadow.

Our little street on the outskirts of the town was unusually restless this morning. As the bells recalled the memories of past Easters to my mind, the neighboring villagers were passing under my window in picturesque costumes on their way to church. I could hear the sound of foot- steps, the rustle of petticoats, even a threat in the loud voices of the young men. A few of them wore red and white flowers with green leaves stuck in their hats.

On the other side of the street, soldiers were leaning out of the window of the Reds' guard-room. A few were loafing about in the street. They looked suspiciously at the peasants and as soon as these had passed they talked among themselves excitedly.

One soldier rang our front-door bell and insisted on being given a suit of clothes, as he was going to a wedding. Gentlefolks had plenty to give him. To give more weight to his claim he began to boast his prowess: "The attack is expected at Uszok. We are going to wipe out the Czechs and unite with the Russians, who have already crossed the Carpathians." He took what he had exacted under his arm and hurried off.

When Aladár Huszár came home he spoke more cautiously than usual.

"There is much ado among the comrades. On the 16th the Roumanians attacked between the Szamos and the Maros. The Red International Regiment fled at the first shot. How the Russian and Viennese Jews ran! They stormed the trains in their panic, and left the poor Széklers to their fate, even before the Roumanians had developed their attack."

We looked at each other: we had never imagined it like this. Even when our sufferings seemed most unbearable we would have wished it otherwise. Where are the British and the French troops?

"The members of the local Directorate suppress the facts," said Huszár, after a long silence. "At any rate it looks suspicious that they should again talk so much about the World Revolution. The World Revolution is always to the front when their own affairs are on the decline. Their newspapers are full of it; Italy and France are seething. Soviet rule has become more powerful in Münich. The proclamation of the Soviet in Vienna is only a question of hours."

How much of this is true? How much lies? Aladár Huszár began to roll cigarettes. He offered me one: they always offer, always give, and I am forever asking and thanking. A match? I should have liked to ask for one, but could not say the word, so I just held the cigarette in my hand. Mrs. Huszár nodded to her husband: "Give her a light..." He jumped up and went to the writing-table and brought back a small cigarette lighter in his palm. "Here is a little Easter present for you."

His wife let her sewing fall into her lap and looked at me. "Well done," she said, "I hate seeing you obliged to ask for every trifle, when you yourself have given up everything."

At that moment I saw behind the lovely cold face the warm heart it endeavored to hide.

Huszár took his hat. "I will go to the railway station for a newspaper." He seemed restless.

"What has happened?" asked his wife.

He hesitated for a moment. "The Directorate has received a secret order by telephone. The Cabinet has decided that hostages are to be taken."

A cloud seemed to pass over the brightness outside, and I felt suddenly cold. This news was the most terrible we had yet heard. Hostages! The foreign race is going to guarantee its life with Hungarian lives!

A very little time seemed to have passed before the door flew open and Aladár Huszár stood there, his eyes shining and his face drawn with excitement.

"They are done for!" He was so excited that he laughed spasmodically, while his eyes were full of tears of emotion. "Look here!" He waved the newspaper in front of us: "The Revolution is in danger!"

In turn we snatched the newspaper out of each other's hands. The General Staff of the Workers' and Soldiers' Council had met on the 19th at the Opera House. It was Kunfi who addressed the crowd:

"The Entente is forging a ring of iron round Soviet Hungary."

We looked at each other. So they will not let us perish after all! Human mercy comes to the rescue at last!

"Just listen! Béla Kun himself admits that they are done for: 'According to reports the Roumanians have taken Szatmár-Németi. The inhabitants at once abolished the Soviet Republic, hoisted white flags and raised cheers for the King. Private property was re-established. The Roumanians are advancing on Nagy-Várad. In Debréczen, however, the workmen managed to suppress the Counter-revolution. Everybody must go to the front. If necessary, we are ready to die for the Dictatorship of the Proletariat!'"

We have learned to read between the lines of 'The Red Newspaper.' They are afraid, and in their fear they threaten furiously. The electrician War Minister threatens the working classes: "Anyone committing acts of indiscipline will be dealt with as if he were a Counter-revolutionary." As for the bourgeoisie, Pogány shook his fist at it during the stage meeting at the Opera.

"Comrades, we must inform the bourgeoisie that from this day we consider it our hostage. (Violent applause.) Let the bourgeois take notice that they will get no respite from any advance the Entente's army may make, because every step which brings the Serbian and Roumanian armies nearer shall be made a bitter trial to the bourgeois amongst us. (Stormy applause.) Let not the bourgeoisie rejoice, let it not stick white flags out of its windows, for we shall paint them red in their life-blood!" (Raving applause lasting for several minutes.)

Then Számuelly mounted the tribune: "The Proletarian country is in danger!" he exclaimed. "Death to all the enemies of the Proletariat! Death to the bourgeois! Although no blood has yet been shed in defense of the Republic, the blood of the Proletarians may yet flow, but then bourgeois blood will flow too."

And the audience, the foreign crowd of the Workers' Council, clapped furiously as the Jew, Számuelly, prophesied the shedding of the blood of the Hungarian Proletariat and the Hungarian bourgeoisie, stirred up against each other. Labour, driven to the slaughter, is to vent its fury and destroy the intellectuals. Magyardom is to crush Magyardom's brain with its own hand.

Madness! They sentence both their slaves and their enemies. Will they last long enough to accomplish the destruction of the nation!

The general assembly on Saturday before Easter resolved that every Proletarian must rise to arms in the defense of the Dictatorship.

One is oppressed by a sense of calamity. The Roumanians in Nagy-Várad! But on the other hand, the horrible Dictatorship is falling. Humanity has pity on us. Even if the Roumanians make encroachments now, peace will restore our territory to us.

There were steps in the street. A man stopped on the curb and looked up at our window. I remembered that I had seen him on the same spot yesterday. Mrs. Huszár pressed her husband's arm. Then the streetlamps were lit, and we watched from the dark room. The sinister shape was still standing at the corner.

*   *   *

April 21st.

THE town remained quiet and the house was wrapped in silence. I could hear nothing but the throbbing of my pulse. Was that man still standing at the corner?

After midnight the roar of a single gun disturbed the night. I waited, but the ominous silence returned. Such must be the silence in a lunatic asylum at night. The lamps burn low in the corridors, and now and then steps pass between the cells. The watchman makes his round... Out there the Red patrols pass under the window. Dawn begins to break: salvation has failed again. And yet the hours are flying for us. If the powers of the Entente delay, the Dictatorship will make us pay for their attempts. Let them hurry, lest they be too late. The Dictators are proclaiming their threat that blood will flow. They are covering the walls with, posters: "To arms!" "Advance, Red soldiers!" "Rise in defense of the Proletariat!" "The Revolution is in danger!"

The fleeing Reds have been re-formed near Debréczen and Nyiregyháza. A number of battalions and batteries have been removed from this western theatre. Trains are running at unusual hours: the Directorate is nervous. The petty tyrants proclaim the victories of the Red army, the reckless courage of the Proletarian heroes. Booty, innumerable prisoners! The newspapers write in the same strain. From the capital come telephone messages and telegrams in cypher. Meanwhile the Czechs are shouting from the other bank: "Hey, Reds, there is a Red Easter in store for you!" It is said that many soldiers deserted this night from the town: certainly there seem to be fewer about than usual. They are disillusioned now; when they enlisted, they were told: "Down with war! Henceforth a soldier's life will be exempt from danger. Red soldiers will have good pay and they can do whatever they like." And now, all of a sudden, revolutionary court martials are established. Béla Kun abolishes the Soldiers' Councils and the 'confidential' system, and behold, the soldiers have to go to war!

Towards evening we went to the bank of the river. Tiny armed figures were visible on the other shore, and single soldiers passed us in haste; they had already removed the red from their caps and a few wore bonnets of the old pattern. A cold wind was blowing, driving back the waters in silvery ripples, and shaking the aspen trees; a shudder passed over the reeds. Another soldier came along from the town. When he caught sight of us he left the road and made quickly for the fields.

"He's deserting!"

The small figures with bayonets on the other bank were gradually absorbed by the darkness. A tree in blossom alone stood out white against the leaden grey sky. Our souls knew hope again. If only the frosty wind does not kill the early spring!

* * *

April 22nd.

NO news has reached us: the telegraph wires are silent: people have even stopped whispering in the street. The soldiers are leaning indolently out of the guard-room windows, and the Czech guns are silent.

No news! Yet suddenly an awful reminder of the times we live in reached my ear. A child was singing in the street. I could not see it, but could hear that it was coming nearer and nearer, so I began to listen. The little songster was just crossing the end of the narrow street and for an instant the break in the houses gave his voice free access to us. "My father... my mother"

It was a small boy and he was balancing himself on the curbstone as he repeated the refrain. Then I caught the words:

"My father, my mother, you may — for all I care..."

The song went on, to the stupid tune of a Budapest music-hall ditty. I have heard many disgusting things told of the new schools established by the Bolsheviks, but I think this was the most disgusting—and the most disastrous. The degradation of the Hungarian schools was not the achievement of a day: it was started unobserved before the war by our Freemasons' educational policy and by Freemason mayors of the capital. Then Károlyi came and prepared the way for Bolshevism in the education of Hungary's younger generation. The mass appointment of Jewish masonic professors and teachers; the Bolshevik reform of school books; the destruction of the souls of the children; the degradation of parental authority; the systematic destruction of moral and patriotic principles; the revelation of sexual matters; all these were the work of Károlyi's Government. The Soviet Government, when it came, had only to change a few men and names, and the whole machine was ready to their hand, to work exclusively, and to their entire satisfaction, in the interest of revolution.

One shudders at the thought of those who have the education of Hungary's childhood and youth in their hands. They all belong to the foreign race. The Commissaries for Education: Kunfi, the morphomaniac; Lukács a degenerate; Pogány, who is openly accused of murder; and Számuelly, the murderer in Russia of captive Hungarian officers. The dictator of the students, or so-called 'young-workers,' is an assassin, the same Lékai-Leiter who had attempted to kill Tisza on the steps of the House of Parliament the day before the outbreak of the Revolution. Murderers and men devoid of moral sense, how should they consider schools as anything but the means of propaganda, as devilish laboratories which may serve to poison young guiltless minds? Normal education is a process of civilization: Bolshevik education is demoralization.

In the dormitories of girls' boarding schools young Jewish masters are made to sleep, so as to accustom the little girls to the presence of men. Jewish medical students accompany little girls to the mixed bathing places that they may kill all modesty with ridicule. Sexual education grows apace.

The purpose of nursery schools has been changed: the teachers have been informed confidentially that the kindergarten must be used to estrange the children from their mothers and supplant the family. All toys are declared common property in order that the children may forget the crime of private ownership. And while our rulers are forcing the present generation of youths into the Red army, they decree that playing with lead soldiers must be forbidden to the coming generation, lest one day the slaves dream of liberation.

An order has been issued that the old reading and history books must be given up: they are being replaced by new history books, written by people who do not even know our language. The workshop of destruction is producing new schoolbooks, for the Commissary for Education has given instructions that in future all schoolbooks must preach the gospel of class-war. Hungarian literature is no longer to be taught; henceforth nothing but 'universal literature' is to be taught in Hungarian schools. Such scraps of our history as are allowed to be taught are falsified and systematically besmirched: "John Hunyady was a mountebank, Matthias Corvinus a charlatan, Denis Pázmándy a scoundrel."

It is not difficult to understand the purpose of the little boy's blasphemous song: let the children despise their fathers and mothers so that even at home parents may fail in their efforts to repair the destruction wrought in the schools.

For fifty years a devilish fiend has been slowly robbing the Hungarian people of its soul. Now that it has attained power it is destroying that soul with feverish haste, lest they should recover their soul when they regain their consciousness.

*   *   *

April 25th.

BLACK and white shapes are circling in the sky: the storks have come back, birds of so many legends and stories. They left us in the autumn, stayed away for many months, and yet they have found their way back to their own ragged nests on the trees along the banks of the Ipoly.

I looked at them as they descended, calm and peaceful. They did not attempt to take possession of a strange nest, of another bird's home. Mysterious, inviolable laws lead them to their own nests, regardless of the fact that in our country, at the foot of their trees, a man may no longer claim his own home. 'Every house becomes common property,' and he who dares to oppose this order is tried by a Revolutionary Tribunal.

Someone had gone out of the room and left the door open. I could see a man in the corridor and heard him say that he had just come on foot, now and then getting a lift on a cart. He brought a letter for Aladár Huszár from his mother at Budapest. I could not help envying Huszár—for me there is never a letter, nor any news.

Huszár showed me his letter: it read as though his mother were taking leave of him on her death bed. They are starving in the capital and are living under a perpetual threat. If three people stop to talk to each other in the street they are promptly driven apart by the former boisterous advocates of the right of free assembly. Nobody is allowed in the streets after ten o'clock at night; even family gatherings at home are prohibited, and after eleven o'clock all lights have to be extinguished in the houses. People are spied on in their own homes by the 'confidential men' who are quartered on them, and anybody who dares to move a hand is denounced. Poor Mrs. Huszár complained bitterly in her letter that a manservant whom she had dismissed for theft had since been quartered on her with his wife. They are her guardrail. Another old lady was compelled to find quarters for prostitutes, who received Red soldiers at night. And these people have to be fed. They get drunk, dirty the furniture, and cover the floor with filth. There are no servants: she herself has to clean up after them, to save the place from pollution. Meanwhile the storks return to their last year's nest. Nature disregards man-made ordinances and continues her eternal laws.

Instinctively I looked at the newspaper. News: the advance of the Roumanians has been stopped. Lower down were three nominations: the Revolutionary Cabinet has appointed the distinguished typewriter salesman, Böhm, Commander in Chief on the Eastern front. The Chief of Staff of this ridiculous and humiliating Commander is to be the Austrian comrade Aurelius Stromfeld, the very man who sent a note to Károlyi informing him that the final victory of the Russian Soviet armies and the World Revolution were inevitable. What new misfortune is this gifted but misguided megalomaniac preparing for us? The third nomination was that of Számuelly to be the President of the Tribunal of Summary Jurisdiction established on the Eastern front. He is to be the absolute judge of all Counter-revolutionary movements behind the front. In his order issued from General Headquarters he stated his intentions clearly: "I do not ask the bourgeoisie for anything, but I should like it to engrave my words on its memory: whoever raises his hand against the power of the Proletariat signs his own sentence of death. As for the execution of the sentence, it will be our business to attend to that."

Who is this man who has the power to speak like that? Whence does he come, he who from this day onwards can dispose of our lives without further appeal?

He appeared in the dark beginnings of the Revolution, at the side of Béla Kun. They crossed the Russian frontier together. Both brought with them the instructions and the gold of Trotsky.

I remember him: it was last winter, and at that time Visegrad street was the well-known 'secret' nest of the Communists. Two figures were coming towards me from the corner, from the direction of 'The Red Newspaper's' editorial offices: one was Maria Goszthonyi, who under the name of Maria Csorba filled important functions in the Soviet and roused the Communist rabble by her reckless speeches; the other was a young man who, although he had no hump yet bore on his face that curious expression common to hunchbacks. I learned later on that this man was Tibor Számuelly.

His grandfather came from Galicia in his gabardine with a bundle on his back. Tibor Számuelly came young to Nagy-Várad, and without possessing any special gift for writing and endowed with a superficial education only, he became a journalist. I may say here that my information concerning him has been obtained from people who knew him personally at that time. In the cafés he used to seek out quiet corners and sit if possible alone at a table. He practically never removed his black gloves—he always wore black clothes and a black tie, and his long straight black hair was combed back from his forehead. His clean-shaven consumptive-looking face was furrowed with blue-black shadows.

Presently this son of a Polish Jew became a Bohemian eccentric, and wore clothes after the English fashion; but the change was only skin-deep, his soul was filled with the ardor of the crowded Synagogue. It remembered the dim lights of the eves of the old faith's Sabbaths, the seven lighted candles, the lust for vengeance of the despised. He mixed little with Christians, and as for the Christian women of bad fame with whom he came into contact, it was only to humiliate them (so he said) that he sought their company. He spoke with hatred of everything that was Hungarian, though he disguised his own characteristic name under a Hungarian form. At the beginning of the war he was writing short unimportant articles for a newspaper in Fiume. Then he joined the staff of the *Catholic Hungarian Courier.*

He was called up for military service when war broke out. For a time he cleverly managed to postpone joining his regiment and then for a while he shirked in various orderly-rooms behind the front. Later on he surrendered to the Russians, and when the Revolution broke out there a sudden change took place in the demeanor of this Jew boy, who till then had been rude and overbearing with his subordinates and cringing to his superiors. He quickly rose above the others. Soon he was seen recruiting for the Red army among the Hungarian prisoners of war. He used threats and every conceivable pressure. The Jewish Czars restored his freedom, and in astonishing proof of racial solidarity, the insignificant little Jew of Nyiregyháza became a commander in the Russo-Jewish army of the Soviet. And then, at last, it seems, he gave the rein to his long-nursed hatred: he ordered the slaughter of ninety-two Hungarian officers, prisoners of war.

Last year, in November, he came 'home,' and soon after met Károlyi at Béla Kun's quarters. Henceforth the two met often, and it was under Károlyi's protection that he proclaimed at Communist meetings: "Death to the Bourgeois!" On the eve of March 22nd he was already Assistant Commissary for war: now he has become President of the Revolutionary Tribunals.

Before he left Budapest for General Headquarters he was sitting one afternoon in the window of Budapest's smartest confectioner's and was looking out on the square. Several people who were close by heard him say: "I am going to build a guillotine on this square. So many bourgeois must be killed that the tumbrils will have to drive through pools of their blood."

Somebody who had been to Budapest told me that Számuelly was surrounded by terrorist guards, that his special train was provided with machine guns, and that an executioner always travelled with him. In the Journalist's Club, the revolutionary 'Otthon,' the once obscure reporter, has become the most important personage among the journalist representatives of his race. One of the most prominent among them, Alexander Bródy, is said to have embraced him at a champagne supper and to have hailed him as "Our prophet!"

Yes, that is what he is, their prophet!... Now that I think of him, the memory of his dark hyena-like features becomes more and more distinct. He grins appreciatively at his new power. I can see his black sleek head and his hand beckoning death. Gallows are erected wherever he goes. And the gallows, like black Hebrew characters, remain in the landscape when his special train has passed on to some other rebellious district. It is in these black characters that this foreigner is inscribing his name upon our history. Tibor Számuelly has been brought up in the secret rites of hatred and belongs to an ultra-orthodox sect of oriental Jews which is stricter in the observance of its ceremonies than any other. The sect of *Chesidem* resembles the Hebrews of the Old Testament, grave, prejudiced and dark. It shuns the light of the sun. Its adherents admit of no other truth than that which is contained in the *Thora*, and that only because it is there. This sect interprets the covenant strictly and to the letter; 'an eye for an eye, a tooth for a tooth' is the foundation of its creed.

Számuelly's degenerate soul has been formed and shaped by these rites and teachings. Thus he has become the most characteristic type of this sect whose ruling spirits for many years have lived and increased stealthily in our midst. Hatred has been given free rein, the type has thrown off its mask, and the thirst for vengeance, stored up for innumerable years, is about to be quenched. In the person of Számuelly the Revolutionary Cabinet has found an executioner for the Hungarian people who is blood of its blood, soul of its soul.

VII

As it was getting dark last night a man crept into the yard. He looked round carefully: the street was empty: suddenly he ran up the back stairs.

Alarming news had been spreading over the town during the day: bands of terrorists are going about arresting people. The Cabinet is issuing open threats, becoming reckless in its fear of overthrow. Strict orders are being sent to the provincial towns. The Directorate of Balassagyarmat has been dismissed, having been accused of weakness and of favoring the gentlefolk. New men are coming forward, a young fellow scarcely twenty years old is to be the Dictator of the proud county. Another of the same type is to command the garrison. Jews have gone, but still Jews are coming. They have orders to take hostages in the county, so that should the Czechs attack these could be thrown to the fury of the mob. Something is necessary to occupy the rabble whilst the Directorate is making its escape.

Lights in the windows disappeared earlier than usual this evening, and the steps of the patrols resounded through empty, overawed streets.

Aladár Huszár is the friend of a people who are of no importance today. The man who stole in by the back door brought a warning: he must escape, they are going to arrest him tonight. So Huszár left his home and went into the dark streets.

The cold penetrated everywhere, even through the walls. We were sitting in fur coats. The candle had burnt to the end, and there was no firewood in the house.

Suddenly we heard the noise of rifle-butts banging furiously upon the door.

Mrs. Huszár looked at me: "Is it for him, or is it for you?"

We put out the candle and opened the window a little. Soldiers were standing outside. "Is anything the matter?"

"No," came the answer; then a face emerged from the obscurity: "We're only making preparations." The face looked scared. "We're looking for the comrade commanders."

"They've gone out."

There was a good deal of swearing. Then: "The good-for-nothing scoundrels!"

I wondered if the officers had deserted too!

* * *

April 25th.

TODAY has been like a nightmare. Bayonets have been glinting in front of our windows. About noon soldiers poured through the main street. They climbed fully armed into commandeered carts, and drove furiously towards Örhalom. The Czechs have opened their attack! At nightfall the clatter of arms was heard in the direction of the prison. Doors slammed and dogs howled in the dark: the Communists were taking their hostages...

The telepathy of common disaster enables us to guess each other' s thoughts; we say nothing, but we are thinking in common; never has there been such sympathy among suffering humanity. On the Saturday before Easter, only a few days ago, Aladár Huszár remarked: "I am so sorry for you. It must be terrible to have to leave one's own home, not knowing whither to go and not being sure of a safe lodging for the night." Today I thought precisely the same thing concerning him. He has gone, with his faithful friend George Pongrácz. Tomorrow they will come here to fetch him and will search the house. We shall all be questioned. And if they recognize me... Well, so be it!

* * *

April 26th.

IT is impossible to sleep these nights, and the lumbering steps of patrols passing in the icy darkness alone mark the progress of time.

Early this morning a Red soldier called and inquired after Aladár Huszár. "He's got to report at once." Then another came and questioned the servants. Mrs. Huszár was unperturbed. They told her that if her husband did not turn up they would arrest her in his place, so she proceeded to pack a small bag, just as I had done not long before. About noon detectives came and held a consultation in the ante-room. Then they went through the house systematic ally, and as they proceeded I fled before them, from room to room. When I could go no further I hid under the staircase, feeling rather like an animal caught in a trap. Would they find me? What good had my efforts been? Again I felt the invisible hand groping around me...

They went, but others soon came. Across the road, at the corner, stood a sentry, his face turned towards the house. In the afternoon posters appeared on the walls—red paper with huge black letters: "He who receives a visitor in his house will be summoned before the Revolutionary Tribunal. Any stranger found within the town after twenty-four hours will be expelled."

Life has fresh troubles in store for me every day. I am resigned to my fate: but ten years' hard labour are in store for those who have taken me in!

Mrs. George Pongrácz came to us, her husband has had to fly for his life. They have only recently been married. Poor girl, she is left quite alone. We tried to devise some plan to escape from this place. Mrs. Pongrácz said at last: "In a village not far from here there's a dear old lady whom I know very well; nobody would look for you there."

We decided on it hurriedly. Mrs. Pongrácz wrote a letter to her friend, Mrs. Michael Beniczky, at Szügy, and told her that Elisabeth Földváry, a poor relation of the Huszárs, with a weak heart(!) begged her hospitality for a few days as she was afraid of the Czech guns. Then she left, and we made hasty preparations. Mrs. Huszár hid her husband's arms and clothes and then we collected all the letters and papers in the house that might have been dangerous and made a fire of them in the nursery. Huszár's desperate counter-revolutionary writings went up in flames—letters, handbills, appeals of the Women's Federation—a sad *auto da fé*: months of hard work, hope and enthusiasm were committed to the flames. However, the children enjoyed it and danced round the unaccustomed blaze; even we ourselves drew nearer and were glad of the warmth.

We were called up again during the night: a cart stopped in front of the house, and the steps of soldiers resounded. Those who will live after us will never be able to understand the terror and anxiety which were conjured up by a few steps in the night, a cart stopping in front of the house... "They are coming...!"

Mrs. Huszár went to the door. They were soldiers—two Red officers come to commandeer night quarters. They marched in and took possession of a room upstairs, and for a time we could hear them moving about overhead.

Are the Czechs going to attack? But the great silence of expectation continues undisturbed under the frigid sky.

*   *   *

April 27th.

THE riverside churches were ringing their bells for Mass, and the town had turned its face in their direction. Our street was empty, except for the Red soldier on sentry duty at the corner. Mrs. Huszár went with me to the door, and when the Red sentry looked towards the town I slipped quietly out. His back was turned to me and I escaped his notice. I carried a tiny parcel under my arm, containing just a few things. How little suffices for our bare needs! Mrs. Pongrácz followed me, and we went quickly across the main street.

I had not been in this direction since the evening when I arrived here, and my imagination had replaced the topography of the town on the banks of the Ipoly by quite a different place. It had placed an ancient town-hall with a venerable tower on the marketplace, where none actually existed. It had placed around it old-fashioned houses with arcades where in reality were tiny shops crowded together and an old fountain' in the middle of the square. I looked round, but reality left no impression on me and the picture of my imagination remained.

Whenever people came towards us I experienced a feeling of terror; I raised my handkerchief and pretended to blow my nose.

"If there are many more people coming," I said, laughing even in my distress, "I'm likely to get a sore nose."

Red soldiers were standing at the railway crossing, and they asked us where we were going.

"We are only going to Szügy, nearby, to spend the day." There came another few yards of street with suburban houses, and suddenly we found ourselves on the main road among endless open fields basking in the sunshine. There was a sharp wind blowing, but spring hovered over the woods of the neighboring hills. The wayside flowers stood in the grass like long-waisted, wide-petticoated little peasant girls. It was like a feast-day, a Sunday of a hundred bright colors. Suddenly I felt an inexpressible desire for freedom. For weeks I had been hiding among friends, stealthily, making myself as small as possible, like one endeavoring to make his way through a thorny thicket. Now at last I had reached the open and the sun was shining on my face. I laughed with sheer joy, and the wind mimicked my mirth as it swept softly over the land.

As if the main road were a church parade, carriage followed carriage in long procession, fat young Jews in service uniform with the Soviet cap lolling within them. Fine thoroughbreds pranced beside them, stolen horses with grooms in stolen liveries. A smart turn-out approached rapidly, the harness and trappings ornamented with the silver arms of a count. The coachmen wore a Hungarian livery. Lolling back on the cushions was a vulgar-looking man, and beside him a shapeless but smartly dressed female was making herself comfortable.

"That is the Dictator of the county and his wife," whispered Mrs. Pongrácz; "I recognize Count Mailath's mackintosh. The dress his wife is wearing belonged to the Countess, she wore it when her husband was installed Lord Lieutenant. These people have taken possession of the castle of Gárdony and have had all the furniture they want sent from it to their own house. The 'comrade' is said to be vastly annoyed because coats of arms and crests 'disfigure' the cigarette-cases he acquired there."

I turned my face towards the fields; the reflection of the sun glittered in a circle round the spokes of the wheel and dust rose in long clouds beneath them. When they had passed and the dust had settled I looked anxiously behind me. Presently peasants on foot overtook us; it is only honest people who walk nowadays. One barefooted old peasant carried his boots dangling from his crook over his back. Poor deluded millions! Do they still believe that everything belongs to the Proletarians? Do they still believe it when the carriages of their former rulers throw the dust into their eyes as their new masters ride by in them? When will the peasantry of this credulous country crush those who have dared to trick it?

I caught sight of the spire of a church beyond the turning of the road, and shingled roofs hiding among the trees. There stood the fine old County Hall, with its double roof dating from the period of Maria Theresa—a red flag floating over it. And plastered all over the walls of the cottages were the joyful posters: "Long live the Dictatorship of the Proletariat."

We left the main road. A red handkerchief waved from a pole on top of a peasant's cottage: the Directorate had resided there. Then we crossed an abandoned cemetery, a tall crucifix standing out darkly above the high grass that covered the tombstones. But the sun was shining and the wind blew freshly. We came to a neglected old garden; within the open gate of wrought-iron Red Guards were loafing; happy or unhappy, whoever liked could go in and out. A large number of munition cases were stacked in the wood shed and on the terrace of the old manor-house. I looked at the inscriptions: *Explosive. No. 15 ecrasite shell.*

"There is enough here to blow up a town with."

Mrs. Pongrácz nodded. "In the next field there's a Red Battery. The Czechs in the vineyard are shelling it." Beyond, above the shingled roof of the manor house, two morose old firs rose towards heaven, their lowest branches touching the young grass. The house with its pillars reminded me of the old garden in Algyest which was my childhood's delight. But here the soldiers had trampled down the grass of the lawn, and the heavy munition wagons had cut deep ruts in the road. Near the gate where the soldiers were, crumpled paper and broken bottles were lying about. But behind the house, on the other side, the garden was practically untouched, and amidst the young awakening of Spring it was beautiful in its wild tangle of growth.

A door opened and an old lady came towards us. She had scarcely looked at me when she said: "You did well, child, to come to me."

She had scarcely looked at me! This was Hungary indeed—the old, hospitable Hungary which today is forbidden by the immigrants!... "Anyone receiving a visitor in his house will be summoned before the Revolutionary Tribunal..."

The overgrown garden peeped in through the grated window; the trees were covered with moss, and old stone seats lined the path. Here was peace. The path was over-run with grass and my feet left no mark on it. I can stop here, even I to whom rest has been so long denied. No search will be made for me here, and I shall be able to sleep at night. There will be no knockings at my window, my dreams will not be haunted by the sound of cartwheels, the ringing of bells, the tramping of feet....

* * *

Szügy, *April 28th.*

THE sun shone into the room; its rays rested on the old furniture and travelled on with soundless steps. Mrs. Beniczky, who was sitting at the writing table, turned now and then towards me and spoke in a low voice, cautiously, for listening ears are everywhere. She inquired about my family, for she had known the Földvárys in other days. My answers became more and more confused. Later on she began to talk of the Counter-revolution and mentioned my name, my real name, spoke of me, of my real self. The blood rushed to my face: she must have thought I had not heard her, for she repeated her question: "Do you know what happened to Cécile Tormay? My daughter met her last winter."

"They say she has escaped to Switzerland..." How ashamed of myself
I felt! I had stolen into this house under a false name, with false credentials.
I had asked my hostess for shelter, though I knew it meant danger to her.
I hated myself, and it was on the tip of my tongue to tell her the truth. Oh,
why could she not see that I was deceiving her, she who received me with
the words: "You have done well, child, to come to me."

We were three at dinner: a visitor had come from Balassagyarmat to
see Mrs. Beniczky. We talked of books, and the guest, who had no more
notion of my identity than our hostess, mentioned *The Old House.*

"What has happened to Cécile Tormay? I am told there is a warrant
out against her."

It was fortunate that I was sitting with my back to the light. Again I
stuttered something about Switzerland. As if speaking to herself, Mrs.
Beniczky said: "But why did she not come here? I would have hidden her
so thot nobody could have found her."

What a burden of self-reproach these words lifted from my
conscience; they told me that it was not entirely by favor of an assumed
name, but to some extent for my own sake, that I was received here.

*　*　*

April 29th.

THIS morning the garden beyond the two tall firs was deliciously
quiet; the trees and shrubs seem to exclude everything that makes life vile
and terrible.

Later in the day one of the maids overheard some soldiers talking near
the pump. Somewhere in the neighborhood a priest has been arrested and
they are going to execute him because a red, white and green flag has been
found in his possession. To the Revolutionary Tribunal with him who
treasures a Hungarian flag! The 'Cabinet' has ordered that every flag, with
the exception of red or black ones, must be given up. Poor Hungarian
flag! Between the black and yellow of the Austrian and the red of the
Bolsheviks, fate has granted it scarcely an interlude in which to float freely
over a free people in a free country. Henceforth the national flag is
proscribed in the land of the Hungarian nation.

The soldiers went on to talk of other things. One whispered: "Have
you heard that Comrade Számuelly is hanging people in
Hajdúszoboszló?..."

Reality has penetrated the garden with all its hideousness. Trees and shrubs can keep it out no longer. Death to everything that is Hungarian! In the county of the noble Hajdú, the Jewish Dictatorship, in flight before the Roumanians, is hanging people—Hungarians. From General Headquarters Comrade Böhm is driving our people to the slaughterhouse. It is said that the pavements of the capital are drenched with rivers of blood. At night there are frequent splashes in the Danube between Buda and Pest. People disappear and never return. The gaols are crowded. Early risers find pools of blood on the chain bridge, with a crushed hat beside them. Who has been murdered? Who are the murderers? There is no answer, but the blood and the news spread.

*   *   *

April 30th.

THE blossoming plum-trees stood like brides in the grass: whenever the breeze rose their white veils fluttered. Time was marked only by the shadow of a slender tree which swept like a giant clock-hand over the lawn and disappeared. Evening fell.

On the main road a soldier on horseback came slowly into sight. He wore the gay hussar's cap of olden times and his dolman swung on his shoulder with the paces of his horse. He looked as if he had stepped out of a picture- book of the past into a strange world of new soldiers with Soviet caps. A Hungarian hussar, a bugler! Remote from the present as his appearance was, the sound of his bugle seemed even more to belong to the past, and the cool evening resounded with the ancient call—a call composed by Haydn, a solemn call: 'To prayer.' The music spread and the forbidden call echoed through the village.

In front of the gate the hands of the Red soldiers went instinctively to their caps. But they stopped halfway, for all prayer is forbidden. On the other side of the road the political delegate to this front, the little Jew Katz, was walking about in patent leather boots. Suddenly he recognized the tune of the bugle call, and his face became distorted with rage. He ran angrily towards the bugler. The soldiers looked down as though to avoid the Syrian eye of the Revolutionary Tribunal.

For some time after silence had been restored and the dust had settled down I stood there, waiting. Nowadays one is always waiting. How many things have failed to come! The ultimatum of the Entente, the French army from Marseilles, British relief troops, the opposition Government in Fiume, counter-revolutions, regiments of officers attacking from beyond the frontiers, relieving Székler battalions... And yet it was good to hope: it helped one to live. But these are things of the past. Now it is only the Rumanians who are coming, and Számuelly is having people hanged...

The night was long and restless. I put out the candle for economy's sake and for hours lay motionless in the dark. Wherever my thoughts strayed they encountered filth and blood.

Then suddenly, out there in the spring night, a nightingale began to sing. I groped my way through the dark room and opened the window. You little artist, the only artist who may practice his art freely in this sad country today! What was it I read in the newspaper this morning? "Order National Council for Intellectual Production... The publication of intellectual products is exclusively in the hands of the National Council..." Art is the vehicle which conveys to us the eternal mystery of the universe. Art is faith wrought into the visible. Art is an aristocracy. Art has precursors, and woe to him who attempts to limit its expanse with shackles. He kills thought, he strikes the image of God as it were in the eye.

Those who have adopted the precepts of Karl Marx speak today of 'party art,' 'mass art,' and 'co-operatives of spiritual production.' What perversely wicked fools are these people whose leader claims to be an author and yet kills literature in Hungary! George Lukacs-Lowinger, the hydrocephalic little Jewish philosopher, son of a millionaire banker, who became a Proletarian apostle through the influence of his Bolshevik wife. As Deputy Educational Commissary of the Soviet he had the book and music shops closed down, and after having thus stopped all literary life and effort, he invented 'the literary register'! He discovered that talent had to be classified, and that each class had to be shut up in a separate drawer, like the goods in a grocer's shop. He therefore decreed that writers were to be divided into three classes, and that the question as to which class a writer belonged was to be decided by a special Directorate. The authors are to receive monthly salaries according to the class to which they are allotted, and for this salary they have to write. They have no other source of income, but the fixed salary is paid to them whatever they produce, so long as it is in accordance with the interests of the Dictatorship of the Proletariat and Class War. Needless to say, the Communist poets all belong to the highest class.

*   *   *

May 1st.

EARLY this morning the sounds of a Gypsy band came from the village, playing the Internationale; thus I realized that this was May Day.

Strict orders have been issued that the village is to be draped in red. A red flag must be hoisted on the town hall, and red ribbons are to float from the windows of the cottages.

The Gypsy band came up to the house and played on the terrace, and the soldiers sang. Mrs. Beniczky and I withdrew to the bottom of the garden. Everything has been commandeered by the Reds: a roast is preparing for them in the kitchen, and other dishes were in process of making. Tonight there is going to be a ball. "Two balls," said the chambermaid, "because we Proletarians refuse to dance with the peasant girls."

Once upon a time May Day was the day of youth, the day of festive excursions for little sempstresses, students, apprentices and children. Then it became the day of manifestations, and, later, of threats. The new saviors of the world promised the millennium for this day. On a blood-soaked land the blood-maddened masses are streaming towards the final battle which is to bring them an utterly unattainable victory. Red flags unfurled in a storm of blood are floating under a sky painted red by incendiary fires.

The first of May has been selected by the Communists for the birthday of the world revolution. Lenin's messages are being scattered broadcast. Moscow has sent its propaganda gold. And the Dictators of the Proletariat are offering their slaves the scent of blood, so that this May shall be their victory.

In Budapest preparations for this festival have been going on for weeks. They hoped to celebrate it with a victory for the Red arms, but for victory they have had to substitute shams. The further the Red army has been forced to retire in the East, the louder they proclaim their Red May.

Panem et circenses! There is no bread, the capital faints for lack of food, so let there be a circus for the people. The last rags are falling from the backs of the destitute millions, so let the town be garbed in red. Entire houses are covered with it; bridge-heads, terraces, walls; even the electric trams have been painted blood-red. The Revolutionary Cabinet has exchanged thirty millions' worth of cattle in Vienna for the red decorations of starving Budapest. The programme of the festivities is so long that the newspapers have no space to report the defeats on the Eastern front.

There are meetings and processions everywhere; everybody has to join in; everybody has to decorate his house; otherwise... May, Spring, glorious feast of freedom, he who dares to remain indifferent to these will be summoned before a Revolutionary Tribunal.

The entire capital has turned red, and on the red background gigantic white plaster statues have been set. On the drill ground a red-covered coffin, two stories high and forty-five yards long, has been erected to the memory of Martinovics, to the leader of the peasant rising, Dózsa, to Charles Liebknecht of Spartacist fame, and to Rosa Luxemburg.

The entrance of the tunnel under the castle hill in Buda is draped in red, and plaster statues of Soviet soldiers with terrifying faces and with rifles raised ready to strike are standing beside it. The naked red giant, hammer in hand, of 'The People's Voice' is displayed at the street corner: "Death to the bourgeois!"

The memorial of our millenary is also covered with red. Over the statue of Arpad, the conqueror, which has been covered with planks, a plaster statue of Marx has been erected. In front of the House of Parliament, like a blood-covered giant bladder, is a red globe. Andrassy's statue has been covered by a red Greek temple, and there again, ten yards high, are the heads of Marx, Lenin, Liebknecht, Engels and Rosa Luxemburg. Plaster, plaster, red cloth (made of paper), red columns, red flag-staffs and flags, wreaths, five-pointed Soviet stars. A sickening red disguise over the deadly pallor of the Hungarian capital. A red rag rouses a thirst for blood in a frenzied bull.

What is it they want, there, on the banks of the Danube? What is it all for? Is it a sudden madness, or is it the accomplishment of the frightful prophecy of the Apocalypse?

I took up my Bible. The prophecy and its realization stood out in red letters before my eyes. But a few days later in the prophecy there comes one on a white horse, dressed in white linen. And the white one vanquishes the red.

* * *

May 2nd.

NEWS has just reached us: the Red army has retired before the Rumanians and has crossed the Tisza. The Serbians have occupied Hódmezövásárhely. The Czechs have occupied Miskolcz and are attacking in two sectors. The population is helping them and there is no resistance; the Reds are in flight. What a terrible position is ours: the invaders fill us with horror, and yet we await them eagerly: we look to assassins to save us from our hangman. And while we bite our lips in helpless anguish our sufferings are unheeded by humanity, which is concerned only with the fact that the Soviet Republic protects foreigners. The Republic of course has decreed that its agents must behave with the greatest courtesy to foreigners, and it has established an 'Office for the protection of Aliens.' Is there not a single foreigner who thinks of asking his own people for help for us, who did not intern them during the war and are now persecuted slaves in our own country?

In past centuries the Rumanians and Serbs fled to us for asylum against their own tyrants, and to us also came the wandering Jew. But now they are all working together to wipe us from the face of the earth. Yet we shared with them everything we had, and they readily received our protection. It is said that only a misguided fraction of the Jews is active in the destruction of Hungary. If that be so, why do not the Jews who represent Jewry in London, in New York, and at the Paris Peace Conference disown and brand their tyrant co-religionists in Hungary? Why do they not repudiate all community with them? Why do they not protest against the assaults committed by men of their race?

*   *   *

A storm is coming, and its breath bends the trees of the garden. The branches of the old firs rise and fall over the lawn like slime-covered oars on a turbulent lake, the leaves of the aspen are thrust apart by the wind as if it were blowing aside the hair from a face walking against the storm. The willow bends as if it were gathering flowers in the grass. The guns thunder near Örhalom. The wind is rising, and already it is roaring like furious giant hounds barking at the setting sun.

The soldiers say that the Czechs are going to attack tonight.

VIII

May 3rd.

A WILD night, like a witches' Sabbath. The nightingale did not sing, the only sound was the roar of the guns. The shells are still stacked on the other side of the wall of my room, out there on the terrace, and if in the dark a shell were to strike here, not one stone of the village would be left on another. But there is so much misery nowadays that no one troubles about such things.

Again the attack did not come off, and during the whole night the garden was wringing its green hands. I was awakened early by excited voices, all talking of the hopeless situation of the Proletarian army. The Rumanians have occupied the bridge-heads at Szolnok and are marching on Budapest. Béla Kun has fallen.

The rumors spread through the villages, and the peasant members of the small Directorates, recruited by force, are saying with pallid lips: "I cannot he blamed, I have only done what I was told. No harm can come to me, I never wanted it." The Communists of Szügy have suddenly become very polite: the Red soldiers actually saluted us. "What is going to happen?" I asked one of them, and as I did so a drunken voice shouted in the yard: "Down with the Dictatorship of the Proletariat!" The political delegates to the front have vanished, and disorderly, ugly indiscipline has taken hold of the men. Sergeant Isidor Grosz shouted his orders in the village street in vain, no one paid the least attention to him. One of the soldiers shouted at him: "Shut up! You left your battery, didn't you, comrade, when the Czechs were shelling us?" I remembered the story of this Isidor Grosz. He went to see his fiancée, having written out a pass for himself and forged his commander's signature to it. When he turned up again his commander brought him before a court-martial. Then the 32nd regiment of heavy artillery began to grumble, and Isidor Grosz ran straight to Béla Kun to complain. The discipline in the Red army is as loose as this everywhere, which explains the feeble resistance it is making.

Meanwhile Comrade Böhm, the Commander-in-Chief, declares that Proletarian self-respect is everywhere victorious.

The door opened; Mrs. Beniczky looked round and then said in a whisper:

"The Counter-revolution has broken out in Balassagyarmat. People are shouting in the street: 'We never were Communists!' Our people have seized a telegram: in it the Soviet Cabinet has disclosed the situation. It has fallen."

Steps came along the terrace. We looked round in alarm. It was Mrs. Aladár Huszár.

What had happened in Balassagyarmat? And her husband? She made a sad gesture, then said that I must go with her. The Czechs were attacking and Balassagyarmat was preparing to receive them. They only want the railway line. Szügy is not going to be occupied, so that if I remained here I should still be in the Soviet Republic. We should have to hurry.

"So they have not fallen after all? And what about the Counter-revolution?"

She told us hastily that a meeting had been held at the square in front of the county hall. Captain Bajatz, who last winter had driven the Czechs out of the town, announced from the balcony that the situation was hopeless. "It is a military impossibility to hold the town." An officer then exclaimed: "Down with the Dictatorship of the Proletariat!" Whereupon Comrade Sugar, the political delegate, elbowed his way to the front on the balcony and incited the people against the bourgeoisie and the officers. "They must be extirpated! Spare neither women nor children! It is they who have brought the Czechs down on us!" The attitude of the crowd changed suddenly: fists were raised and, bayonets pointed towards the bourgeoisie. Blood flowed. Captain Bajatz fled: he was last seen riding towards Kóvár, and as he reached the bridge the Reds opened fire on him. That was the gratitude of Balassagyarmat for his having saved it once. However, he spurred his horse and with two other officers rode over to the Czech lines. Since then the other bank of the Ipoly has livened up. And in the streets of the town the Proletarians are clamoring for our death and shout that they are going to kill the hostages if the Czechs enter. "The whole town is in an uproar, and the railway barriers are guarded. Let us go!"

I was loth to go, and Mrs. Beniczky looked affected too. She said nothing, but she must have wondered that I should leave her now, when it was fear of a Czech bombardment that had driven me here.

"I must explain... It was not because of the—of the bombardment that I came here."

"I knew that much, Elisabeth; it was not fear that brought you here. But I did not question you, I just enjoyed having you."

The assumed name suddenly became unbearable.

"Dear Mrs. Beniczky, I am not the person you think."

She stepped back and looked at me in surprise. "But who are you then?"

Her eyes sparkled when I told her. "Goodness me! But then..." She kissed me and her face showed clearly that she was anything but displeased. "Mind you come back if things turn out otherwise than you expect." And she looked after us as long as her eyes could follow.

Most of the soldiers had removed the red ribbon from their caps and had replaced it by a white flower. By nightfall whole troops of them were going off. A bandy-legged, unkempt young Jew was hurrying towards Mohora. "There goes Béla Kun's soldier!" the Reds shouted. They laughed and one of them spat in the dust.

As we approached the town the country became more and more deserted. We could hear the sound of rifles in the distance. The poplars along the Ipoly were bent as though the weight of the leaden sky pressed them down. Everything bowed to the wind, the dust raced along, and petals were swept in showers from the fruit trees. When we had reached the streets two soldiers, pale as death, came running past us. They glared at us suspiciously, with frightened eyes. Others followed them, carrying rifles and haversacks. They shouted excitedly at us:

"Into the houses. Nobody must remain in the streets."

Another group came running along, dragging a little fair-haired lieutenant with them. They were holding his hands, and pulling him along so that he should not escape. They even implored him: they needed him. Opposite some railings they knelt down, the raised stocks of their rifles pressed against dead-white cheeks.

"The Czechs are here!"

We reached the house and banged the door behind us. Machine guns rattled and a gun roared, making the windows shake. Opposite, under the palings, soldiers bent low and ran feverishly towards the barracks at the end of the town. "There they are, near the wood. They have crossed the Ipoly!"

No human being was now visible in the streets. The rattle of the machine guns continued, and the guns fired more rapidly, the shells whining through the air above our heads and bursting in the vineyards towards Szügy. A cloud rose wherever they struck the earth.

"The church spire of Kóvár has been hit, it's disappeared altogether."

On the main road some cows were rushing along in a wild stampede, the heavy coat of the cow-herd swinging right and left as he ran. Everything was dashing for shelter.

The street became darker and quieter, and the rifles alone broke the silence of the night. The electric lights were out, the current had failed.

Hours passed, then heavy fists were heard banging at some door. Armed men clattered past our window and went on towards the prison. The unsuccessful Counter-revolution had disclosed the honest people. Another door banged in the next street: they were taking hostages. And in every part of Hungary doors are banging like that tonight...

* * *

Balassagyarmat, May 4th.

WE are still ascending our blood-covered Calvary; later on its stations may show up clearly. There, at that corner, did they put the cross on our shoulders, there did they smite our faces, there did they spit into our eyes, there did we collapse under the cross, and nobody came to help us to bear it. We had to rise and drag it further.

Yesterday we thought we had escaped. Yesterday the news came that the Cabinet had fallen and that the Red armies were everywhere on the run. Today they have shunted the ill-success of their arms and the people's fury onto the bourgeoisie. The game of the Károlyi revolution is being repeated. Instead of pogroms, let there be massacres of Christians. They spoke of it at the marketplace: Számuelly is coming to restore order. The lives of the fallen Red soldiers must be revenged.

Mobilization!... The newspaper seems to be composed entirely of exclamation marks. 'To the factory-workers!' 'Order!' 'Appeal!' 'Decree!'

Comrade Pogány has sounded a tocsin of alarm: "The news from the front is bad. Our defeat at the front means the return of the Dictatorship of the Bourgeoisie, our victory means the conservation of the Dictatorship of the Proletariat. Everything depends on organized labour. Today the position is this: the revolutionary Proletariat of Budapest can no longer trust the front, on the contrary, it rests with the Proletariat of Budapest to save the front by its revolutionary impetus. The Dictatorship has reached its crisis..."

Only after this confession did the newspaper give a belated account of the May festivities of the capital. The town in scarlet; hundreds of thousands in the streets; an exodus to the woods; illuminations, fireworks... And the poor people who expected to be fed on the festive

104

occasion staggered back like madmen to the great incertitude, hungry, and their eyes sore with the scarlet glare.

The deadly color of the red madness was still on the walls of the houses when at 2 p.m. the trembling Cabinet met in the great room of the Town Hall. Meanwhile rain had begun to fall, and the thirty millions' worth of red paper-cloth was soaked; red streamed down the houses, the walls, the plaster statues, the pavement. Everything was painted red. It is said that the town looked like a huge blood-covered slaughterhouse. And then the news spread that the Dictatorship had fallen.

The newspapers reported the details of the emergency meeting of the Workers' Council. Béla Kun shouted to the audience that "The masses of the Red army are fleeing before the hireling armies of Imperialism. Looking now," he said with raised voice, "at Soviet Hungary, I remember a story by Gorki. Gorki went to Paris in search of the spirit of Revolution, seeking its aid for the struggling revolution of the Russian Proletariat. He searched for the ancient Revolution, crowned with the good Phrygian cap, he searched and inquired, and at last was led to a hotel where he found a courtesan, a woman fallen more or less to the level of a street prostitute, and he asked her not to give herself to the Czar, but to help the Revolution. But the woman the Revolution had turned into a courtesan gave herself none the less to the Czar; so Gorki ends with these words: 'I wanted to spit my bloody, purulent saliva into her face.'"

That is the kind of thing Béla Kun remembers when he looks at 'this Soviet Hungary' and he dares to say it to a race to whom Louis Kossuth once said: "I prostrate myself before the greatness of the Nation." Kossuth prostrated himself while Béla Kun thinks of expectorating. I read the report to the end: nobody seems to have risen to choke the words in his throat. In his awful Ghetto-lingo Béla Kun went on:

"...It is not the Rumanians, it is our own troops who are a danger to Budapest. We had to disarm the units which returned from the northern part of the Tisza, so as to save at least their weapons for the Proletariat. The morale of the troops is such that Budapest is helplessly at the mercy of a Rumanian attack. The question arises, comrades, shall we give up Budapest, or shall we fight for Budapest? I have always told my comrades that I know neither morality nor immorality. I know of only two things; those that are useful to Proletarianism and those which endanger Proletarianism. And I declare that it is dishonorable to tell the bourgeois the truth if this truth is to be hurtful to the Proletariat. But, comrades, I will not deceive the Proletariat. I will tell you that the workers' battalions are wanting in the fighting spirit which would entitle us to think of the salvation of Budapest..."

Thus does this man speak of his own character, the man who in his absolute power admits that: "We were a small group, in opposition to the majority of working men, when we started the fight for the Dictatorship." And he reveals the terrible secret of his success: Károlyi's high treason. "I feel somehow that if the Dictatorship were to perish now, it would perish only because it gained a bloodless victory. It was too cheap, it was given us for nothing..."

I fact, it cost nothing except Judas' money and perhaps the existence of Hungary. For now Béla Kun has renounced the whole of Hungary and is ready to satisfy any territorial demands the Czechs, Rumanians and Serbs may raise, on condition that his power is left to him, and "Budapest, where the protest against capitalism can make a stand."

His is no longer a human thirst for power: it is an insatiable animal greed, which allows the limbs of its prey to be torn off as long as it can devour the heart. After having bartered away the land which the nation has held for a thousand years in exchange for a single town, he has telegraphed to our hungry neighbors, offering them the ancient soil of the nation. And all he has to say to his comrades about this unexampled deed is this: "It was not for our pleasure that we sent those telegrams to the surrounding bourgeois states..."

A stranger soul has never used stranger language in Hungary.

While Béla Kun was declaiming: "I am not in despair... I do not want to make you despair, comrades... you will never hear despondent words from my lips... I shall never give it up... I say we won't be downhearted... bad times, but not hopeless..." news was brought to the assembly: the position in the field is not hopeless! The attitude of the meeting altered at once. The orator became truculent once more.

"If possible we must defend the Dictatorship before Budapest, through the Bakony, to Wiener Neustadt... We must not resign our power!"

The Workers' Council then adopted a resolution—that it is the duty of organized labour "to defend to the last drop of blood the achievements of the Dictatorship of the Proletariat."

How this defense is to be conducted was revealed by a comrade called Surek:

"Honored Workers' Council... The bourgeoisie is grinning and rubbing its hands everywhere. We must freeze this grin on its face! Tomorrow we must go to the factories and our first duty will be to exterminate the bourgeoisie effectively, in the strictest sense of the word. We must keep our pledge that when the Entente comes here it shall find nothing but mountains of bourgeois corpses and a determined Proletariat.

Enough bourgeois must not be left alive to form a Government."

In deference to foreign countries this speech was not reported in the papers; but political agitators are spreading the words of Comrade Surek.

Now and then a bowed female form passes the window, her face set towards the prison, carrying food for some hostage. The observation post of the Reds has been established on the prison roof, just above the hostages. Let the Czechs shell it! Soldiers stop the women, inspect their baskets and take whatever they fancy. Then they say, as a parting greeting: "That is the last dinner you need bring! If the Czechs enter, we shall hang the swine."

* * *

May 5th.

THE bombardment has ceased, and the town is creeping out of its holes. But people pass each other stealthily, without exchanging words, as if they dared no longer talk. And above the county hall the wind is toying with the red flag. A blood-red shawl is floating in the spring breeze: Szolnok has been retaken.

In the afternoon Gregory, the Huszárs' coachman, came running horror-stricken from the town: the Reds have declared that instead of Aladár Huszár they are going to arrest his wife.

It was about ten o'clock when there was a knock at the door.

"Let me go," I said to my friend. Are they coming for her, or has her husband come back, or are they searching for me? The candle guttered in the wind, and at the garden gate three men with fixed bayonets emerged from the dark. They pushed me aside without saying a word and marched up the stairs into the room. I ran and got in front of them.

"What do you want?"

They strode towards me menacingly and suddenly I found myself surrounded. They looked round suspiciously, and the leader said roughly:

"Why is there a light in this house?"

I gave some explanation. One of the soldiers, a long, angry-faced man, leant over me threateningly:

"This is no time to have lights burning. Just you look out! If we catch you again we shall hang you on that lamp-post there, at the corner."

When they went I felt as if a throttling hand had released my throat.

* * *

May 6th.

I HAVE been thinking of my mother all morning. This is her name day, and I cannot be with her. Fate is continually pushing back the hands of the clock that will strike the hour of our reunion.

The town is beflagged with red flags. What has happened? Szolnok? Or is it some other victory?

The Powers of the Entente have ordered the Rumanians back, and now they are standing waiting beyond the Tisza. Meanwhile we perish here.

Számuelly has no time to come here, luckily: he is restoring order in the towns which put out white flags on the arrival of the Rumanians. Six Hungarians were hanged on the 3rd of May. Mrs. Huszár received the news, one of the victims being a relation of hers, Béla Batik, an only son the war left to his mother. Számuelly sat in judgment over him. "Off you go to the gallows!" said he, and he himself put the halter round his neck. Then he lit a cigarette and clapped Batik on the shoulder saying: "It will be all right, my hangman has the knack of it. Listen, you dog! I grant you the time it takes me to smoke this cigarette. If you will tell me meanwhile the names of your accomplices, I will let you off." He then sat down on a chair and smoked while the other stood under the gallows with the rope round his neck. The cigarette was finished. "Long live the White army and Hungary!" Batik shouted, and Számuelly released the trap with his own hand.

Bloodstains multiply everywhere. We now know the names of at least two of the victims whose blood has been spilt on the chain bridge. They were Alexander Hollán and his father. They had worked hard all their lives and they were slaughtered by those who called themselves the leaders of the 'workers.'

It happened on the 27th of April. All over Budapest it was forbidden for anybody to be in the streets after 10 p.m. The window blinds had to be drawn and if a light was visible in a window the 'Terror Boys' fired at it. Armed lorries were continually rushing about in the dark streets. The town listened with bated breath: hostages were being taken. Motors were racing up the castle hill: it was a hunt for human victims. When these had been collected a car crossed over to Pest and stopped on the bridge. The two Holláns were hustled out on to the lower quay. Probably it was there that their captors intended to do the deed, but for some unknown reason they ordered their victims back again into the car. They started off but stopped again at the pillar and obliged the tortured men to get off. The motor-car waited nearby and those in it heard a violent altercation going on in the dark. Shots were then fired and there followed two splashes in the Danube.

Nobody has seen the two Holláns since. The story of the happenings was told by Karátson, a Secretary of State and one of their fellow prisoners. Then, one does not know how, the news filtered out and is being whispered today behind the closed doors and windows of Budapest. Many know it, only poor Alexander Hollán's wife is in ignorance. The Communists declare that her husband is in gaol, and at noon her little grey shadow waits day after day amongst the other women at the prison gate. She brings food and linen to her husband and sends messages, and thanks the terrorists at the gate for transmitting them. Meanwhile the Danube carries her dead gently towards the sea.

The prisons are crowded with hostages awaiting their fate. Death perpetually hovers over them, for they are threatened daily with execution and daily one or another of them is led off to the prison yard. They blindfold him and fire over his head-for fun. The hangmen of today greatly enjoy gloating over their victims' fear. Yet to produce terror is the delight of degraded souls. Hearsay reports hundreds who are the innocent inhabitants of prisons, but names cannot be ascertained. Yet we know there are Archduke Joseph Francis, Bishop Count John Mikes, Alexander Wekerle, the former Prime Minister, the president and the vice-president of the Hungarian Academy of Sciences, several former Ministers, court dignitaries and members of parliament, generals, lord lieutenants, landlords, and many others, among them the aged Count Aurel Dessewffy, Lord Chief Justice, who was dragged by Red soldiers from the side of his wife's deathbed to be cast into prison. There is the elite of the Hungarian nation, with many others whose names have not reached me. Many unknown people, students, women, farmers, manufacturers, even some workmen. They are all hostages—prisoners in their own country— pawns for the lives of Béla Kun, Számuelly, Pogány, Landler and other comrades.

* * *

May 7th.

NOW and then comes the sound of distant gunfire. Whence does the wind bring it? The Reds have beaten the Czechs back all along the Ipoly. A new poster has been stuck on the wall of the house opposite, it is an appeal to the inhabitants of Balassagyarmat by Comrades Riechmann, the political delegate, and Singer:

> Comrades! We have vowed on our ideals that if any among you who
> want to restore the old order raise their sacrilegious hands against us, we
> shall strike them down with our iron fists and smite them like a hammer
> smites the anvil. What do they want? To bring back the old criminal
> order? Do not attempt the impossible, because henceforth the slightest
> attempt will mean paying with your lives, and we will deal with you as
> with ordinary assassins who are a danger to human life. Behold, your
> heroes, sitting in gaol and waiting for the sentence of justice for their vile,
> incredible treasons... What does the country mean to the bourgeois?
> You have seen how it created happiness and comfort for them, while
> our share was misery... And we declare to the bourgeoisie of the whole
> world that we will not give up our town and our country, because *now*
> *they are ours, it was we who defended them for fifty-two months...* Long
> live the world revolution! Long live Béla Kun!

Comrades Singer and Riechmann! They cannot even write the Hungarian
language, and yet they dare to claim not only our country but its defense
during the war which they successfully shirked for fifty-two months. Let
them behold from their graves, those who have fallen on distant
battlefields, those whose feet were frozen in paper boots...those whose
wives hungered and shivered in the queue! Among my relations fourteen
followed the call. All of them were young. Eight of them will never return.
Do they behold these things from their graves?

At the end of October the disbanded soldiers came back from the
world-war clamoring for pogroms. In November they were already
demanding the blood of their own kin. The air was full of secret
promptings: 'Everything shall be yours!' Later on there came the shout:
'Plunder the gentle folk!' Those who first whispered saved thus their
fortunes and their lives. And the people chose as its leaders the owners of
the gin-shops and declared the landlords their foes. And Comrades Singer
and Riechmann declare today that our country is their country and no
longer ours. The leadership of the nation which was once Széchényi's,
Kossuth's, Deák's and Tisza's, is now theirs.

*　*　*

May 8th.

BÉLA KUN has asked the Rumanians for an armistice. His offer expresses deadly fear. If he can retain the rest of mutilated Hungary in his grip he will renounce any territory, is ready for any sacrifice.

Madarescu, the commander of the Rumanian troops in Transylvania, answered three days later. In his conditions, he never mentions the Soviet but always speaks of Hungary He insists on the disarmament of all Hungarian forces. He requires that the Hungarian Command shall acquiesce in the execution of the ultimate conditions whatever they may be. He requires the delivery of all arms, guns, ammunition, means of transport, equipment and provisions. He demands all railway material and armored trains, and orders the return of all prisoners of war, hostages and civilian population carried off by the retiring army. This reparation is to be done without any obligation of reciprocity on Rumania's behalf. That is how Hungary is spoken to today! And the Dictatorship of the Proletariat, which has helped the advance of the Rumanians from the Maros and Szamos to the Tisza, may count this humiliating tone among its achievements. It is we alone feel the pain. When on the 1st of May the Rumanians crossed the Tisza, Béla Kun prepared for flight. The families of the People's Commissaries were packing up. Big sums were smuggled out of the country. Then the Rumanians were stopped by the Entente, so Béla Kun gained time. He organized the workers' battalions and today he answers Madarescu's armistice proposals by mobilization. So we continue in agony.

New orders have been posted up in the streets of Budapest:

> To save the Proletarian Revolution we order the general mobilization of the Proletariat. Budapest will from this date be under martial law. We appeal to the Proletariat to do its duty to the last.
>
> The Revolutionary Cabinet.

And the hated and persecuted middle classes are ordered to pay the blood-tax for the salvation of their executioners: "Every officer of the reserve who is under forty-five years of age must report for active service. Those who refuse to obey this order..." If the middle-classes do not obey, they are threatened with the Revolutionary Tribunal; the Proletarians, however, if they enlist, "will receive in addition to their pay the usual wages of workmen."

No, it is not yet over, indeed it is beginning once more.

In Budapest the comrade Commissaries and their wives are reviewing the troops, and the electrician Commander-in-Chief is starting in the royal train from his Headquarters to inspect the troops in the provinces.

The Galician Neros are now quite at home in their bloody and fantastic role. Their chronicle, 'The People's Voice' which until lately has spent all its energies in undermining authority and in attacking militarism, now reports in rapture:

> Comrade Böhm inspected the troops and expressed his complete satisfaction at their appearance. After the review the Commander-in-Chief travelled with his whole staff to the front, where he inspected the advance line and received the reports of his generals. Comrade Böhm has expressed his confidence...

It is an old familiar text, only the name of Comrade Böhm has been substituted for that of the Archduke. 1914... 1919!

Here in this place it is not very easy to hold a review, for the greater part of the garrison has evaporated. The place of Captain Bajatz has been filled by a local butcher's assistant who commands the army from a coffee house. Comrade Riechmann is the chief of the general staff.

Towards evening the news spread that the Czechs are going to surround Balassagyarmat tonight. A nightingale was singing in the moonlit garden, and voices rose in the garden next door:

"If the Czechs do not come tonight it will be the end of the hostages. The soldiers have been shouting all day under the prison walls 'You are going to die, you swine!'"

At that moment a cannon roared in the vineyards. "Bless your sweet little throat," exclaimed the voice of an old woman.

"Don't bless it so loud or you will find yourself in prison."

"But the nightingale!" stammered the old woman.

"Of course," someone laughed; "I thought you referred to the Czech gun."

Wild firing came from the Ipoly, and bullets whistled right and left. We ran towards the house. Near the shed a bullet passed so close to me that I felt the wind of it: it passed over my head and struck the wall like a mad wasp. The shutters of the houses were closed rapidly, they give one at any rate a feeling of shelter. Bullets continued to spatter on the walls. Every now and then we rushed out, looked round in the—moon light, and then rushed back again. All the while the wasps are buzzing round the house.

* * *

May 9th.

ON the sunny side of the street, tired, ill-looking, prematurely aged people came slowly from the direction of the prison. The hostages have been released. The order came from Budapest:

"The Soviet takes hostages when danger is imminent. As the Soviet is at present in no immediate danger, we order their provisional release."

The wife of a railwayman came into the yard with eyes red with weeping. The soldiers had deserted their post, so Comrade Riechmann and the butcher's commander ordered the railwaymen out. They at least love their country, and last winter they opposed the Czechs. Now they have driven them back again, having made forty prisoners. But thirty-eight railwaymen are missing, and Comrade Böhm is going to credit internationalism with this victory won by Hungarian nationalism.

A carriage rattled down the street. Nowadays whenever a carriage stops anywhere all the windows and walls of the neighborhood are on the alert. We noticed that everybody was looking in our direction.

Gregory the coachman put his head through the door:

"Here they are!"

Detectives. I hid my notes in the sofa cushions and fled before them from room to room. They requisitioned uniforms and field-glasses. They also inspected the library and told us that the piano was public property. Even sewing machines are taken by the Government, and it makes no difference if the owner is a tailor. Thus are they killing home industries. They took all the tobacco they could find, nor did opera-glasses escape; "The army needs them. We give no receipt. These things no longer belong to you, nothing belongs to you." And they took them. As they left they questioned the maid in the corridor:

"And where may your master be?"

I heard the girl reply mockingly, "In town!"

"Don't play the fool!" the detective shouted, "we know he has run away. We are searching the whole county for him."

Again the girl chaffed them. "What an idea! How can he have run away? They are pulling your leg. He comes home every night."

"Well I never," said the man to his companion, and they whispered among themselves. The maid thought herself very clever and laughed contentedly.

When they had left, Gregory the coachman came in.

"They said they will come back and watch for him every night."

Mrs. Huszár advised me to go back to Szügy till this zeal blew over.

In the afternoon the sky became clouded. The fusillade died down.

The stuffy heat preceding a storm weighed heavily on us. In town they were burying some soldiers, unfortunate victims of the Red war. The passersby stopped on the curb and stared at the funeral, while the procession passed slowly under red flags. A red cross was borne in front of it, then came the coffins, draped in red, followed by two vulgar-looking girls, in red dresses, carrying wreaths of red flowers tied with red ribbons. Under the grey sky, on the grey road, death, dressed in red, proceeded towards the cemetery. And among the green fields, in verdant peace, the garden of Szügy was waiting for me.

IX

SINCE I left Szügy the almond trees have blossomed; so beauty came to meet me, and my heart lost some of its wildness and I felt less lonely and sad.

When I reached the bottom of the neglected garden I saw that someone was sitting on the stone seat leaning his elbows on the table and staring towards the sun. For an instant I was taken aback: who was this man? Then I remembered: he must be one of the officers quartered on us. Abject distress was depicted on his downcast face.

It was despair that drove many patriotic officers through hunger and poverty into the Red army, and among the humiliated they are the worst; trampled, threatened, insulted, hungry, shivering and watched; the helpless prey of a typewriter-agent commander-in-chief, of the delegates to the front, of scum.

So the pathless garden has appealed to another unfortunate. He too would like to escape, but cannot; he too would like to hope, and there is nothing to hope for. What is in store for us? Every attempt we have made has broken down, our hopes from abroad, our hopes from our own efforts. The Red press is howling for blood. "Death to the bandits of the Counter-revolution!"

The greater part of Hungary's aristocracy fled abroad in March: the Hungarian peasantry keeps obstinately silent on its isolated farms, in its sequestered villages. So there are none left for a counter-revolution but those who for a thousand years have borne the weight of our destinies. Once they were the electors of kings, when they were known as the gentry, later as the educated classes, and today as the middle classes. They have always been to the fore when death or toil was demanded of them, and always in the background when royal favors and grants were distributed; but never have they been mediocre in fibre. This class will be forever the trunk of the oak, the power that supports the tree and stands up against the blows of the axe, yet does not receive the rays of the sun. Now the axe has fallen. Men were wanted who dared to die, and in Budapest the first attempt at a counter-revolution flared up. But somebody betrayed it, and those caught were sentenced to life-long imprisonment and their leaders executed.

Then came the news that the 'Cabinet' had sent to the Hungarian Legation in Vienna one hundred and forty million crowns to finance a revolution; whereupon Hajób, the Secretary of the Legation, and the patriotic Hungarian employees stormed the Communist Legation. The money fell into the hands of the counter-revolutionaries.

'The Red Newspaper' foamed as it reported the matter. Our hopes rose. It was said that over twenty thousand Hungarians, able to bear arms, were in Vienna, and in our imagination the right bank of the Danube was already aflame. People whispered: "the Hungarians of Vienna have started, it is only a question of days and they will knock over the Dictatorship." Then one night about fifty officers crossed the frontier—and were disarmed by the Austrian frontier guards.

Still there was hope. The ideals of the Budapest conspiracy survived its martyrs. The thread was not dropped. Brave men began once more to organize. It was decided that the aeroplane which was to give the signal for the rising was to fly over Budapest on the 4th of May at three o'clock in the morning. On the eve of the event a few officers, confident of victory, appeared in a restaurant with white roses and with restored decorations and insignia of rank, and made the gypsy band play the national anthem. This stupid demonstration naturally aroused the attention of spies, and the same night Colonel Dormándy, Captain Horváth and several brave officers and officials were arrested.

When I reached the house a letter was waiting for me from Mrs. Huszár. A clergyman of the reformed church is going tomorrow to his parents who live on the other bank of the river, and he will take me with him. One has only to ford the river and one is safe.

*   *   *

May 12th.

I HAD a curious dream last night. I dreamt the moon was shining on the manor-house. I had to escape, and was implored to hurry. Somebody hastily pressed a bundle tied up in a handkerchief and a staff into my hand. Then I found myself on the main road along the river, alone in the silvery light of the moon. The water was visible between the trees and sparkled brightly. Then I noticed that the bundle in my hand became heavier and heavier. I looked at it and found that it was all covered with blood; blood was streaming out of it and running down my staff till it covered the road.

Later I told Mrs. Beniczky my dream. "Don't go," said she; "a better opportunity will come." So I stayed. In the afternoon the commander of the artillery in the village came to take leave. The Czechs are retiring all along the line, the Reds in pursuit. The Rumanians also have lost the initiative. In Germany the awful conditions of peace have provoked an outburst of Spartacism. The Germans are making an alliance with the Russians. France does not care; she requires her troops for troubles at home. The domination (such as it was) of the Entente in Hungary has come to an end. The gunner looked down in despair:

"The Soviet is going to rule the world," said he.

If this is true I shall not escape; I shall go back to my mother and report myself. One gets tired of being a fugitive.

There was a knock at the door and in came Mrs. Huszár. She too was pale and spoke in whispers:

"Bad news. It is all over, and the town is full of detectives. You mustn't stay any longer—you must leave here immediately."

"And your husband? Supposing it's true that things are going to continue like this for years?"

"I've just heard from him," said Mrs. Huszár, "he's hiding in the woods. He's having a bad time of it too, but then he is a man." She had no thought for herself, only for others. "There's no need for you to stay with us."

So we agreed that I should be informed as soon as the clergyman returned and get ready to start.

The moon was filtering through the trees and in the blue light on the lawn the white fluffy dandelion clocks swayed like tiny Chinese lanterns on the ends of miniature poles. The breeze swept across the grass and extinguished the lanterns. The fluff floated in the moonlight: the image of our torn hopes.

* * *

May 13ᵗʰ

THIS morning a soldier I had not seen before came in through the garden gate, bringing the officer's dinner in a canteen. He put down the canteen on the steps of the terrace and went into the kitchen. The men have ordered roast veal for their own dinner. When he came back he saw that a dog was licking the officer's food.

"What does it matter?" said he; "dogs can feed out of the same trencher."

* * *

May 14th.

THE last frost was shimmering on the grass, and machine-guns were clattering away as if needles of steel were sewing a shroud in the air.

A cloud rose on the main road, as if raised by a whirlwind: a carriage came racing along at a mad gallop. A young man was driving, giving the horses their head, and as he leant forward, I saw that he had a gentlemanly appearance. That was all I could see through the dust; the carriage passed in a flash.

Shots were fired at it. "Stop him!" howled a hoarse, thick voice from a cottage.

They are going to arrest him; already a mounted trooper is galloping after him. But his horse shied at the shooting, rose on its hind legs, and then swerved with his rider into the fields. Meanwhile the carriage had disappeared, and my heart followed it. The fate of the driver is mine, his escape is my escape. I do not know who he was. I could not even see his face clearly, but he is 'wanted,' so we are friends. It is only thieves and malefactors who are not hounded in Hungary today. They are free, they judge, rule, and speak in the name of the country. Those who are hunted are my brethren.

* * *

May 16th.

THE garden has never attained such supreme beauty; it seems to open in the morning as for an embrace. Its silence was interrupted this morning, however, by a sound like a giant blue-bottle humming in the distance. It flew fast, came nearer and nearer, its hum became a roar. A motor-car was racing along, a grey, luxurious field car, like the one the King used to have. I looked out between the shrubs. The car stopped near the path, and the driver in his leather coat leant forward, adjusting something near the steering wheel. There were three passengers in the car, the one on the right, lolling back among the, cushions, a fat, high-shouldered, short-necked, broad Jew, whose very attitude was unpleasant. Under his flat Soviet cap greasy black hair curled over his neck. His clean-shaven face reminded one of a music-hall artist.

The car started and disappeared in a cloud of dust. I shrank back with disgust. Why had that face come here? Where had I seen it before? I shuddered. It was as though a soft slimy toad had suddenly appeared on the surface of a clear sylvan pool. The garden closed over the vision and the flowering lilacs effaced its impression. In the evening I was told that the man in the princely motor, with his suite, was Joseph Pogány.

I suppose I ought to be amused. Here am I, outlawed, sentenced to death, and sleuth-hounds have been let loose upon my tracks. The chauffeur is probably our housekeeper's fiancé, the same who was set to spy on our home. And these people who have been searching for me for weeks were standing just now a few paces from me; they, openly, free, while I was hiding in the bushes. May the same fortune attend their search for others.

*   *   *

May 17th.

YESTERDAY a newspaper was thrown from the train. The old middle-class newspapers have stopped publication even in their new Communist disguise. Following the Russian example there are now only official papers; 'The People's Voice,' 'The Red Newspaper,' 'The Red Soldier,' 'The Young Proletarian'; *Világ*, the old newspaper of the Freemasons, has remained, though it disguises its identity under the name of *The Torch* and serves as official mouthpiece of the Commissary for Education; and there is the old capitalistic *Pester Lloyd* used by the revolutionary Cabinet as its semi-official, German mouthpiece.

The newspaper went from house to house through the village and at last reached us. It proclaims in gigantic type: "Victories of the Proletarian army. Lenin congratulates Béla Kun by wireless on his victories." So Lenin is speaking once more!

The sun is shining and yet the horizon appears dark and sad. Is it really possible that they should triumph in the end? Suddenly I laughed: Comrade Landler has published an article in 'The People's Voice,' telling the story of how he visited a workmen's battalion with Béla Kun and Pogány. To quote him verbatim:

When they saw us they cheered. Then a curious thing happened—our comrades asked for our autographs. We were obliged to give our autographs, not to one, not to ten, but to half a battalion. He who cannot interpret this incident must be afflicted with blindness. An army which is on such a high level of culture that its men, a few miles behind the front, ask for nothing but autographs, *an army like that cannot fail to be victorious!*

The paper was still in my hand when I came to a little plot of land below the garden known by the name of 'the parson's green.' It used to be glebe land but Mrs. Beniczky had rented it for many years. She has just been informed by the Directorate that this is to be her last year of tenancy. However, they are graciously allowing her corn to grow there. John Kispál, the gardener, a member of the Directorate, was hoeing in it, and behind him a small girl was sowing corn in the furrows. When Master Kispál perceived the newspaper in my hand, he leant on his hoe and sucked at his pipe so violently that he drew his cheeks in. Then he sent the girl for tobacco and looked round cautiously. That is the way people have nowadays when they want to speak openly.

"Tell me, Miss," said he, "what is going to happen?"

"How should I know? "

"Well, the gentle folks always know more than we do; they get it out of their brains. Brains can't be taught." He gave a long pull at his pipe. "Nowadays they put a man up against the wall if he says what he thinks. Mistress Bakalár has been carried off in chains, because she could not keep her mouth shut. She said that the Reds were greater enemies than the enemy. It was no help to her that she was a first-class Proletarian, rifle-butts played havoc with her head." The gardener looked down pensively. "Even that is not the worst of it. What's worse is that they are forsaking the country. How can any Hungarian do such a thing?"

"Those in power today are not Hungarian."

"What? You don't mean to say that Béla Kun is not a Hungarian? "

"Why, his real name is Cohen!"

Kispál's mouth opened wide. "If that is so, the gentle folk have treated us very unfairly. Why did they allow such a thing? Believe me, if he had come here under his true name the people would have had none of him."

When I reached the house the soldiers were making a great noise in the kitchen. They told the maid that an army order had arrived: the 32nd Artillery would have, to leave this place. A small battery would come in its place with a hundred and fifty men. But they were not quite sure about obeying this order yet: Sergeant Isidor Grosz has a sweetheart nearby, and

Katz, the political delegate, does not want a change, either. So they have sent to Budapest to ask Béla Kun to change the gunners. They will stay on with the 8 c.m. guns, and if they do not get their way, they are going to blow up all the ammunition. Comrade Pogány was in a temper when he left here. In the morning when he rushed into the commander's office he shouted and did not say "good morning" to anybody.

He asked an officer:

"How many recruits, and what stuff are they made of?"

"Eighty men, poor fellows, mostly flat-footed." "Why did they join up?"

"For pay, clothes and boots," the officer answered. "Not for the ideals of the Proletariat?" Pogány insisted.

"I can't tell. The matter was never mentioned."

The People's Commissary turned his back on him furiously and ordered the officers to parade in front of the men; then he asked the latter: "Are you satisfied with the comrade officers?" After that, though the Red press describes his indomitable courage at the head of storming troops and gushes over his self-sacrificing heroism, he retired to a safe distance behind the front.

And the gunners are going to remain another day because they want to have a dance as a send-off. The men say that Isidor Grosz has come to an arrangement with Belo Kun—he came back with his pockets bulging with money, so now he does not mind leaving. It is to be hoped that none of the others will take the thing amiss: there is a lot of ammunition in the woodshed and on the terrace. The gate stands open, and there is nobody to guard it. Even children steal in and break the boxes open, stealing the cartridge cases and the cordite to make fireworks with.

The maid went to the dance tonight. There was a Gypsy band. The soldiers danced and "the Proletarian army, as a sign of its great, self-respecting discipline," emptied several barrels of wine.

* * *

May 19th.

THE Red press is shrieking with sarcasm, mixed with hatred! "The parody of a Government in Arad!" What is it, an opposition Government? Surely not a Hungarian Government? But it is. It was formed in Arad on the 5th of May, two weeks ago, and we, living in the same country, have received the news only today! That is how The Terror deals with our news.

CÉCILE TORMAY

At last...! I read the manifesto of Arad over and over again. "The real leaders of the nation being now in prison or banished, we assume the leadership provisionally."

A Hungarian voice, after a long silence. It does not boast, it has none of the conceit of the distributors of autographs, it is manly and modest like the man who is at the head of this provisional Government, though for an instant his name repelled me. Károlyi! Awful memories are connected with that name, and an irremovable curse. After Michael Károlyi comes another Károlyi; but Count Julius Károlyi's personality stands high above the name, as if in expiation of the crimes which another bearer of it has committed. The Foreign Secretary, Baron Bornemissza, has been for years the leader of the Hungarians whom fate has cast among the Rumanians. The Minister of War is not a typewriter-agent or a second-rate journalist, but a real soldier. And all the names are of this stamp but one: Varjassy has been Károlyi's and Jászi's man. But that matters little now, and the more 'The People's Voice' fulminates, the greater is my joy. "Who are these nobodies?" the Communist paper asks. "Hungarians!" replies the air, replies life, replies morning and night. And hope made golden promises.

Dense masses of soldiers came from the village this afternoon, and the gunners of the 32nd came to harvest in our garden. They are leaving this evening and flowers are required for the train. So they made a dead set at everything that blossomed in this quiet realm of green. Branches cracked, the garden moaned. Within an hour the dreamy little shrubs were changed into scarecrows, the grass was purple with the blossom of lilac. Branches were twisted and cut down to stumps, wounded plants were stripped of twigs and leaves. They have trampled Spring to death. I raged inwardly; let them have the flowers, but why this mad destruction? I went into the house: I could not bear the sight of it.

* * *

May 20th-21st.

AFTER the tepid rain in the night the sun has come out from among the clouds, and the ill-treated shrubs look less hopeless, laden as they are with glittering drops. The rain has made the grass raise its head and some forgotten lilacs have opened their blossoms.

Ever since break of day the air has been humming above our heads. Steel moles are mining the clouded sky. They are invisible till they fall with a terrific crash and raise mole-hills on the ground.

The Reds have retaken Miskolcz from the Czechs. Eleven counter-revolutionaries have been arrested in Budapest. In the 'Frankel Leo' barracks a memorial tablet has been unveiled to the French Communist leader of that name who was born in Old Buda.

In other countries there is peace, there is a future. They awake daily without fear, their dreams are not nightmares; they have doors they can close, cupboards that are not searched, a hearth which is not shared by uncivilized, spiteful strangers. There one may sing and laugh. One may even speak openly, happily. They have music, pictures, and books, and no one comes to take them from them. Man is allowed to create, their minds produce songs and sculptures and pictures, scholars pursue their studies, and women have not forgotten to smile. And in the stifling fetid atmosphere of ugliness, humiliation, reckless brutality, restraint, slavery, and hatred, I am homesick for an hour's beauty. Just for an hour to have things as they used to be!

Mrs. Beniczky had a visitor today, an elderly lady who lived in the village. I escaped quietly to my room, and although the visitor spoke in whispers, now and then she forgot herself and then her voice reached me. Suddenly she became aware that she was raising her voice and pulled herself up.

"I understand that a poor relation of the Huszárs is staying with you, where is she?" she asked anxiously. "In the next room? Goodness, then I ought to... "

"Don't worry," said Mrs. Beniczky, laughing quietly, "she is hard of hearing."

Since I have been in hiding goodness knows how many things I have been. First an escaped teacher, then a nurse, then a poor relation; now I am deaf. Yet under false names, under all sorts of disguises, almost invariably I have met with kindness. Of course some people naturally tried to impress me with their own importance, and I shall be forever grateful to them, for they have taught me what it feels like to have to put up with other people's conceit. There was a 'comrade' officer of the Reds who used to make me feel fearfully small—I was only a 'poor relation.' He scarcely ever took any notice of me, and when I said anything he looked ostentatiously bored. O poor relations, unwanted superfluities, you have been my teachers, once I was one of you, and when these times are over never shall I forget that I am of your kin.

When the visitor left, I sat before the fire and read Petofi's poems to my hostess. Slowly the day closed in and when the light failed we sat talking quietly in the dusk.

"It was lucky that I did not let you go with the parson," said Mrs. Beniczky; "God has preserved you."

The news had reached us in the afternoon. Although I had refused to go with him, the Reverend Sebastian Kovacs had started off to see his parents, but while he was fording the river both the Czechs and the Reds had fired on him from the banks. He threw himself into the water—a woman who saw the whole thing recognized him and came to tell us. That was the last that was heard of him.

"If you had been there, if they had arrested you, or... Do you remember your dream the previous night?"

I shuddered: once more I saw the white moonlit road and the little bloody bundle of my dream. Again I felt the groping hand around me. For two months it has reached out for me, missed me, come closer, missed me again.

"There was no reason why you should go," said Mrs. Beniczky, "this is a sequestered place, and you are as safe here as if your mother were watching over you."

Then, all of a sudden, I saw my mother again. She was not visible, yet I could see the poise of her head, her blue eyes, and the wonderful smile on that delicate, narrow face.

Petofi's book was lying open on my knee: "Mother, our dreams do never lie..."

And in the dark the smile was still present.

*　*　*

May 22nd.

LAST night two officers staying in the house came into the dining-room bringing maps which they spread on the table. Their faces were the picture of despair. Their position has daily become more insufferable and orders from General Headquarters have now reached the political agents at the front that all officers are to be watched by 'reliable individuals'—the said reliable individuals being Jews in every case. This routine was begun yesterday, and two soldiers with fixed bayonets are posted in front of every officer's quarters. They take it in turn to follow their officer wherever he goes, they eat at his table, they sleep in his room. This is in strict accordance with the Russian plan, only Trotsky favors Chinese soldiers for the job.

Voices sounded at the door and the officers snatched up their maps.

A soldier with his bayonet fixed stood in the doorway. The shade of the hanging lamp cast the light low on the table, so that the soldier's face remained in the dark; only his repulsive, protruding eyes shone as they passed inquisitively round the room. Then he shouted to the officers: "Come along, comrades!" So we were left alone once more, and only the roar of guns broke the silence of the night.

At dawn the little village became a swarming camp. A.S.C. carts covered with tarpaulins came clattering from the direction of Balassagyarmat. The banks of the Ipoly are being evacuated and the soldiers are hastily packing. Camp kitchens and mounted troops clatter along the main road. Dust, clouds of dust. Buglers sounding the 'fall-in' and nobody paying the slightest attention.

Mrs. Beniczky and I held a council this morning. If the Czechs are really going to occupy Balassagyarmat, nobody would think of looking for me there. What shall I do? Finally we decided that I could go, and we took leave of each other; but it was with a heavy heart I left the old house and the garden behind me.

John Kispál, the gardener, a member of the Directorate, proposed to help me reach the town. As we came to the barrier at Szügy an armed soldier barred our road and pointed his bayonet at me. "Where are you going? Have you got a pass? No? Then back you go!"

"Steady, man, steady!" said John Kispál with an air of importance. "Don't you see she is with me? I am a member of the Directorate, and don't you forget it, my boy!"

The soldier looked at me. "'Why are you going into the town? What have you got in that parcel?" Then he growled: "Well, you can go to hell if you like, so far as I am concerned."

John Kispál stepped out proudly and his face showed clearly the satisfaction he felt at being such an influential man that even Red soldiers got out of his way. I couldn't help chuckling: in Soviet Hungary a member of the Directorate uses his influence to help me to escape and carries my bundle on his back. Meanwhile the warrant for my arrest lies on my writing table at home.

"What's going on here?" John Kispál asked two passing farmers. The men shrugged their shoulders contemptuously: "The Directorate of Balassagyarmat is on the run," said one of them. "They are afraid of sharing the fate of their colleagues in Fülek." He made a circle round his neck with his finger and looked upwards.

We had been walking for some time when the gardener suddenly turned to me:

"I should like to ask you, Miss, what you think about it all? Shall I come to any harm when things come right? That is always on my mind, because I don't think a man ought to assume that things will always remain as they are. They may, but they may change too. It is wise to arrange matters so that whether things remain as they are or whether they change one may always be nice and snug."

Guns thundered from the vineyards and a shell shrieked across the Ipoly and fell near the road, raising a cloud up to the sky. Not a single carriage was visible on the road now: the motors of the delegates-to-the-front, the members of the Directorate and the 'reliable individuals' have all been swept from the landscape by the wind raised by a single shell. In the distance behind us they were tearing along at a wild gallop, off the road whenever possible. I began to feel safe. There is less danger in shells than in Bolsheviks.

Bugle calls could still be heard in the direction of the town, and my pulses began to throb. What if the barriers on the other side were to close and I should have to stay on in my Red prison!

"I haven't any papers," the gardener said; "you'll have to go on alone. Go straight through the High Street." He was pale and obviously afraid. So presently I found myself alone. I jumped over the rails: people were running towards the houses so nobody took any notice of me, and I reached the Huszárs' house in safety. Mrs. Huszár and the children welcomed me with open arms.

A soldier was following me down the street, stopping at every corner to sound the alarm. I noticed that his bugle was ornamented with a huge red tassel which the rising wind blew against his mouth. And as I looked back in the twilight it seemed to me that the bugler was calling blood.

X

May 23rd.

I HAD hurried in vain. The Directorate has come back, so I have to remain in my Red prison. The battle last night caused many casualties, and the towns near the front are bewailing their dead. Everything that is Hungarian sorrows. The wheel of Fate is turning in blood, slowly, terribly. It is turned by the Powers, but it is our blood.

Noon came, then afternoon, again the enchanting hour of sunset on the banks of the Ipoly. The sun stands on the hills above the bank and pulls at the golden net which he cast over the valley in the morning. Like a fisherman he pulls the light, glittering net over the fields and crops. The net glides on, fast, without a sound. Now and then its gold is arrested for an instant by a shrub, by the verdure of a poplar, by the aspen of the river banks. Then the net glides on, and the trees, the crops, the water, the meadows, grow dark. The net has reached the horizon. For an instant, like a golden line, it lingers on the blue crest of the hills, then suddenly it dips into the west on the other side and is gone.

I love this light: it has touched the steeples of our churches, the thresholds of our cottages, from one end to the other of our country. For a thousand years it has come to us with dawn, over Transylvania, over the Carpathians, the Great Plain, over the waters of the Tisza and the Danube, over the fields of Banat, over the Carso, over the blue, salt bay of Fiume, over all our ancient, humiliated counties, over Buda and Pest, over Pressburg and Trencsén. All that has been torn asunder is united again in its net. But the catch of the great fisher is scanty now: he carries naught but another Hungarian day, a day of anguish, of blood, and of tears.

Only occasional rifle shots sounded round the house now; the town was going to rest. The electric light went out early tonight, so Mrs. Huszár and I sat facing each other by candlelight.

Shells screeched through the air above the roof. What is happening to our country? For days we have had no newspapers. Tribunals of Terror sit at night. Racing motors spread death and Béla Kun speaks of plans for tens of years.

The clock on the wall has stopped; goodness knows how long we have been sitting like this. Better to do something than sit and think, so I fetched my patience cards. Tiny cards, the colored toys of an old world. Crowned kings, ermine cloaked, powdered little queens, haughty young knights, they all look as if in their vanity they were leaning over a mirror to see their reflection. When I left home my mother packed these cards in my bag, and they have become my only luxury. Whenever I look at them they tell me something gently, in whispers, of my home. Soothers of worries, prophets, fortune-tellers! We laid the cards slowly out on the table, collected them, started anew. How thin my hands have grown...

Over the roof, high up, another shell whines. Then a splintering crash. Now the other side answers...

"The Reds..."

"That one came from the Czechs." Silence.

"There's another Red."

We spoke mechanically, for by now we had got to know the voices of the guns. Meanwhile the little queens and kings on the table came and went by the light of the candle.

"The Czechs..."

Three weeks! For three weeks it has been like this. Yesterday, today, tomorrow—it is always the same. There are no longer nights and days; there is nothing but monotonous, continuous explosions.

What if it is to be always like this? What if this is to continue forever? The very air seemed to shudder. From the opposite side of the table a pair of wide-open, fixed eyes stared at me.

"The Czechs..."

Machine-guns were rattling somewhere near the Ipoly, and the dogs barked. Another bullet struck the wall.

"The Reds "

Again the windows shook with the detonation. At the end of the room the door opened by itself, making room for hopeless despair, which entered and sat down to keep us company.

* * *

May 24th- 25th.

IF after the bloody battles of the war the victorious generals had occupied our country their conquest would have put an end to the slaughter. But Hungary was occupied without fighting by twenty-four Jews. The state of war has become permanent, the slaughter continues, and—worst of all misfortunes—for months there have been continuous executions. Sentence of death is everywhere. Some take a long time to realize it, but it is there none the less.

Dreadful news reaches us from Budapest; the city is starving; and in answer to that, Béla Kun declared at a meeting of the Workers' Council: "There are enough supplies to prevent the Proletariat of Budapest from going hungry." He forbore to speak of the inhabitants of the city, only of the privileged Proletarians, which for him means the Jewish intellectuals and, possibly, those who profess to be Red Proletarians. They will not go hungry. If Hungarians do... Béla Kun shrugs his shoulders.

The cruel ingenuity of the People's Commissaries is inexhaustible. Whatever they do not dare to do themselves is done by the Workers' and Soldiers' Council, and as a silent means for wholesale executions food tickets have been introduced. The inhabitants are divided into classes, one class receives bread, the other is denied it. Those who receive red tickets—the workmen performing manual labour, Red soldiers and all the Red elite—will still be able to eat their fill. The recipients of blue tickets—officials, teachers, widows, pensioners—may continue hungry. Those who receive no food tickets will have to die of starvation. Thus, it is possible to carry out executions merely by the use of colored scraps of paper.

"*The classification of the head of the household will apply to all those members of the family who live with him.*" This order reveals the intended extermination of a class: the children of the Hungarian educated classes are to be exterminated with their parents. The Dictatorship of the Proletariat, which carries its class war into everything, even into its administration of justice, its 'First Reader' and the nursery schools, uses daily bread as a weapon of war. Never has cruelty been displayed with such cynicism. Not only does the Dictatorship of the Proletariat make a distinction between adults, but it extends its favoritism to the children. It distributes food with discrimination, the children of the ruling class enjoying a preference. Let the miserable little ones who had the misfortune to be born in the grey, modest homes of officials or other intellectuals instead of having seen the light of the world as offspring of laborers or Red soldiers, let those poor little children starve and perish. Since Herod nothing so wantonly cruel has been known in human history.

May 26th-29th.

For two months the blood-reeking news has been coming. At first we shook our heads incredulously. Rubbish! Visions of a distracted mind. Terror inspires mad tales. Then the news died down, and now, all of a sudden, it has returned with proofs and names.

It was at the beginning of April that I heard that a sailor in Budapest was recruiting a band of terrorists among freed convicts and Russian Jews. Next we heard that these people had occupied the palaces of Counts Batthyány and Hunyady. On the first of May they hung out a huge sign over the palaces: THE LENIN BOYS, and ever since then they have been known by that name. The Lenin Boys, armed to the teeth, clad in leather coats, appear at night in the streets of Budapest or in those provincial towns where the miserable population dares to show signs of dissatisfaction. The other day they carried off the organizers of the Counter-revolution, Colonel Dormándy and Victor Horváth, who are said to have been tortured atrociously. They were tied up in the cellars of the Batthyány palace, burning cigars were stuffed into their mouths, water was forced in enormous quantities down their throats, and nails were driven under their fingernails. Whether they still live no one knows; there are others too. Last week we heard that a counter-revolution had been attempted at Makó and that the former President of the House of Commons, Louis Naváy, had been killed. We could not believe it: all his life he had been an advanced Liberal who had fought for universal suffrage, and he was a gentle scholar and philanthropist; moreover after the Revolution began he retired from all public affairs.

But the news persisted: the terrorists had gone down to Makó to take hostages and amongst others they had arrested Louis Naváy, his nephew Ivan and the mayor of the town, and had taken them by rail to Budapest. When the train stopped at the station the terrorists shouted into the compartment where the prisoners were: "Let the Counts and Barons step forward!" Nobody moved, then a man who as an orphan had been brought up by the kindness of the Naváys shouted: "This one's a Right Honorable and that one's an Honorable, take these." The Lenin Boys dragged them from the train and forced them to dig their graves at the bottom of the embankment. There was no time for a tribunal, so they fired at them without any preliminaries, stabbed them repeatedly with their bayonets, and crammed them into the half-dug graves. One of them was not quite dead when they were buried, and his poor protruding hand waved feebly for a time. The picture of it haunted me for many nights. It was impossible! Incredible! But the news was repeated and proved to be true. Other news followed.

A young ensign named Nicholas Dobsa, eighteen years old, suddenly disappeared in Budapest. He was asked by the Terror Boys for his identity papers, and he laughed. He said nothing, just laughed. Poor boy, he disappeared behind the door of the Batthyány palace never to reappear. Others disappeared too, and more pools of blood were found in secluded places. Many other violent deaths were reported, though rumor could not give the names.

Meanwhile Számuelly's special train is on the move all the time, and wherever it stops there are executions. It started at Szoboszló, a long distance from here, and the news came to us by an eye-witness, Antony Szatmáry, a railway man. It happened on the 23rd of April, when the Red front was at Debréczen. During the morning a hussar suddenly stepped out of the ranks and shouted: "Let us run, the Rumanians are coming!" So the International Battalion started off at once. The remnants of the army fled on the last train to Szoboszló, and my informant, Szatmáry, was pressed in to act as stoker. An armored train, advancing cautiously, met them, and a black-haired, red-nosed young man leant out of the window: "What news, comrade?" "We are the last to leave," the stoker answered.

The young man was Számuelly, and when he stopped at Szoboszló he was mad with rage. He ordered the station master to be flogged, as well as some workmen, and when his train reached the signal-box and saw that a white flag had been hoisted on the church spire he ordered the train back and ran into the town with his terrorists, accompanied by a fair-haired, blue-eyed woman on horseback. He arrested three men at random, Körner a mill-owner, Joseph Tokay a police officer, and Ladislaus Fekete the mayor, and had them hanged on trees in front of a chemist's shop. "Be quick!" he said, and cleaned his nails while the execution was being carried out. Then he boarded his train again and went on. In Kaba he had the curate, the notary and the magistrate hurriedly tortured, and moved on again, because the Rumanians were coming. Thence he went to Szolnok, where he took hostages and had them hanged. One hundred and fifty were executed. They were all Hungarians—and Christians...

Steps approached the house and Mrs. Huszár exclaimed in alarm: "The parson!"

The Reformed minister, Sebastian Kováks, looked frightfully thin in his black coat. His face was ashen and fresh furrows played round his mouth. He spoke pantingly, as if he had been running hard, and turned to me.

"God protected you that you did not come with me. When I reached the Ipoly both Reds and Czechs came rushing towards me. I had no choice, so ran into the river and threw myself into the water, which was simply swept around me by bullets. The Reds fired volleys after me."

That was the history of the journey I should have had to share.

"You would undoubtedly have been shot or arrested," the minister went on. "The Czechs wanted to intern me, and the Reds were hunting for me. For three days I hid among the crops before I dared to come home. I hear that a Czech shell struck the church; we had arms hidden under the roof."

Bullets were again whistling in the street. The minister shuddered and looked anxiously round, then he smiled, embarrassed: "Since then my nerves won't stand it. I had rather too much of it." He sat down almost in a state of collapse, and although he was a young man he looked very old.

* * *

May 30th-31st.

The banks of the river were unusually silent this evening. Just as it was getting dark the soldiers rolled a hogshead into the museum garden—the museum serves as a barracks. We heard one of them saying under our window that there was going to be a distribution of rum. What does that mean?

The patrol passed. Then the strains of a Gypsy band filtered through the night. Silence followed. It must have been about two in the morning when a voice mingled with my dreams. I woke, but could not at once grasp its meaning.

"Attack..."

"Who?"

"The Reds!..."

That was not what we had hoped for! For an instant my heart stopped beating. Doors were carefully opened and closed. The little girl came into the room and sleepily dragged her pillow behind her, like a white ant carrying a load too heavy for it. She lay down on the couch and fell asleep.

Wild firing was going on, so we opened the window. Suddenly the rifle shots seemed to come much nearer. The dawn was full of explosions and the deadly arpeggios of the machine-guns ran into one another, their staccato notes running in endless sequence up and down the banks of the Ipoly. Someone was playing the dance of death in the grey light. Shells passed so rapidly over the roof that it was impossible to tell which side fired them, and stray bullets thudded against the walls of the houses. Not a soul was visible. The house shook and every sound echoed through it as it does when one is under the arch of a bridge.

This went on for several hours: the vague grey objects regained their outlines, and things assumed their natural colors. The golden sun shone on green trees and on the brown tiles of the roofs. The artillery went on firing, but the rattle of the machine-guns seemed to get further and further away. The fight was now beyond the Ipoly, somewhere among the vineyards. It was not the other bank that had come to break down our prison, it was our prison that had spread to the other side.

A young boy doubled up on a bicycle passed under our window. "The Reds have crossed the river!" he shouted. "The Czechs are running along the whole line." People began to appear from the houses and a peasant girl stepped aimlessly into the middle of the street. The vineyards became silent; the Red guns alone went on firing and there was no answer from the other side. But it was not the silence of the living; it was the silence of death. Under the tension the dam which kept the Red waves in bound has broken, and the wave has spread and flowed over little hamlets, villages, and castles, hitherto untouched. God help the people on the other bank, for they are all Hungarians and their share is suffering and death. The victory remains with Trotsky's agents. The long road of homelessness has become longer in front of me, stretching into the unknown, even beyond the frontiers.

Presently the guns on our bank stopped firing too and on the main road little figures, bent under heavy loads, could be seen approaching. When they got nearer I saw that they were soldiers—the victorious Reds returning from the villages on the other bank among the vineyards, laden heavily with loot. They had captured the entire camp of the fleeing Czechs and brought bundles of rice, matches, tobacco, sacks of dried prunes, barrels of rum, wine and honey. A Jewish front delegate had even obtained a carriage, which he had loaded high with plunder, and the soldiers roared with laughter as he drove down the street. Let Béla Kun run after the Czechs himself if he wants to! They were very merry and some of them very unsteady on their feet.

About noon, however, their merriment was unexpectedly interrupted. Firing broke out suddenly and machine-guns rattled in the vineyards. A soldier without his cap and his face white with fright rushed towards the Museum garden. "The Czechs have come back!" he shouted, and his voice rang down the street. "They're in the vineyards again and have captured our people!"

The Czechs had, in fact, returned to the vineyards and caught sixty Reds pilfering there. The buglers sounded the alarm in vain: the Red army was busy cooking rice and drinking rum. Some Proletarian women, who had had no share in the booty, stood there, arms akimbo, and scolded the soldiers: "Of course when there's a distribution of meat or of milk you're always in the front row. Then you shout that you are Reds and steal the milk from the kiddies' mouths. But when it is a question of driving away the Czechs you run home with what you have stolen. You let them take the hill."

Most of the soldiers were drunk, in fact they had got tipsy before the attack began, for while they were falling in Gypsies played to them and rum was distributed.

"Mental degradation by means of alcohol was one of the weapons of the bourgeois," shouts the Red press. "Alcohol is the Proletariat's greatest foe," is posted by the Communists on all the walls. Yet the Dictatorship of the Proletariat makes the class-conscious Red army drunk whenever it wants to drive it to face unnecessary death.

*   *   *

May 31st.

WHAT hast thou done, Michael Károlyi?

When morning came the Czechs had stealthily, quietly evaporated from the hills, fleeing before a miserable handful of Reds. They are the same Czechs who five months ago descended from the mountains of Zólyom and took undisputed possession of Pressburg and Kassa, impregnable Komárom, a third of our country. How they would have run if they had had to face the hussars of Limanova and the territorials of Gorlice! But Károlyi's minister of war did not want to see any soldiers, the same Linder who recently, at a review, exclaimed to comrades Böhm, Pogány and Landler in front of their armed servants: "You see we had to break up the old army to create this."

Two towns and all the heights above them have been taken by the Reds, who have captured machine-guns and two heavy guns. The Czechs were surprised in their sleep and fled half-naked, all the prisoners being taken in their night clothes. Peasants' carts laden with Czech uniforms and boots rattled over the bridges all night. I could not sleep: I thought of the people on the other bank of the Ipoly, whom I do not know and yet for whom I fear. When they wake, they will find the train of the plunderers which brings the awful Red epidemic of tyranny and terrorist tribunals. And when it comes back it will carry away hostages...

The clock struck. Half-past one... A long train whistle; buffers knocking together; coupling-chains clanging in the dark. Fetters and skeleton keys...

May the Lord have mercy on us all!

* * *

June 1st.

A DRUM is being beaten in the village and the sound echoes from street to street. The Revolutionary Cabinet has decreed general conscription, and a small minority of alien race disposes of the nation's blood by simple decree. I shuddered. Henceforth they are going to force everybody to take up arms for them against himself.

An aeroplane flew over us. "An Italian machine," said someone in front of the house. The airman was reconnoitering the Ipoly valley—eyes from another world looking down on us, indifferently, without sympathy. To him we appear only as black spots, swarming ants. Does he know that the ants are suffering, that the ant-hill has been kicked to pieces and that strange vermin have invaded it? He flew on—a dragonfly passing across the prisoner's window.

The catafalque of the fallen Red soldiers has been erected in front of the county hall; red flowers, a red cross. (Why the cross?) Red shrouds showed under the lids of the red coffins. Only the little son of Stefanovic was not among them—the only child of a counter-revolutionary railway man. He was the best pupil of his school, a fervent little patriot, but was called up and had to go. He was wounded under the vineyards and implored the soldiers in vain to take him back to Balassagyarmat. They had no time—they were carrying rice. So the boy dragged himself to a field of oats and when the Czechs came back they found him and clubbed him to death with the butts of their rifles—"the little red vermin." His parents brought the corpse back, and the Directorate sent them a red coffin. "That is enough," said his father, "he shall never be buried with such tomfoolery."

Among the dead Reds there are many little Stefanovics. Passers-by stop reverently at their graves, for they hated the Directorship of the Proletariat and loved their country. Two soldiers came into the yard, two sad-faced boys, and asked for red flowers and red ribbons for their comrades. Out there, unmarked graves; in here, propaganda funerals.

In front of the county hall Comrade Singer pronounced the valedictory discourse:

"We take leave of you with the promise that we will fight with merciless hatred against the bourgeoisie, and, should we perish, the very blades of grass will continue the fight, animated by our hatred."

In the cemetery the minister spoke:

"My brethren in the Lord, standing at these open graves, let your last word be that of love..."

In these two speeches Christ and those who had crucified him met.

* * *

June 2nd.

SOMETIMES the candle flares up before it goes out. So with the news today. In this morning's paper we read:

> Szeged is in the hands of the counter-revolutionaries. The opposition Government has removed from Arad to Szeged and is in communication with the Hungarian counter-revolutionaries of Vienna. Western Hungary is organizing and in Szeged Hungarian White Guards are being formed under French protection.

It is actually in the Red papers! Have the Entente Powers stopped the Rumanians on the banks of the Tisza to give us a chance of saving ourselves by our own efforts? That would at least be human justice. A nation, deadly humiliated, could thus regain its self-respect. If only this were the case! Then we could bless our two months' sufferings. Not Rumanians but Hungarians would retake Budapest from the Red tyrant.

I noticed this morning that the soles of my boots were worn through. What a shock! What shall I do if they give way? We had frozen, black potatoes for supper and when we rose from the table Mrs. Huszár told a story about some bread and butter. The little girl began to cry: she was hungry after her supper and wanted some bread and butter.

Torn boots, black potatoes, what do they matter? There are Hungarian soldiers in Szeged!

XI

June 3rd.

I'VE got a fever of some kind and it frightens me—it would be terrible to be ill at such a time and in a strange house. I must try to keep going, but oh! how I long to go to bed.

A man came in from the village this morning and reported that when the Reds made their advance on Friday morning the houses of all Jews were at once surrounded by Jewish Red soldiers with fixed bayonets—to prevent them from being looted. This was corroborated by one of the owners of the protected houses himself.

Thus even after the abolition of private property the Dictatorship officially protects all Jews' belongings. Beyond the Ipoly Red soldiers have plundered Sztregova, the ancient castle where Imre Madách wrote *The Tragedy of Man,* but the Jewish Red soldiers protected the house of Fischer, the land agent of Leszeny...

*   *   *

June 7th.

I'VE had to give in: I can hardly distinguish things and am unable to move.

Baron Alexander Jeszensky came to see me, bringing messages from Bercel. Charles Kiss is with the Kállays and is coming to fetch me in a couple of days. He has made all preparations for my escape to Vienna.

*   *   *

June 8th.

THE Reds have retaken Kassa from the Czechs. Poor city. It received the victors with red, white and green flags, thinking they were Hungarians. Orders promptly came that the flags were to be removed.

Two days ago someone knocked at our window late at night. Anxiety spread through the house; men's voices were audible from the corridor. Aladár Huszár had come home! He looked like an apparition, a man of the woods, for his dress was torn, his shirt was in shreds, and his beard and hair had grown inordinately long. For six weeks he had been hiding with his friend George Pongrácz in the wild hills of Börzsöny.

They, too, were expecting the fall of the Dictatorship and were waiting for the intervention of the Entente. Then came the offensive of the Reds. As the battle was progressing northwards they concluded that the Reds were winning and that there was no escape; and as they could not ask for asylum from the Czechs, whom they had formerly helped to drive out, what was the good of waiting any longer?

"So we came home," said Huszár, and despair was in his eyes. "We shall give ourselves up to the Directorate and stand our trial."

The Directorate had ordered proceedings to be taken against them, but miraculously had failed to arrest them.

*　　*　　*

The doctor came to see me this morning—I've got rheumatic fever, and in the afternoon the children brought me some forget-me-nots from the river. Dusk came, then darkness. When I woke up a candle was burning in the room and Charles Kiss was sitting at my bedside. He brought me news of my mother, after all this time; she is alive and well, but fretting about me as she has not heard from me for weeks. She was questioned many times by the Red agents and they forced her to swear that as soon as she knew where I was she would report to them. Once a detective said to her: "How must you have brought up your daughter for her to behave like this?" "I brought her up as a Hungarian," my mother replied simply. Whereupon the detective hung his head and then said, as if ashamed: "I, too, am Hungarian," and he kissed my mother's hand. Since then there have been no more inquiry agents to see her.

Then Charles Kiss talked about himself. Most of the time he has been hiding in Western Hungary, where the whole region is in a ferment, counter-revolutions breaking out here and there. But as soon as ever there is news of one Számuelly makes a sudden appearance. In Devecser he had the counter-revolutionaries hanged round the church; with the exception of a young teacher they were all peasants. He forced the women to look on. In Nagygenes he had a farmer hanged in front of his children. The farmer did not die at once and when he was in his coffin he sat up. The wife and children ran to him sobbing. But the Terror Boys know no pity: they finished him off in his coffin.

Charles Kiss is going to escape to Vienna. To do this he has to go through Budapest—a long way round. I watched his face anxiously, afraid he might say that I should have to take the same road, but to my relief he said nothing. I raised my arm to shake hands with him when he went, and had to clench my teeth to restrain a cry of pain. Then I lay for hours motionless, and all through the night made preparations. In the morning I was as tired as if I had wandered along endless roads.

* * *

June 11th.

THE newspapers are howling victory—the delivery of Kassa. The Internationale is played and the Red Guard of Honor (?) cheers as Garbai and Béla Kun pass before it.

Far away I seem to hear wild Kuruc songs... and see the Kuruc horsemen waving their caps to their prince[2]... Our lovely town, longing for deliverance from Czech captivity. What a different home-coming you must have expected!

And this is how (according to the reporters) Béla Kun held forth:

Dear comrades! Now, comrades, the Dictatorship of the Proletariat is a fine thing, is it not? You have scarcely tasted it, but you will soon see what a beautiful, good and reasonable thing the Dictatorship of the Proletariat is, from the workers' point of view. The Proletarian who labors, who was oppressed, cannot understand how anyone can want anything else but the Dictatorship of the Proletariat. It is so simple. We do not mind what language a laboring brother Proletarian speaks, we have but one enemy—the bourgeoisie, whatever language it may speak...

---

[2] Francis Rakoczi, the leader of the Kuruc rising against the Hapsburgs, in the early years of the 18th Century, a national hero, is buried in the Cathedral of Kassa. His body was transferred from Turkey to Kassa in 1907. [Transl.]

Above the words of Béla Kun and the other 'comrades' I seem to hear a thundering voice rising from the depths of the Cathedral crypt:

" *Why did you bring me home? I listened in peace to the murmur of the sea.* "

*   *   *

June 12th.

IT has been rumored for days and now it turns out to be true: Clemenceau is negotiating with Béla Kun in the name of the Peace Conference. His Note came by wireless from Paris to Budapest "to the Hungarian Government."

This Note, which declares to the Hungarian Government that it has just been decided to summon its delegates, calls upon it to stop its attack against Czecho-Slovakia, otherwise the Governments of the Allied and Associated Powers will take the firmest measures to force Hungary to do so. The Note reminds Béla Kun of the gratitude which he owes to the Allied Powers because:

> ...*on two occasions they have stopped the advance of the Rumanian armies which had crossed the frontiers fixed by the armistice, and had prevented them from advancing on Budapest, and had stopped the Serbian and French armies on the southern front of Hungary.*

Clemenceau, the President of the Peace Conference, is ready to sit down at a table with Béla Kun. His blind hatred is ready for anything so long as it leads to the poisoning of the open wound in the side of poor Hungary, fallen in a gallant fight. And we, poor fools, expected human charity from the victors, who by this very document certify that for months they have been responsible for the prolongation of Bolshevik misrule in Hungary!

Béla Kun, the Communist of 1919, thus answered M. Clemenceau, the Communist of 1871:

> Monsieur Clemenceau, President of the Peace Conference. Paris.
> The Hungarian Soviet Government has observed with pleasure the intention of the Allied and Associated Powers to convoke Hungary to the Paris Peace Conference. The Hungarian Soviet Republic has no hostile intention towards any people in the world, it desires to live in friendship and peace with all of them, all the more as it does not insist on territorial integrity.

Then he goes on sarcastically:

> We are delighted to hear that the Allied Powers have ordered the Czecho-Slovak republic, the kingdoms of Rumania and Yugo-Slavia to stop their attacks, but we are forced to emphasize the fact that the States in question have paid no heed to the orders of the Allies.

Finally he offers the help of the Red army "to enforce the orders of the Allies."

* * *

June 13th.

WE only heard of it today, although it happened at the beginning of the month: the Directorates of Szombathely and Celldömölk had attempted to use the military to enforce the enlistment of railwaymen of military age in the Red army. They, however, decided to stop work and overthrow the Dictatorship of the Proletariat by a strike. All honest railwaymen joined the rising one after the other, and on the 2nd of June all trains between the Austrian frontier and the Danube stopped. The train of Számuelly with its Lenin Boys alone was running. As Budapest had refused to join in, the railwaymen did not succeed in stopping the traffic throughout the country, and after a struggle of six days they returned to work. The trains started from gallows-trees and with them the halting circulation of the Dictatorship of the Proletariat was restored. Another hope gone. Then followed the fulfilment of Béla Kun's promise: "I shall hang a few railwaymen in every station and then order will be restored. I have done the trick before in Russia."

But meanwhile the smoldering fuse had again blazed up and counter-revolution broke out in Sopron. Other towns followed, but it did not last long, for in a few hours the Reds came in from all sides. In Csorna the Terrorists of Györ collected the counter-revolutionaries and crammed one hundred and fifty into a small cell, then closed the iron shutters to suffocate them.

Then Számuelly arrived in the town. In front of him armed guards ran shouting: "Into the houses!" and those who did not manage to get out of the way in time were shot. When Számuelly with his Lenin Boys actually entered the town the streets had been cleared, so the black hyena in his armored car raced amidst a deathly silence to sit in judgment.

141

A table was placed in the open, and the prisoners were led before Számuelly one after another. He examined nobody and only asked who was possessed of property. Then he ordered some to the left and some to the right. No witnesses were called: Számuelly alone represented the tribunal. "To death!" he shouted to those on the left, and eighty started for the square in front of the church.

One of the men sentenced, a journeyman bootmaker, collapsed on the way and was left there. The others were beaten with rifle butts and spat upon by their hangmen. The eye-glasses of Lieut. Takács were thrust into his eyes until the eyeball was forced out of its socket, and while he walked on they even tore his handkerchief away so that his eyeball hung on his cheek. They boxed the ears of Gyula Akics, a mill-owner, while he stood under the gallows, and then Stephen Tárcsay, Louis Laffer, Gyula Németh and Francis Glaser were hanged. No doctor was present at the execution. Before the corpses were cold the Lenin Boys stripped them and made the other prisoners bury them. Számuelly watched the execution and made jokes.

Next day he went to Kapuvár and entered the place with a band of a hundred and fifty Terrorists armed with machine-guns and hand grenades. All he asked the prisoners was their name. "Hang them!" he cried. The mayor, the police sergeant and three others were led in front of the Catholic Church. He reprieved one of them on the way, because he was told he was the president of the Jewish congregation. In this place, too, the prisoners were beaten on their way to execution. The rope broke when police sergeant Pinter was hanged. His two little children ran up and implored mercy, but Számuelly would not relent. He then imposed a fine of millions on the town, and all the cattle he could lay hands on were driven away. Then he went on, without remorse, calmly, in his princely special train.

This death train passes through Hungary day and night, and wherever it stops men are hanged on the trees and blood is spilt on the pavements. Along its track people often find naked and mutilated corpses. In the Pullman car Számuelly sits in judgment. I heard this from a reliable man, who had gone over with the Socialist party to the Communists to save his own skin. He had to report to Számuelly in Szolnok, and it was then that he saw the train.

Számuelly lives permanently in this train, and even in Budapest he sleeps in it, being surrounded by thirty selected Terrorist guards. His special executioner travels with him. The train consists of two parlour cars, two first class carriages in which the Terrorists travel, and two third-class carriages for the victims. The executions take place in these, and the floors of the cars are covered with blood-stains. The corpses are thrown out of the windows, while Számuelly sits in his Pullman car surrounded by tapestry walls, beveled mirrors, and fragile gilt Louis XVI furniture covered with pink brocade, and seated before his delicate, feminine writing table, he disposes of people's lives.

Through every action of practical Marxism, through all its ordinances and institutions, even through the communication of its news, there grins cruelty—the repulsive, morbid cruelty of sensuality.

The brave kill, the cowards torture. The Hungarian people can be wild, ruthless, coarse and even vindictive, but through all its history it has never been cruel. It is not a sensual race. It expresses sensuality neither in its ancestral religion, nor in the conception of its gods of pagan times, nor in its legends, stories, folk-songs, humour or art. The cruelty of the Bolsheviks, on the other hand, is imbued with the sensuality of pathological aberration. Its origin is neither Slav nor Turanian, but of another race living in our midst. The history of the Hebrews, the Covenant, the Talmud and the Jewish literature of the various languages of the world, everything that originates with Jews, is overflowingly sensual. Cruelty finds its fantasy and energy in sensuality. The bloody invasion of the Turks, the merciless oppression of the Austrians, were incomparably milder than the cruelty of the Bolsheviks.

Számuelly's train races on without a stop, past trembling little guards' houses, through torpid, insignificant stations, through plains and over hills. It rushes through the country from end to end, to forge, with the cruelty of the conquering race, permanent shackles round our ruined country. No other sound is heard throughout the land; just the shriek of a train.

*　*　*

June 14th.

THE town was smothered in a stifling white heat. Under the window the little street basked lifelessly in the sun. As far as I could see from my pillow nothing was happening. Our fate was as stifling and as motionless as the street.

The first national congress of Soviets is meeting today in Budapest. On the previous two days the Communist party held meetings in the Hungarian House of Parliament. I began to read the report: "There was a red shine in the eyes..." Then I stopped: a grimy old wall in Budapest came to my mind, a glaring red poster sticking to it... And under a blue sky a giant laborer was furiously painting the House of Parliament red with a brush that dripped...

I continued to read the account of the Communists' general meeting. The reporter, with the traditional rapture for everything that is new, gushed over the aspect of the altered assembly room in the House of Parliament. The old frescoes have disappeared, and instead of the sacred crown above the chairman's seat,

> ...a fierce-looking laborer with a Phrygian cap is contemplating the place, with the Soviet's five-pointed star above his heart. On the wall there are no longer pictures of 'historical celebrities,' nor of 'glorious battles'—new strokes of the brush have transformed them into symbolical, grandiose decorations.

How they hurry to cover and efface everything that was ours! Yet even while they are painting their ordinances with our blood, every successive beat of the country's heart is louder and louder, more and more threatening. What have you done with our country? With our language, our honor, the purity of our children, the memory of our greatness? The throbbing of the Hungarian blood bodes ill, but they hear it not, though the anger of a deeply insulted nation is boiling up around them. They will not hear; they plunder and murder as before and hold meetings in the stolen house of our stolen country. Their newspaper chroniclers record with satisfied racial self-consciousness the arrival of the delegates: "They entered without the slightest embarrassment, without emotion, without fuss."

The strength and misfortune of the Jewish race are that it is surprised by nothing and does not believe in the aims which it professes.

I thought of the great hall where once the noble figure of Stephen Tisza dominated so many storms, and I thought also of those who could never have invaded the place had they not passed over his dead body. They do not know it, but they are going to their ordeal, for even as they speak the blood begins to ooze out of the country's open wound.[3]

"As they passed before the red draperies their faces showed up against the red background." Many of the People's Commissaries have escaped from gaols and lunatic asylums: is the background of these faces a fitting place for the Hungarian laborer, painted above the presidential stand with a Phrygian cap and a Soviet star? If this laborer could articulate, his cry

---

[3] It is a common belief in Hungary (and in many other countries) that if a murderer approaches the corpse of his victim the blood will flow from the fatal wound. [Transl.]

would sound the knell of this 'assembly.' I have spoken with many real Hungarian laborers during the last few weeks, on shaky, springless carts, near railway embankments, in the fields, near the hills, on the main roads, and how many of them have cursed those who deliberate this day over our ruins. But they were not there in the great hall among the speakers. It was Béla Kohn, Richard Schwarz, and William Böhm who spoke. The committee is composed of: Moritz Heller, Rabinovits, Vera Singer, William Lefkovits, Elias Brandstein, and Arpád Schwarz.

What did they discuss during the two days? Did they raise the question whether it was fitting to shed blood in order to accomplish their universal brotherhood or whether they should attain their aim by starvation? Did they mention that round the green table in Paris foreign hands are squeezing our thousand-years-old frontier, while others are standing by eager to tear off such parts as have not yet been distributed?

Not they! The Dictators discussed a proposed change of name of their party and debated the expediency of tightening or relaxing the pressure of the Dictatorship. In this the hand of Lenin appears, for a few days ago the Russian tyrants sent a message to their Budapest branch that henceforth it must call itself 'the United Communist party of Hungary.' Many members obeyed, but the more cunning ones advocated the advantages of the 'Socialist' sign. They look ahead and hope that should Communism collapse somehow in Hungary it might be possible to save the Jewish domination by returning to the old conditions. That is the only thing that matters to them; everything else is of secondary importance—the schoolbooks, the gallows, the prisons, the keys of the safe-deposits, the fresh soldiers' graves, the new casualties, the recent mutilations. Henceforth it will be unnecessary to characterize the Dictatorship and its tyrants; their deliberations have disclosed their nature.

"The power of the Dictatorship of the Proletariat is now in the hands of an active minority," said Béla Kun. In giving the list of the delegates' names 'The Red Newspaper' and 'The People's Voice' show what this active minority is. Practically every member of it belongs to the foreign race. In his programme, Béla Kun clamors for the application of merciless violence:

> The quotation of pacificism has suffered a slump, and the quotation, not of the imperialistic war but of the revolutionary class war, is soaring... The army is nothing but the armed Proletariat. It is a class army... this does not mean that we intend to limit our recruiting to the industrial Proletariat of the towns. It would be rank folly to expose to the risk of death none but the *elite* of the Proletariat. The self-conscious

Proletarians must be distributed among the Proletarians who possess self-consciousness in a lesser degree. We must be sparing with the class-conscious Proletarians.

This is meant for the educated classes, the manufacturers, and agriculturists. Never have words contained more calculated iniquity. The Israelites have redeemed their blood with that of the Canaanites. Let him bear the cross who is about to be crucified on it.

Béla Kun continued to outline his programme. He had but a few words for the land question: "That my programme does not say much about it is quite natural. It is a question concerning which we are still groping in the dark. I admit that."

They will talk about it later, when the peasant has paid the blood tax. Till that is done, let him live in the illusion that his land is his own and is not appropriated by the Co-operatives of Production belonging to the Government.

"The Dictatorship must apply stricter measures!" Pogány exclaimed. He spoke of the Counter-revolution in West Hungary. "There is only one road open for us: Forward, to the left!"

Comrade Horváth, of whom it is common knowledge that he has stolen his clothes from Count Joseph Károlyi's castle, declared that the prestige of the Dictatorship ought to be improved and expressed himself disparagingly of the Soviet delegates: "I declare and am ready to prove that in Szekesfehervar one evening there were sixty political delegates in the coffee-house whose Polish-Jewish origin was unmistakably written on their faces."

Vágó-Weiss, a People's Delegate, interrupted: "How dare you talk like that?" and Számuelly banged his desk with his fist. How hurt they are if we touch anything belonging to them; but if we express pain when they destroy our God and our country they hang us.

All references to gallows, all threatening and blood-thirsty speeches were suppressed by the newspapers, out of consideration for foreign countries. The meeting was concluded by a speech by Béla Kun in which Hungary's Dictator furnished some further characteristic details about himself and his order.

"First of all I want to deal with Comrade Schwarz's interruption," the Commissary for Foreign Affairs said, and then proceeded to answer the comrade who had proposed: "if our party's old programme contained the abolition of capital punishment, its present programme ought to contain it too." In his answer Béla Kun made some humorous remarks concerning capital punishment and said that the old Socialist programme had claimed the right for everyone to install and operate small stills (loud laughter). Richard Schwarz interrupted: "I was not joking!" Béla Kun continued:

I know full well that Comrade Schwarz was not joking, for he is not a humorous man (laughter), and yet there was some unconscious humour in his proposal (hear, hear). When a programme like ours is under consideration... a programme which forms the foundation of the Dictatorship... it is unseemly to discuss such trifles. This settles, as far as I am concerned, the proposal made by Comrade Schwarz, and I propose its rejection. (Signs of approval.)

Finally, to complete his self-characterization, he expressed his ideas on intellectual production:

It is in the nature of things that the Dictatorship is not over-favorable for the development of personal liberties, it is not propitious to the assertion of individuality; but if our intellectual life has declined, bear in mind that it is not our intellectual life but the remnant of the bourgeoisie's organization of physical tyranny which it was pleased to call literature.

(Shades of Goethe, Arany, Shelley, Andersen, Flaubert, Dostoyevski, masters of your art, know you all that you are naught but that part of the bourgeois organization of physical tyranny which is called literature.')

The window near my bed is open. The birds twitter and I can hear the concert of frogs by the Ipoly. A dog barks. Birds, frogs and dogs all speak their own language: why do not the Budapest Communists debate in Hebrew?

* * *

June 16th.

THE Soviet assembled yesterday in Budapest and meetings were held from morning till night. The national delegates of our county's Soviet attended. The Red newspapers this morning are bursting with pride, with ecstasy over the opening festivities.

"The laboring people of Hungary have gone to Budapest to lay the foundations of a new Constitution which will create a new atmosphere and bring happiness in its wake."

As a matter of fact the laborers of Balassagyarmat are indifferent and miserable. Nobody bothers about the Soviets. They have no part in it. The whole thing is strange and distant to them.

"The will of the millions," say the newspapers. And there it meets, this curious assembly, elected by orders of the People's Commissaries, by the privileged fraction of the population, with lists prepared in advance, under the supervision of soldiers with fixed bayonets.

A theatre was the scene of the opening ceremony. The First National Assembly of Hungarian Soviets met in a suburban theatre in the neighborhood of the old clothes' market. "Red walls and wreaths, arranged by inspiring, artistic hands," the Red chronicler reports. "Silence dominates the audience of thousands, the crowded boxes, when the curtain is raised." On the stage there is a red tribune ornamented with artificial red flowers and a long table where the People's Commissaries assemble. "A historical, grandiose gathering," says the reporter of 'The People's Voice.' "The stage is inundated with a flood of light. The strains of the Internationale rise. Everyone feels that this is the beginning of the second thousand of Hungary's historical years." (A pity it's begun on the stage, though.) "You are burying today this country's thousand-years-old Constitution," said Alexander Garbai, the President of the Council, in his opening speech. But a People's Constitution grows from its soil, like the crops, and no executioners can kill the soil. Today the soil is suffering in silence: it is the apotheosis of Béla Kun. "The Congress rose for him and applauded him madly for several minutes." His will is done. He imposes the 'Constitution' he likes, and the Soviet joins the Third International. Its leader then produced a message from Red Russia's leader: "Every Proletarian will fight like a tiger; we shall win or die!" The factory workers swore fidelity: "We will be the pillars of the Soviet Republic."

Steps came along the quiet street and somebody said "good day": it was Mrs. Huszár speaking through the window. The local schoolmaster was outside and wanted to borrow a copy of Marx's works. He has to give a lecture on the Communist Declaration. He doesn't want to, but what is he to do? He will get two hundred crowns for it, and if he disobeys he will be dismissed; besides, he has so many children...

I remembered a tale of the country where the hunchbacks lived. Once upon a time there was a country which was inhabited exclusively by hunchbacks. If by any chance anyone with a straight back happened to enter the country he was at once put to death. Everything went on all right till one day it pleased God to give an exceptional year for wine. Hills and vales resounded with the music of the grape harvest, and it so happened that many people got drunk on the new wine. In the land of hunchbacks the ground was shaking with dancing and the air was filled with songs. Then it happened that a drunken young fellow snatched the hump from his back and waved it with joyful shouts above his head. Others imitated him—all had regained their courage. So they shook their false humps from their backs and finally it turned out that there was only one genuine hunchback in the whole of the hunchbacks' country.

The steps receded from the window: the teacher went off with Marx's writings under his arm.

Wait till the grape harvest, land of Hunchbacks!

*   *   *

June 19th.

THIS is Corpus Christi but I know it only by the distant sound of the bells. Now the procession is passing with doffed hats, gravely, silently, under the church banners. The villagers have come to town, there is a sea of people and the organ sounds in the distance. In a cloud of incense, the Host is floating down the church, out under the open sky, and it glitters in the sun. As it passes the people kneel. Christ walks among His people. He walks everywhere in the country and they dare not, interfere with him. Only when the procession had returned to church did little Jew boys rush up and throw thousands of handbills among the people. One of them flew to me through the window.

> Proletarians of the world, unite! Read this and pass it on! The Revolution cannot indulge in sentimentality and must not know pity. *Gallows or bullets!* It will be wise for the bourgeois and hooligans not to try to attack the Revolution, because at the first attempt iron fists will stifle their souls in them with unrelenting deadliness. The Revolution is prepared for everything, all means will be employed by her to preserve her glorious purity as an eternal purity. Woe to those who attack her treacherously!

*   *   *

June 20th.

IN Budapest, too, the victors made preparations for Corpus Christi day.

It happened in Buda, in front of St. Matthias' church during the

149

procession. I have it from an eyewitness. Round the banners thousands of children were thronging, among crowds of their elders. A motor-car came racing down Tárnok Street, a Commissary's car, the son of a political delegate sitting in it. His sweetheart, a waitress, stood in front of a shop and waved her hand to him. The young Jew wanted to show off his power, so he shouted to the chauffeur: "Run them down!" The car made straight for the procession, which fled in panic. When the car reached the Host the Jew boy spat on It. The crowd raised a shout and would have lynched the blasphemous wretch if Red soldiers had not rescued him, dragging him under a doorway. The crowd attacked the door, but before the Terror Boys could arrive the soldiers themselves had settled the aggressors with their bayonets.

And at the same time a similar incident took place at the bottom of the castle hill near St. Christina's church. A Jew drove through the multitude and before he could be prevented spat on the Host. In this case the crowd fell on him and beat him to death. Later on shots were fired into the church. News of this kind comes from all quarters.

XII

I LIKE to listen to the children when they talk about the banks of the Ipoly. The dragonflies have made their appearance over the slow, warm water. The golden maple has withered in the garden. The crops are hot between the furrows. I like to hear that summer has come, the terrible time is passing.

In the name of the Entente, Clemenceau has sent a new ultimatum to the Soviet.

> The Hungarian army fighting on Czecho-Slovak territory must be withdrawn at once behind the frontiers fixed for Hungary... The Rumanian troops will be withdrawn at once as soon as Hungarian troops withdraw from Czecho-Slovakia. If within four days after the 14th of June the Government does not comply with this demand, the Allies will take punitive measures.

On the other hand the powers of the Entente declare "in the name of peace and justice" that the frontiers to be fixed in a subsequent message will "permanently separate Hungary from Czecho-Slovakia and Rumania and that these Powers will be obliged to withdraw behind the fixed *natural* frontiers."

An hour must have passed since wo began and we are still reading the names of towns and villages cut off by Clemenceau's line in the name of" peace and justice."

The name of every lost town, every little village is a stab. They want to take the sky above our heads, the ground under our feet. They want to take our ancient Hungarian towns, which we have not conquered by arms but which we have built with the sweat of our brow. They want to take the region of Sopron, where the giant of Hungarian music, Francis Liszt, was born; Czenk, where the builder of modern Hungarian culture, Count

Stephen Széchenyi, sleeps his eternal sleep; Pressburg, the ancient coronation town, whence the cry of Hungarian fidelity "*Moriamur pro rege nostro!*" rang out over land and sea. They take Kassa with the grave of the champion of Hungary's freedom, Francis Rákóczy; Munkács, the birthplace of our great painter, Munkácsy; Gyulafehérvár, the resting-place of Europe's savior, John Hunyady, the scourge of the Turks; Kolozsvár, where stands the birthplace of the great prince of the Renaissance, Mathias Corvinus; the field of Segesvár, the cemetery of our national poet, Petöfi. They want to take Arad where thirteen martyrs of our independence, including Count Leiningen, died within an hour for their country. They want to take Szalonta, John Arany's purely Hungarian birthplace, the district where the oldest and purest Hungarian is spoken. They want to tear from us our brethren the Vends, Ruthenians and millions and millions of Hungarians. They want to take two rivers, the Drava and the Sava, and three mountain ranges, the Tátra, the Mátra, and the Fátra, which adorn and form the armorial bearings of Hungary. *And all this never belonged to those to whom it is given.*

They want to rob us of our cradles and graves, "in the name of peace and justice...." My God! "Natural frontiers..." Are they making fun of our sufferings? Dare they call the wound cut into the country's body "Natural frontiers?"

Somebody in the room laughed gruesomely.

"Here, we overlooked this: the frontier is only fixed till the conclusion of a definitive peace treaty..."

I clung to the words, supported myself with them as with crutches.

"Of course these frontiers are meant for the Bolsheviks only. They are threats to induce them to surrender..."

Aladár Huszár shook his head sadly:

"You will see, all this will remain..."

*   *   *

June 22nd-23rd.

THE days when something happens to us are not always the worst. The long dragging hours of eventless days are just as terrible. To stand roped to the mast of a wreck, to wait passively, to gaze at the hopeless horizon and to fancy that every white wave is a sail. To see the lights of phantom vessels, to hear imaginary voices. There is nothing to see, nothing to hear: all this is as much torture as the catastrophe itself.

June 24th.

THE blossoms of the acacias have faded, but this year I have not seen their beauty. Now they have fallen to the ground and something else is in the air—a rich scent which floats through my window. If it had a color it would be white, if it were visible it would smile—the limes are blooming. Somewhere, everywhere.

Books are less heavy to my weary hands, and I can now sit up in bed. The shrill whistle of the trains no longer pierces my brain, and there are many trains running, more and more every day. The troop trains are coming back: something is happening.

The Soviet meeting was suddenly broken up and Budapest is under martial law. The Soviet members of Balassagyarmat have already come home, and judging by their reports the triumphant Soviet must have been a strange gathering. During the proceedings the comrades unfolded their greasy parcels and began to eat, filling the place with the smell of garlic and the litter of food. Not-withstanding prohibition there was a good deal of drinking in the dining-room, and while the comrades in the House of Parliament were gushing about Proletarian happiness, outside, at the entrance to the former House of Lords, the leather-jacketed Lenin Boys were brutalizing pale and starving people.

Béla Kun presided autocratically over the assembly. Whenever anything began to go contrary to his desires, a motion of his hand closed the debate. On the last day but one ninety-seven members had put down questions, but he shouted at them that he was fed up with their talk and in twenty-four hours he hustled the Communist Constitution through. The Soviet members of the capital attacked those of the provinces; they clamored that it was their fault that the capital was starving, why did they tolerate all the counter-revolutions? The provincial members, on the other hand, declared that the Communist administration was bankrupt, was worse than any other, and finally left the place as a protest. The wind was already veering and only Béla Kun's terrorism saved the Directorate. The Commissaries were shouting: "We won't stand the preaching of pogroms in the Soviet!" There was great excitement. William Böhm declared that an anti-Semitic pogrom putsch had been started in Budapest two days ago.

The Commander-in-Chief held forth in gloomy strains: "Though the Red army is gaining victory after victory, the situation is not altogether rosy..." On the 2nd of May, he declared, amidst frenzied applause, the People's Commissaries and the members of the Workers' Council were to proceed to the front. "Our publicity agents have spread the news over the country, yet the comrades still stick tight to Budapest. If Eugéne

Landler with his twenty stone can climb hills and lie in trenches under fire, surely the others can do their duty too, otherwise the Proletarian soldier will no longer believe in Proletarian equality." Then the Red Commander shouted in despair: "The reserves have not turned up. If this goes on for another four weeks, Vágó, Landler and Pogány can go into the trenches under my leadership if they like, but there won't be any soldiers left..."

I pictured the scene and could not help laughing at its absurdity. I could see the twenty-stone mass of Landler, and Pogány's terrific circumference protruding from the trenches, while Comrade Böhm, the typewriter agent, with his Field Marshal's baton elegantly held to his hip, stands over them, the shadow of his legs throwing an O on the deserted landscape. "A grandiose historical group," 'The People's Voice' described it. Just so.

My friends heard me laughing, came into my room, and laughed too. The children, who hadn't seen anybody laugh for a long time, could not understand what had happened to us, so they, too, burst out laughing.

"And this is the gang which rules over us!"... The laughter stopped suddenly and there was silence—the same silence as yesterday and the days before that. The children stopped laughing too, and shyly left the room...

Another train whistled beyond the trees and a former artillery officer ran in for a moment to see the Huszárs. Strange rumors are flying about: the army is falling to pieces an along the front: the soldiers are threatening to shoot their commanders: Béla Kun promised peace and bread and now they have war and paper money: at Branyiszkó the Székler battalions and workmen-soldiers demanded the national flag to be brought out and others left the front: yesterday a victorious regiment retreated from Léva to Ipolyság: on the Danube the Reds are retiring too, without any cause, dispersing in an directions: the men at the front have sent an ultimatum to Béla Kun demanding that the "comrades should come out into the firing line too," or they will fight no longer: all the soldiers are saying the same thing:—"the Jews swagger about in patent leather boots behind the front while we die."

It was not the ultimatum of Clemenceau and the Allies that stopped hostilities with the Czechs, it was this attitude of the troops. "Why did we beat the Czechs?" the soldiers grumbled. "What was the good of shedding all that blood if we have to come back?"

"Our blood is cheap to the comrades!" others answered.

The soldiers who are passing through the station talk about marching on Budapest: they are going to brain the People's Commissaries! Huge inscriptions are chalked up all along the trains: "To death with Béla Kun!" "Kill the Jews!"

A poster has been stuck up opposite our house: it represents a Red soldier with Semitic features holding a rifle; his raised hand points in front of him and his mouth is open as though he were pronouncing the inscription: "You! Counter-revolutionaries, lurking in the dark, spreading false reports, *Tremble!*"

'The Red Newspaper' shouts in the same bloodthirsty strain:

> We demand martial law against the Counter-revolution! We demand that the administration of martial law should be placed in the hands of the only man fit for the position—Comrade Tibor Számuelly. Tibor Számuelly is a brave and energetic man, who dares to be ruthless for the sake of the Revolution... With ten men he crushed the Counter-revolution in Western Hungary... All honor to him who, in the interests of the Revolution, recoils from nothing, who has enough culture and courage to choose with energy and revolutionary faith the only path that is possible, the path that is inevitable, the path trod by Saint-Juste and Marat. The right system for every emergency, the right man for every job! Martial law for the degraded Counter-revolution. Tibor Számuelly for the suppression of the Counter-revolution!

Today's 'People's Voice' reports that martial law has already been proclaimed; its administrator, however, will not be Számuelly but Commissary Joseph Haubrich, the Red Military Commander of Budapest, who is a Christian. But it is obvious why the choice fell on Haubrich and not on Számuelly. The Jewish race is short-sighted where the lessons of history are concerned, though it is not lacking in prescience. Számuelly's gallows, set up in the Hungarian villages, are not discernible in Paris and Rome, hut foreign countries have their eyes on Budapest. So as far as Budapest is concerned let it be a Christian who sheds the blood of the Christians that rise against Jewish tyranny. The Red press proves this assumption to be correct. Számuelly's slaughters were passed over in silence, but the first execution under martial law in Budapest is announced in huge type: "COUNTER-REVOLUTIONARY SENTENCED TO DEATH!"

In Budapest and in the provinces small hand-written and typed handbills are now being circulated, marked "Copy this and pass it on!" These handbills set forth the aims of the foreign race which, under the aegis of the Dictatorship of the Proletariat, has come into power, and appeal to the Hungarian people to be patriotic. Among others who undertook the distribution of these leaflets was Géza Herczeg, a young man of the clerical class. He was caught and "On Monday night the Revolutionary Tribunal sentenced him to be shot."

So a Hungarian has died because he distributed bills inciting his compatriots to rebel against the Jewish terror. On the feast of Corpus Christi a young Jew spat on the Host, another fired at the altar, and in another place a volley was fired at the procession. Számuelly favors the proximity of churches for his executions, but in Béla Kun's Soviet Republic there has been no conviction for persecuting Christians. The cup has now overflowed, the millions are beginning to see. The eyes of the soldiery have been opened by the useless deaths of their fellows and by the acts of the champagne-drinking delegates-to-the-front. Recruiting is announced to begin in our county tomorrow, but village after village is sending messages to the Directorate that it will not permit it. The peasantry is fairly aflame. 'Comrade' nowadays means Jew in the minds of the peasants.

On the other bank of the Ipoly they have beaten the political delegate to death; his name was Ignace Singer. I remember seeing the red-haired Ignace Singer, the torturer of Balassagyarmat, and the rest of the Directorate bolting in coaches from the Czechs; it was he who, after the defeat of the local Counter-revolution, shouted from the balcony of the county hall: "Slaughter the bourgeois and don't spare their women and children!" His voice will be heard no more—nor will that of his friend, Comrade Riechmann, who has chosen the wiser part and has absconded with five million crowns in cash.

One more storm and the fury of the betrayed people will break through the dams. The people has recovered its memory; it remembers who exploited it during the war, who enriched himself by Hungary's disaster, who dragged it into the terrible peace, into civil war and death. The air is resonant with this new consciousness, conceived in blood. In the great plain one can hear metallic clicks which bode danger: with set teeth the Hungarian peasantry is sharpening its scythes; and the edge is not meant for the crops, for the peasant looks towards Budapest. The news has been spreading for days. In the county of Pest counter-revolution has flared up. Aszód and Pécel have risen, Cumania and the whole length of the banks of the Danube are in ferment. It started on the 19th of June, on the feast of Corpus Christi, and the tocsin carried the news from village to village along the banks of the Danube. The peasants took their scythes, tore up the railways and cut the telephone wires. The Directorate took to flight, and the Red Guards surrendered and ran for their lives.

Kalocsa, Dunapataj, Dömsöd, Tas, Lacháza... names that sound like ancient Hungarian music. They are ringing with the sound of Hungarian hopes... Hungarian scythes.

*　*　*

June 25th.

IT was long after midnight when I heard steps coming from the direction of the railway station. A voice said in the street: "There will be no trains for Budapest tomorrow."

The news spread in the morning—nobody knew who had brought it, it just came suddenly. *The Counter-revolution has broken out in Budapest!* Imagination supplied the rest. The Hungarians working for us in Vienna... a railway strike... the names of villages and counties... all along the Danube... the whole of Western Hungary, Szeged... The Whites are marching with fifty thousand men from Szeged towards Budapest.

Stories inspired by hope.

Then somebody came from Vácz, bringing news. Yesterday at four o'clock in the afternoon four cannon-shots were heard in the direction of Budapest. The cannonade increased. People ran down to the banks of the Danube and listened with their ears to the ground. Many stuck ribbons of the national colors in their coat. There is a counter-revolution in Budapest! The barracks rose against the Dictatorship of the Proletariat, and most of the factories joined in. The monitors on the Danube shelled and destroyed the Hotel Hungaria, which had become Soviet House. The ships hoisted the national flag, and white flags are floating from the castle, from Mount Gellert, from the houses of Buda.

A fierce joy seized me and I wanted to get out of bed, I felt ill no longer. Then... nothing especial happened and yet things began to lose their brightness. Evening came. We laughed no more and suspense became pain.

No newspapers arrived. The train was very late; there was a passenger from Budapest—Comrade Frank, Dictator of the County, and once again he talked loudly under the porch, and he wore a red tie. A gentleman passed with a white handkerchief protruding from his pocket. "Remove that counter-revolutionary badge!" shouted Frank. My friends sat around me in silence, none of us dared speak of plans. Hope dried up in our hearts. Then the door was cautiously opened and somebody came in. It was a railwayman—they always have the latest news. The Counter-revolution in Budapest has been defeated, and those who were caught are to be hanged!

In Budapest everybody knew about it beforehand, people talked openly in the streets. The signal was expected for three o'clock, when the monitors would open fire. The moving spirits of the rising were Captain Lemberkovics and a military chaplain, Julius Zákány. Haubrich, the Red commander of the garrison, appeared to side with the rising and declared that in case of success, he would assume the military dictatorship; in case of failure, however, he would deal mercilessly with the—organizers. He also informed the credulous counter-revolutionaries that the Soviet had ordered him to declare martial law. He had managed to postpone it till the 26th, but could hold out no longer. Let them therefore have the rising on the 24th, on Tuesday. Thus it was Haubrich himself who fixed the date and on Tuesday morning his posters appeared on the wall. Martial law! The carrying out of the Counter-revolution was entrusted to a Red brigade of Hungarian soldiers composed of about three thousand men, and they had thirty guns and a few armored cars. Haubrich knew of this, and just before the rising he dispatched the brigade to the Northern front. From that moment the Counter-revolution was reduced to a forlorn attempt, supported by the men of the artillery barracks, the monitors, the military academy, and the patriotic workmen of a factory in Ujpest.

When the signal was given in the harbor of Old Buda, the three monitors came forth under the national flag and began to shell Soviet House. Fifty pupils of the military academy occupied a telephone exchange and meanwhile people were gathering at the appointed places. Officers, citizens, students and policemen met under doorways. The workmen, however, forsook the rising at the last moment. Many of the officers were late. In places where four or five thousand armed men were expected, only ten or twenty appeared, and of the twenty thousand hoped for only a few hundreds turned up.

The men in the artillery barracks were restrained by Communist orators, who appeared suddenly and informed them that the Counter-revolution had already been defeated everywhere, and made them arrest their officers. The monitors gave up their useless cannonade and fled down the Danube to the south. The workmen of the factory were persuaded to surrender to a band of terrorists who had hurried to the spot. Shots were exchanged between Buda and Pest. The colors on the masts of the ships on the Danube and on the soldiers' caps changed from red, white and green to red as events took this turn. Terror Boys on lorries with machine guns raced through the empty streets, shooting into the windows and firing volleys at the houses, occasionally breaking into houses and carrying the occupants off. They tore down the national colors wherever they found them, and corpses began to strew the pavements. When evening came the unfortunate town knew that it had not yet freed itself from the tyrant and that there was seemingly no hope left. By its organization, the Red power had swept away in a few hours the rising of the barracks, the monitors, and the factories. The whole thing crumbled away in blood, misfortune, and retreat. Everything was lost.

Not everything! In the general collapse a handful of Hungarian boys kept the flag flying. The forsaken cadets of the military academy held out. Till next morning these boys in white uniforms defended the telephone exchange which had been entrusted to them against the assaults and machine-guns of the Reds. They also defended the building of their academy, besieged by a whole regiment. The attacking Reds were reinforced in the morning, artillery was brought up, and Haubrich sent a message to the effect that if they did not surrender, he would have the whole place blown to pieces. Then only did the gate open and the heroes of the Counter-revolution lay down their arms. Soldiers with fixed bayonets drove a group of boys in white uniforms to the condemned cells.

Everything is lost. Yet there has been this ray of light in a town wrapped in darkness and shame. Our honor, which the men could not defend, was saved by a few boys; and through our despair there appeared a vision of a new generation worthier than the old. What will be their fate! The nights are nights of terror and nobody sleeps; some fight with horrors, others hope and pray.

Poor boys! I think of them and their mothers, of unknown, pale, sleepless women, strangers to me yet closely kin. I, too, have a mother.

*   *   *

June 26th.

THE Red press rhapsodizes today.

> The Counter-revolutionary plot has failed. Capitalism attempted to regain its power. It was led on by a tricolor flag. The mean, cowardly bourgeois mob of priests, bankers, aristocrats, officers, *Jew boys*, has crept out of its lairs to incite pogroms.

This is a cunning attempt to twist the truth. The persecution of the Christians must be screened, and as there is none to contradict it, Béla Kun's press boldly calls executed Christians 'Jews' so as to persuade the grumbling people that the Dictators do not protect their own race. And it accuses the Jewish bankers of sympathy for the Counter-revolution so as to throw sand in the eyes of the peasantry led to the scaffold. Géza Herczeg, to whom they allude, was a Hungarian, and the Jewish bankers have nothing in common with Hungary's struggles.

I have it on the authority of one of the noblest figures of the Counter-revolution, a friend of mine, that when in desperation the organizers of the Counter-revolution asked for a loan from the Hungarian Jewish bankers abroad, and the Hungarian aristocracy, for the present deprived of all its means, offered to guarantee it, they refused with derision; for although the Dictatorship of the Proletariat is causing them temporary losses, they are ready to sacrifice themselves for the final triumph of their race and declare proudly that "This Béla Kun is, after all, a wonderful fellow!"

The written materials for the history which is to be compiled tomorrow is already being intentionally falsified by the newspapers of today. The Counter-revolution was not a fight of Capitalism against the Proletariat, it was a fight of the Hungarian nation against the foreign race. Its victims are not bankers and capitalists, but the poor Hungarian middle-class, starving intellectuals, struggling manufacturers, poverty-stricken officials, and artisans, while its butchers are not Proletarians but Számuellys, Joseph Pogánys, George Lukács and Béla Kuns.

"Bad news..."

It is cold. The door rattles and the wind comes in at every crevice. Out of doors under a leaden sky the trees are blown nearly to the ground.

Someone says in a whisper:

"There is an old saying that when there is a wind like this in June it means that the gallows are busy."

They are hanging Hungarians everywhere. Brave Captain Lembrovics and his friend, Lieutenant Filipec, have been killed. They have hanged the leaders of the factory workers, Ladislaus Orszy and foreman Martinovics. Other factory workers and bourgeois have been shot in front of the factory by terrorists.

'The People's Voice' reports the news with satisfaction:

> The Court martial has sentenced Stephen Kiss, Joseph Grasse and Ladislaus Szabó, former officers, and Zoltán Oszváth, a captain on the active list, Antony Waldsteinbrecht, a former lieutenant of the reserve, and Francis Imrey, a former captain, to death by hanging.

The Terror tribunal is now trying the pupils of the military academy. And who will count the corpses thrown into the Danube, the dead bodies lying in the streets? Now and then one hears a name from among the many. Madarász, a young medical student, was beaten to death because he had the temerity to study with a candle burning in his room. To the shame of humanity, they have also murdered Dr. Nicholas Berend, the famous children's specialist.

Comrade Haubrich proclaims proudly: "Order reigns in Budapest," and has the following proclamation posted up:

> After June 26th the doors of all houses must be closed at 8 p.m. No one is allowed in the streets after 10 p.m. More than three people must not be together in the street. All theatres and places of amusement are to be closed." And the Dictators order the city, distracted with sorrow, to hoist red flags on its houses. The walls are covered with orders.
>
> Any counter-revolutionary attempt, or offence, will be punished by hanging. Any counter-revolutionaries caught armed will be shot on the spot.
>
> Budapest. June 25th, 1919.
Joseph Haubrich, Béla Kun,
Commander of the Garrison. Deputy Commander-in-Chief.

They give orders, sentence, and murder undisturbed. The wind is howling. Trees are blown nearly to the ground. And all over Hungary there are hangings.

*   *   *

June 27th.

Now that it has passed we begin to realize that even in our despair we had still hopes. It is no good to tell us we were wrong, we persisted in believing in the success of the heroic inhabitants of the banks of the Danube. That is over too, for there also the Counter-revolution has been defeated. A political delegate boasted loudly in front of the county hall of Balassagyarmat: "We have settled the whole lot. While Béla Kun and Haubrich worked in Budapest, Számuelly dipped the peasants' rising in red. He took his revenge on the farmers. Any village that had injured the Jews was simply exterminated."

People are fleeing from those parts, coming in our direction, and escaping over the Ipoly into the hills, where the Czechs are. The Czechs take our people to Olmütz if they are officers and to Pressburg if they are civilians. The fugitives know the fate in store for them, yet they go there; anything is better than the gallows.

People escaping from sentence of death are continually ringing at the door, seeking Aladár Huszár. Somehow those who are in trouble know his name, and they come to him pale and exhausted, even as I came. Often they cannot speak, yet he understands them as he understood me. The Directorate keeps an eye on him and his house is watched—detectives swarm around it. But he manages frequently, when night has come, to conduct anxious shadows through the quiet streets of the town to the living bridge across the Ipoly. Meanwhile the Red sentry loafs at the corner and glares at our windows. Hours pass. Mrs. Huszár walks quietly up and down in the next room. She stops suddenly, resumes her walk, then stops again. The whole house shares her vigil. Then the small gate opens... so he has come home at last. The wind covers the tracks of the fugitives, the news of blood alone remains. The banks of the Danube are one continuous death rattle: for a whole week Számuelly has been hanging. The Revolutionary Cabinet dispatched him and he arrived with his terrorists at Kunszentmiklós the day after the rising. With him came his two Russian Jew hangmen, Itzigovic and Osserovic, and, dressed in black and with leggings, a little Jew hangman called Kohn-Kerekes. The latter was overheard having an argument with Gustav Nick, a freed murderer and terrorist, as to whether one could hang two or three within five minutes.

Számuelly toyed with his elegant chamois gloves. He wore patent leather boots, a Soviet cap, and on the breast of his Russian blouse a red Soviet star. Ignace Fekete, a telegraph operator, was dragged before him. Számuelly inquired why his orders had not been obeyed? "Hang him!" Somebody told him that Fekete was a Jew. He made a sign to Kohn-Kerekes: "Let him go!" Jews are only hanged by mistake.

In Tass he had two men hanged on a mulberry tree in front of the town hall because they carried sticks. "Where did you buy those sticks?" "Somewhere," the men answered haughtily. "Hang them!" ordered Számuelly. In Solt he had the notary and the innkeeper hanged. He spat on Lieutenant Azily when he was already on the gallows. And on he went with his hangmen. Csengöd, Öregcsertö... everywhere he hanged.

In Dunapataj he met with resistance, so he attacked the peasants, who had only scythes, with guns. Yet they stood their ground for five hours. Hundreds and hundreds perished. In today's 'Red Newspaper' Számuelly reports in Dunapataj alone three hundred counter-revolutionaries killed. When his Terror Boys got possession of the village he had sixty men, old and young, hanged and shot without questioning them. He himself fixed the rope round several of the victims' necks and kicked the corpses with his patent leather boots. In Dunaföldvár also the trees were turned into gallows. After a desperate battle Kalocsa was forced to surrender. Számuelly erected his gallows in front of the house of the Jesuits. During the execution a priest in full canonicals, with a crucifix raised high, appeared in one of the windows and from a distance gave absolution to the martyrs, Poor Hungarian peasants, unknown yesterday, now immortal! They were thrown naked into pits—the Directorates did not even register their names. Számuelly, with disgusting callousness, certified 'suffocation' as the cause of death.

A single gesture on the part of humanity would have been sufficient to save us from all this shedding of Hungarian blood. Instead, the victorious powers encircled us and pointed us out to their own working-men as an example of the blessings of practical Marxism. They talked of 'peace' in Paris. And to satisfy the more sensitive of their citizens their representatives in Budapest now and then entered a formal protest against the shedding of blood.

A traveler came with the evening train from Budapest and he brought news. The Revolutionary Council had fixed Thursday for the executions, which were to take place in public, in one of the finest squares of the town, the Octagon. All preparations were made: the military cordon was posted early in the afternoon: the Lenin Boys were there. The whole town was trembling with excitement and a crowd of some ten thousand people assembled, waiting and murmuring. There were no gallows—it was intended to hang the counter-revolutionaries on the lamp-posts. The carts for the corpses arrived, and the excitement of the crowd increased. Six o'clock struck. Somebody shouted: "They are bringing the condemned!" Then it was given out that the hanging would not take place. At the last moment Colonel Romanelli, the head of the Italian Military Mission, had sent a note of protest to Béla Kun, which was reported in the newspapers:

> I address to you the demand that you respect without exception the lives of all the hostages and political prisoners who have fallen into your hands in consequence of the late events, including those who were taken after armed resistance. I warn you and every member of your Government that you will be called jointly and severally to account if you execute the sentences mentioned above.

Béla Kun answered as follows:

> The Hungarian Soviet repudiates all threats which render the members of the Government responsible for events which are the internal affairs of the country." He appealed to the "friendly feelings testified by Italy towards the Soviet" and expressed his doubt whether Italy could be the protector of "gangs of assassins who, in the interest of the Counter-revolution had intended to murder women and children and exterminate the Jews" and who had been sentenced by judges of the Soviet "according to their own laws.

Számuelly goes on hanging people in the provinces, but in Budapest the execution on the Octagon was prevented by the manly and determined attitude of the colonel. But while Italy saves a few lives with one hand, what action does she take with the other? Why does Italy refuse to know who Béla Kun is and what it means in the eyes of Hungary that he can boast of his friendship with Italy and that the Red army can proclaim "We are smashing the Counter-revolution with Italian guns and Italian arms? "

It is said that the pearls from the lovely white necks of Hungarian women go abroad, and that fine thoroughbreds are driven from the Hungarian prairies in exchange for guns sent to exterminate us.

If this is true, there will be no blessing on the exchange. Spilt blood will ooze out from under the pearls and from under the hoofs of the horses.

XIII

THE Counter-revolution has been beaten everywhere. The power of the Dictators seems never to have been greater. When they first came they had to share their power with the trade-unions, the Soldiers' Council, the 'confidential men,' the Peasants' and Workers' Councils and later on with the National Soviet. Within three months they have freed themselves of all these. First of all the peasants disappeared as a deciding factor. They were followed by the 'confidential men 'and these by the Soldiers' Council. The Workmen's Council was reduced to a shadow, the trade-unions were transformed and subdued, the Soviet was sent home, and of the remnant of these three they made a dummy, the 'Economic Council,' in whose hands the new constitution was placed. The beginning and the end of this Constitution is the domination of their race over the ruins of the destroyed power of the State. The edifice of tyranny has been perfected. All means and all power are in its hands. It has absolute sway over life and death. Law-giver, executive, judge, gaoler and executioner, all in one.

The red flags of victory are floating over seas of Hungarian blood. The Dictators are reveling. Complimentary addresses and telegrams are pouring in. Among the first, Comrade Frank pays his homage to the Cabinet in the name of the Directorate of Balassagyarmat. The County of Nográd! Its people bite their lips with shame and hatred. At the recruiting meeting of Balassagyarmat not a single man presented himself for enlistment, so the meeting had to be closed, and the Directorate asked the Government for Terror troops, so that violence and rifle butts may be used to force men into the army.

Meanwhile the Red press reports a sequence of congratulatory addresses. The women raise their voices too. What may they have to say? In the name of the national organization of Communist women, Sarah Goldstein, Mrs. Elias Brandstein, Maria Csorba-Goszthony, Ida

Josipovich and Vera Singer, the women whom the unfortunate inhabitants of Budapest called 'Lenin Girls' after the defeat of the Counter-revolution, "greet with love Comrade Haubrich and request him to present their heart-felt gratitude to the others." Meanwhile demented mothers and sisters weep for the captive pupils of the military academy and the shadows of horrified women roam under the acacias on the banks of the Danube.

"The country honors the victors of the Counter-revolution." So the comrades of the Frank type swear to fight to the last breath for the victory of the Revolution, and Sarah Goldstein and those of her kin send their "loving thanks," their warm gratitude. Otherwise there is silence. Awful silence. And the summary tribunals of the Revolution are sitting permanently.

Colonel Romanelli prevented the executions at the Octagon, but hostages are strangled secretly, quietly, on out-of-the-way building plots, in the deep recesses of dark yards. There are frequent executions in Parliament Square: the rabble hangs about there for hours on end; women sit on the curb and wait.

"What are you waiting for?" someone asked. "For an execution," a surly woman answered.

It is so simple, the Entente sees nothing of this. Soldiers with fixed bayonets bring a victim. The hearse follows. The crowd turns to the steps. A volley is fired. The stones beneath the lions are battered with bullet marks. The hearse goes off slowly and the square becomes empty. There is nothing more to be seen.

In the House of Parliament, on the side reserved for the Peers, are officers of the Political Investigation Department, modelled on the Russian Cheka, and Otto Korvin-Klein sits there in judgment. Since the representatives of the Entente have invited Béla Kun to disband the terror detachments, the Lenin Boys have transferred their quarters from the Batthyány palace to this place.

In the adjoining houses people only sleep in the daytime: at night they look trembling towards the House of Parliament from behind their darkened windows. Above the entrance of the House of Lords shines a huge arc lamp. Motors pass incessantly. This is the time when the terrorists collect the hostages, the material for Korvin-Klein. The cars stop under the lamp. The light shows leather-coated men dragging along their miserable victims, whom they push into the entrance. Now and then a scream filters through the walls of the House of Parliament. Then, as if by word of command, the engines of the motors begin to purr, the horns are blown to drown every groan, every death-rattle. Armed Lenin Boys emerge from the gate, dragging a form with them. The group proceeds to the lower quay. Arms clatter, the steps die away in the distance. There is a splash. Then the black group returns, but there is no longer anyone in their midst. Romanelli has protested against public executions. But near the House of Parliament people cannot sleep at night. The streets are dark and empty. In the whole town there is but one other doorway lit up: under a red canopy an arc lamp burns above the door of Soviet House. Beside it is a small trench mortar and terrorists stand on the pavement in front of it. On the balcony a huge red flag hides the machine-guns, and the entrance is vividly illuminated. The People's Commissaries arrive in motor-cars. The terrorists line up. Present arms! Mrs. Béla Kun receives the same honors. And within the walls of Soviet House the comrades insist on being called 'Excellencies.'

A country gentleman told me about this; ignorant of the change he went straight from the station to the Hungaria Hotel. The guards mistook him for somebody belonging to the place, and only when he wanted to pay his bill did they discover that he was an outsider. Afraid of being punished, the frightened servants smuggled him out and the news of the orgies in Soviet House escaped with him. Michael Károlyi and his wife spend an evening there now and then. For a long time I had not heard of them. In the first week of the Dictatorship of the Proletariat Michael Károlyi stood as an invisible power above the Revolutionary Cabinet. The People's Commissaries treated him with respect. But after the Soviet elections, when Béla Kun and his followers had obtained full control, Károlyi was thrust into the background. They wanted to send him to Gödöllö, the former royal residence, as Commissary of Production, and later they placed their former protector with a Communistic co-operative society. For appearances' sake Károlyi pays occasional visits to his office, but he does no work whatever. He has had a gramophone installed in his office. Detectives guard the peace of his villa in the hills of Buda, while motor lorries pass between the starving houses to carry food and ice to him. But the hospitals have no ice for their patients. His wife is often seen in a glaring red hat, driving through the quiet streets in the car of the People's Commissaries. At night they partake of the festivities of Soviet House behind locked doors, in company with Béla Kun, Comrade Dovcsák, Pogány, Landler and their womenfolk. The Gypsies who play to them spread the tale. The revels go on and the music never stops. Disregarding prohibition, French champagne flows freely. Tibor Számuelly pours some into Countess Károlyi's glass, pouring it with the hand that fixes the rope round his victims' necks. They drink to the eternal prosperity of the Soviet, and costly banquets are consumed in illuminated halls while the dark town is starving. The evening ends in voluptuous dancing. Then the music dies away...

*   *   *

July 2nd.

PEOPLE are being stopped in the street.

"Your purse!"

The 91st order of the Revolutionary Cabinet is being put into execution:

> The banknotes of the Austro-Hungarian Bank, of the denomination of 50, 100, 1000, and 10,000 crowns, are withdrawn from circulation on the 1st of July of this year. Anyone using them after that date for payment, accepting or proffering them or exchanging them, will be charged before a revolutionary tribunal. Besides the punishment, all notes found in the possession of the culprit will be confiscated. The informer shall receive half the value of the confiscated amount.

Detectives are about and the Red soldiers are confiscating on their own account. They present their bayonets: "Your purse! Get it out of your pocket! Blue money is prohibited!" and they take the notes of the Austro-Hungarian Bank. Some of them keep the purse too—as a souvenir. But the white-backed Soviet money is returned with derision to the owner. Red posters on the walls proclaim: "Social production is the source of prosperity!" The Soviet system, after despoiling the treasury, the safe deposits and private dwellings, has now started to 'produce' from people's pockets.

Just as Marxism was incapable of realizing its political conception, so it is incapable of realizing its economic ideals. In its attempt to alleviate the want of small change the Cabinet ordered six locksmiths' shops in Budapest to manufacture two-penny iron coins. The cost of production of each of these coins was over a shilling. The Marxian pamphlet theory has collapsed in the light of the sun; its political application has resulted in unheard-of tyranny and slaughter, and its economic application in bankruptcy and robbery.

The Jews have been spreading the news for days that the 'blue' money of the Austro-Hungarian Bank is going to be valueless. This morning at dawn their wives went to the bridge over the Ipoly and stopped the peasant women who were bringing their baskets to town. An old woman from the other side came into the yard and told us that the Jewesses were, after all, kind to the poor people. They read out at the bridge the new law about the 'blue' money. Those who did not turn back at the news had theirs exchanged by the Jewesses, out of sheer kindness, so as to save them from the Revolutionary Tribunal. For three two-hundred-crown bank-notes they had given her a thousand-crown Soviet note. Of course it was a 'white' note and her husband would not have such things in the house, but in any case the soldiers would have taken the blue notes and the white ones are better than nothing.

Aladár Huszár came in.

"What has happened? Anything wrong?"

"No, nothing." He was looking for his wife. They talked for some time, then came back. I felt that they had read the anxiety in my eyes.

"A reliable carriage has come from the other side of the Ipoly. You can escape by that."

So we need worry no longer. Fate has decided.

"We have no right to detain you. You are safer there." And tears stood in their eyes too.

Aladár Huszár went to bring the carriage to the door while I packed my meagre belongings. It was slow work; every trifle reminded me of something and every movement reminded me that I was still convalescent. Where shall I rest tonight? To part from good friends, to go on the road again, further from home, to knock again at strangers' doors? To ask the Czechs for protection? I shuddered.

When I had finished packing I sat down on a chair and held my breath. I wanted to think hard what I should have to do. I had little money and my boots were worn. Yet, somehow I must get to Nyitra, whence I could escape to Vienna. If I got well I might find some work. Or perhaps at Szeged... It tired me out to think of it.

Noon came, then afternoon: Aladár Huszár came in with great glee, a smile in his eyes. "You've got to stay with us! The carriage has gone, I could not find it. Fate has decided."

"You stay at home with us," his wife said softly.

Fate's carriage had gone. Goodness knows where it is now. It may be a good omen, it may mean that these things will not last much longer.

"We have lived through bad days together," said Aladár Huszár. "We will share the good ones that are coming as well."

We smiled at each other. We know by now that sufferings unite people more than joys.

*   *   *

July 5th.

EVERYBODY says that Balassagyarmat will be in the neutral zone. Us military evacuation is expected for today and people are so excited they hardly know what to do with themselves. They stroll about in the street with their hands in their pockets. There is no work, no food; the shops, even the chemists, are empty. Women gather at the street corners. And from the other bank there comes an uninterrupted stream of heavily-laden carts. Fine old furniture, bedding, mattresses, old family portraits, are heaped pell-mell on them. On one, amidst torn silk curtains, on empty bags, I caught sight of a beautiful bracket clock, the jolts of the car making its soul hum.

"The famous Balassa clock from Kékkö Castle," said Aladár Huszár.

There came a flock of sheep, followed by a troop of singing soldiers, then a herd of pigs, and some cattle. Valuable Swiss milch cows with huge udders were being driven to the slaughter-house.

The people glared gloomily at the plunderers.

"The main roads are littered with books," a young man said in front of the window. "Everything you see has been stolen." The loafers shook their heads and swore. "The whole of the highlands is mined. They did not rob the gentry only!"

"Who is all this going to belong to?" an old peasant inquired.

"Who?" said a frightfully shabby man with a gentlemanly appearance. "Listen to this! It tells you who: 'The Red soldiers' Ten Commandments. 10th commandment: Don't take rich people's houses, cattle, land or jewelry. Leave those to the Soviet.'"

*　　*　　*

July 6th.

THEY are coming! Somebody said so and the news ran through the town and blossomed out in every little house.

They are coming! How often have we said these words with horror within the last terrible nine months. The soldiers are coming from the front and are no longer defending our frontiers. The French, the Czechs, the Rumanians, the Serbians, are coming. The Communists, the Red soldiers, the searchers, the detectives, are coming. They are coming, the terrorists. Then again we said, 'the Rumanians are coming.'

And now the words are in our mouths again and they sound joyful and great. Hungarians are coming! From Szeged! Everybody says so. It is simply a question of days.

The Red press splutters with rage. It foams with vulgar, coarse words against the Entente and Count Stephen Bethlen, because it has heard that even in occupied territory Hungarian White Guards are allowed to be enlisted. But, according to 'The People's Voice':

> The comic-opera Government of Szeged has not strength enough to organize the rabble of the bourgeoisie, it has not even the power to form an armed force from its hooligans, cut-throats and gutter mob, for the realization of its sinister projects.

We really know nothing at all, we do not even know whence the news came, yet we keep saying to each other: "They are coming..."

When darkness fell I took a walk in the little back garden. Suddenly somebody rose from among the shrubs, it was the wife of Gregory, the coachman:

"Do tell me, please, Miss, what is happening?"

The question came suddenly, and I answered instinctively: "Our own people are coming! The Hungarians have started from Szeged!"

The old woman looked me straight in the eyes, as though seeking confirmation. It was obvious that she had something to say. Then she folded her shrivelled old hands, and, in a devout, humble attitude, which words cannot express, her voice rose through the silent night:

"Our Father, which art in Heaven, hallowed be Thy name!"

*   *   *

July 7th-10th.

THE fleeing Directorates from the Highlands are flocking in and requisitioning houses for themselves. Female detectives have come from Budapest. The escaped Directorate of Losoncz has quartered itself on Balassagyarmat. Its chief, Comrade Szijgyártó, terrorizes and issues orders right and left. He wants to dismiss all the officials who had been left in their places and threatens that he will not allow any bourgeois family more than one room whatever be the number of its members. He commandeers whatever he wants—take everything from the bourgeois! They are taking even from the poor. Orders have been received that sixty head of cattle have to be sent Budapest; they will not even leave the milch cows.

There is no food: the Government has stopped all supplies for Balassagyarmat, it being in the neutral zone. For days the bakers have baked no bread, nobody will cart wood, and there is no salt. A peasant offered four chickens for two pounds of salt, although he would not sell them for two hundred and forty crowns. One cannot buy anything for money. Our Sunday dinner cost us a towel and a sheet: everything is done by barter, money has disappeared from circulation.

In vain has the Cabinet decreed under the pain of severe penalties that the 'blue' money (of the Austro-Hungarian Bank) must be exchanged within nine days for their own 'white' banknotes. At 'The People's Bank' of Balassagyarmat the people of the whole county have so far exchanged twenty crowns. The peasants hide their money and say: "What good is it to pay it into the bank if it is worthless? Let the worthless things remain in our trunks." The other day a soldier stuck the white money he had received for pay on the wall. It has no purchasing value.

The peasants laugh among themselves. They are hiding their crops, they did not enlist, and they will not give their money to Béla Kun. As for the propaganda speakers, they say: "We sent them back to the Government—in blankets."

Since things have taken this turn, the three hundred crowns daily wage fails to revive the enthusiasm of the Jewish agitators engaged by the Dictatorship of the Proletariat. The Commissary for Education has now decreed that henceforth the teachers will have to speak to the people in the villages.

*   *   *

Voices in the next room. Railwaymen, postmen, simple citizens now frequently slip in by the back door; they come for advice and bring the news.

The Czechs have again entered Kassa, but the Rumanians have not withdrawn from the Tisza, whatever Clemenceau may have promised. The heroic pupils of the military academy escaped death at the last moment: the Terror tribunal sentenced them to hard labour. This is to Romanelli's credit. It is said that it was he who delivered Baron Perenyi and his patriotic companions from gaol whither the Counter-revolution of Juno 24th had brought them.

A deep sad voice spoke: "Fourteen counter-revolutionaries have been sentenced to death in Budapest."

I strolled out into the little back garden but even there I could not breathe. The trees did not move. The soil was hot and above it the air trembled like leaves above an open fire.

*   *   *

July 12th.

THEY came slowly round the corner, talking with an air of importance. Then they stopped, as though quarrelling. They had Soviet caps on their heads and were dressed, regardless of the heat, in leather coats and black leggings. Then I noticed the hand grenades in their belts. They had a bestial look about them, with faces that betrayed a familiarity with gaol. The hand of one was covered with black hair and he had a costly ring on his finger. Where did he get it from? I shuddered.

They have been coming for days, their number has increased since the Entente insisted on the evacuation of Balassagyarmat. The forsaken town listens trembling at night when their nailed boots clatter along the pavement and stares at them with horror from under doorways, from behind drawn curtains. They laugh, boisterously, their mouths wide open...

I looked after them. As they lifted their feet I saw the heavy nails on their heels. How many human faces have they crushed?

The Lenin Boys, escaped convicts, miscreants ready for any mischief—these are the props of the Dictatorship of the Proletariat. These are the men who take hostages. These are the judges presiding over the terrorist tribunals of Bolshevism. They judge and hang when and where they like. They can do as they like. Their commander is a sailor called Cserny who was a leather-worker before the war. His car is constantly racing through the streets of Budapest. Several people have described him to me. He always wears a cap drawn deeply over his face and goes about in a leather waistcoat with long sleeves, a red scarf round his neck. His face is clean-shaven and his eyes are animated by the soft, greedy expression which is characteristic of a bloodthirsty feline playing with its prey. There are many rings on his red hands and he uses scent. His appearance is that of a footman dressed in his master's clothes. His decisions are rapid, he does not waste time on his victims, and when he has finished with them he spends hours looking at the artistic frescoes of the House of Parliament. He is sentimental and without mercy. He purrs and claws.

It is said that this man got to know Károlyi when the sailors mutinied in Cattaro. After the mutiny he fled to Budapest. He was given money by his friends and sent on a tour of instruction to Bolshevist Russia, where he made the acquaintance of Számuelly in a school for agitators in Moscow. Soon after the October revolution he came to Budapest and during the whole Károlyi regime he agitated undisturbed among the sailors. On the night of March 21st he commanded the plunderers.

And since then this brigand is the absolute master of the nights of Budapest.

*   *   *

July 13th.

IF bread runs short in a town the Revolutionary Cabinet at once dispatches a propaganda speaker to the place.

Comrade Soma Vass has arrived.

The people taking their Sunday walk stopped in front of the town hall. Comrade Vass (Weiss is his real name) appeared suddenly on the balcony, near the red flag. But he wasted his time with his threats and incitements, the public remained cool and indifferent.

A laborer shouted to him: "Give us bread!"

The speaker waxed hot: "That is not the question today. The question now is the preservation of the Dictatorship of the Proletariat. We will not tolerate the Counter-revolution!"

"Is bread a counter-revolution?" the laborer heckled.

"Don't interrupt, comrade! We shall crush the Counter-revolution. We shall exterminate it. We shall hang every bourgeois. If there are not enough gallows in this Soviet Hungary, we will grow them. Yes, comrades, we will grow them!"

The heckler swore. One man lit a cigarette and several cried, "Shut up," but Comrade Soma Vass went on talking. Nobody paid any attention to him, the people chatting among themselves. "He will grow gallows... a nursery of them... grow them, shape them... Well, at least he has a programme of a sort."

And thus, after all the destruction, Béla Kun's spokesman has nailed down the only creative policy of Hungary's Socialist production. They are going to grow gallows.

*   *   *

July 14th-20th.

BÉLA KUN has sent a note to Clemenceau asking for the evacuation of the Tisza as promised in compensation for the abandoned offensive against the Czechs; he received the following answer:

"Béla Kun, Budapest. In answer to your wireless which you sent on the 11th inst. to the President, the Peace Conference declares that it cannot negotiate with you as long as you fail to observe the conditions of the armistice."

For a time I stared at the text of the telegram. How much blood, shame and suffering would have been spared to humanity if the victorious powers, instead of sending propositions through General Smuts to Béla Kun's band of murderers and dangling before the Soviet's eyes the possibility of its admission to the Peace Conference, had sent from the start a reply to this effect. Let the spilt blood and the inhuman tortures fall on the heads of those who wanted to bargain when conscience, honor and charity forbade any bargaining.

It is all clear now. The victorious Great Powers did not enter into negotiations with Béla Kun because they were pressed to do so by their own Proletariat, for that pressure would still exist, but simply because he made light of the integrity of the country to which he had not the slightest title. This shame can never be wiped out. The frigid, tardy note cannot restore the lowered dignity of the victorious States.

Béla Kun answered, his reply couched in provocative, ironical terms. He made little attempt to disguise the doubt he had of Clemenceau's veracity and derided his impotence to impose his will on the Rumanians and Czechs. Orders for mobilization are again covering the walls of the town, and the village criers are walking the streets and beating their drums. Huge posters have made their appearance, representing the running figure of a sailor, his mouth wide open. His head is about two feet long, his arms about three yards. Above his head he stretches a. red cloth inscribed with the words: To ARMS! And while this frightful poster-sailor overruns poor, truncated little Hungary, deprived of its seashore, Béla Kun puts out his tongue at the peace conference. At the meeting of the 'Committee of 150' he rang the tocsin with one hand: "The Proletariat in Hungary is going through its crisis!" The other he waved in triumph: "Today the Hungarian Soviet is an important factor in international affairs, more important than old Hungary ever was! This is proven by Clemenceau's last despatch..." He had a word for everybody, but through his boasting one could hear the chattering of his teeth. The Bavarian Soviet has died, the Austrian Soviet was never born, the armies of the Russian Soviet did not come to the rescue. And throughout Hungary his enemy Counter-revolution raises its head. It is there on the edge of the scythe as the stone sharpens it, it is in the glaring emptiness of the recruiting offices, at the idle writing desks of the offices, in the movement which hides the blue banknotes and refuses the white ones, in the stroke of every oar that crosses the Tisza at Szeged.

The Dictatorship is groping about, seeking something to cling to. As a last hope it is clinging to the phantasmagoria of world-revolution, which, after all, was from the beginning the foundation of its politics. So the Soviet Cabinet has addressed an appeal to the Proletariat of the world, calling on it to demonstrate in favor of the Hungarian and Russian Soviets and to proclaim world revolution on July 20-21st.

XIV

July 21st.

PEOPLE call revolutions 'youth' and 'dawn' But revolutions are not daybreaks, nor are they the chaos out of which comes the beginning of all things. They are not the first hour of a new age, but the last decaying hours of a senile age in which the features of the times have become distorted.

This is not dawn! Revolution is the midnight agony of a passing age, when the vision of the future appears only through the blood and sweat of the dying. The senile age dies in the revolution. And when the disorder of dawn has passed and morning breaks, man becomes a child again and an autocratic power takes it by the hand and leads it back to order, to law, to church, to early Mass, into the presence of God. Then comes the youth of the age, the period of dreaming idealism, of fights for freedom, of Art. This age gathers flowers, ploughs and reaps, sings and follows the footsteps of the beloved. Then comes the age of manhood. It creates industry and commerce, it goes on board ship, weighs anchor and brings treasures from beyond the seas. The treasures increase, the superfluities accumulate and flow into a few hands, the reign of gold raises its head above the misery of millions.

The evening comes over a pale world of ill omen. The nauseous scent of faded flowers pervades the air. In saturnalian revelries the cups are emptied to the dregs. These are the hours of wild, dissolute orgies, old faces painted to look young, derisive laughter. The bells of the churches only mark time, law is only respected by the simple and regarded no better than stupid, traditional nursery tales by the cunning. The tired incapable crowd is ruled by degenerates, hereditary wrecks, criminals and lunatics. Respect disappears, the hand that worked drops its tools and the hour of midnight approaches.

Then comes the agony of the senile age. Blood is shed, flames rise to the sky and between fire and blood the age dies. Revolutions are not mornings. They are the death-struggles of the midnight hour. And we poor

Hungarians have been for months the witnesses of such an artificially provoked agony. It ends the age, but, above my sufferings, I feel that the real dawn is coming towards us.

* * *

July 22nd.

THE day of the heralded world-revolution has passed. The Red press gushes over the strikes in other countries, but reports that the Dictatorship will summon before the Revolutionary Tribunal any Hungarian workman who dares to stop work. In a fortunate country like Soviet Hungary there is no longer any need for strikes. In Russia, where happiness has been attained to an even higher degree, workmen who strike are executed. None the less there is no work being done in town today. Nor is there any on other days. Why work? For forged bank-notes?

World-revolution! That is the word which is being whispered today at street corners. A mad hallucination! Yet, if it were to come? What if man's evil spirits were powerful enough to send million in the same hour to the assault of their God, their country, their home and humanity? Or if Béla Kun's word is just successful enough to induce the Proletariat of the Western Powers to tie their Governments' hands so that things may continue here as they are for months and years, till the fire has burnt out?

A solitary figure came through the silence, came quickly, with an elastic gait, though the bag on his back seemed heavy. He turned his head constantly to right and left, and his eyes, widely opened, had a stare in them which reminded one of the demented. He looked round, then again started quickly towards the Ipoly. Then he disappeared.

This stranger passes here frequently nowadays, though he is not always the same. Sometimes he is young, sometimes old. He is fleeing from gaol and death, and dreams of Szeged. Two friends of my brother Géza escaped this way, across the river. They came to the house, on their way to Szeged. They had no idea I was here, but they brought news of my brother. He is hiding in the hills of Buda, like the others who have not escaped abroad and are not yet in prison.

They also told us that Stephania Türr had been in Budapest in June, looking for Count Stephen Bethlen and me, to take us to Italy.

One evening there was a knock at our gate at an unusual hour and a newcomer stood in front of us like a shadow—Count Stephen Keglevich, fleeing from his property in Abony. His wife and children are coming to us too, they have had to flee separately, so as not to attract attention. They were driven out by hunger and the children were, on the verge of starvation, for the only food they could obtain was what the peasants succeeded in bringing them by stealth from Count Keglevich's own farm. Since May, when Számuelly suppressed the Counter-revolution in Abony, that region has been like a mortuary, and now war is beginning again there. So they are escaping to Ipolykürt, beyond the Ipoly, to the plundered castle. There they will, at any rate, be able to sleep on the bare ground— the one thing the Reds and the Czechs could not take away.

The patriotic Counter-revolution of the faithful Vends, in Western Hungary has been defeated by the Reds and the Vends have fled into Austria. They have been interned in Feldbach and many Hungarian officers have joined them. Baron Lehár is their commander. In Szeged the legendary hero of Novara, Nicolas Horthy, is Minister of War. Paul Teleki is Foreign Secretary. General Soós and Gömbös are organizing the national army. When I took leave of the latter in March, I knew that I should hear of him if I lived.

It is said that Colonel Julier, the new Chief of Staff, who was forced to take Stromfeld's place at the point of the revolver, will be Red only till he has crossed the Tisza. It is also said that whole battalions of the Red army are deserting to Szeged. In our imagination that town, like a mirage, is floating amidst national colored flags on the banks of the Tisza, above the Great Plain. We see the three colors, we hear the National Anthem whenever we think of the town. Our proscribed flag, our proscribed hymn! I am a beggar, for the property of the dead and the condemned reverts to the Soviet. But when my imagination sees the three colors floating against the sky, when the great prayer of my race echoes in my mind, I am the richest woman in Hungary.

A hand has put 'The Red Newspaper' on the table—big type again: "Revolutionary outbreaks in Paris, Berlin and Turin. Demonstrations of the foreign Proletariat in favor of the world-revolution." Then, set in small type, a short notice: "Kiel... The demonstrations have passed without the slightest disturbance."

That is the history of the world-revolution. It is finished and the door is still open.

*　*　*

July 23rd.

THE news is in everybody's mouth: the Reds have won a decisive victory on the Tisza and the members of the Directorate have regained their confidence. It is from the attitude of these people that the town reads the position of the Dictatorship. Their star is in the ascendant and the Proletarians treat us with more rudeness than ever. Red color has again blossomed out on the soldiers' caps, but they do not feel too sure about it, and instead of ribbons they wear geraniums. That generally means that the position is doubtful: a ribbon cannot be removed suddenly, a flower is quickly torn off.

Goodness only knows how often I have wandered round the little back-garden. If it is really true that the Reds have crossed the Tisza! Those who have seen their bestial destruction in their own country, and observed them returning with booty stolen from people of their own blood, must falter when they think of their victims.

"What news?"

In Huszár's hand the journal's yellow, mean paper rustled. "They have crossed..." he paused, then went on: "... On July 20th we crossed the Tisza at various points... From Tokaj to Csongrád we are pursuing the beaten Rumanian troops everywhere..."

So they have won a victory with our blood against our own blood; for this is not a question of Rumanians. A defeat of the Rumanians, the reoccupation of the torn-off territory, the release of our Hungarian brethren, were not the objects of the Dictatorship's ambition, but a new larder and a new field for robbery, new slaves and new legions. And we cannot even deceive ourselves with the belief that the news is untrue. It is true, it must be true, because Béla Kun, who loses his head when in despair and is impudent after success, has sent to Clemenceau, the President of the Peace Conference, the following ironical, provoking message: "We have been obliged by the Rumanian attack, which was undertaken against the wishes of the Entente, to cross the Tisza, and to enforce the wishes of the Entente against the Rumanians."

Our thoughts travel wearily to those parts where, behind the receding Rumanian flood, foreign energy will set against each other the few remaining Hungarians. Számuelly's train is under steam, and if it starts it will plant the further shore of the Tisza with gallows.

A tightly-shuttered house has been burning here in Hungary for months. Nobody tried to extinguish it. At last the smoke choked itself, the fire burnt itself out. Who troubled about those who were in the house? Those outside cared only that the fire should not spread to the adjacent houses. Now the windows of the house on fire have burst, the fire has been revived by the air, the flames lick the palings, spread, flare up, run. What if they were to ignite the Great Plain and unite with the Russian conflagration?

Evening came. Hours dropped into space. One of us picked up the paper and we now noticed something for the first time. Below the news of the passage of the Tisza, three words darkened the page: "Sentence of death." At Saint Germain the victors presented their peace treaty to the remnant of Austria.

Our quarrel with Austria has lasted for centuries, and she brought us hard times, yet there is no people on earth to whom her fate causes as much pain today as to us. We have fought and fallen together on the battlefield. Now they hang a beggar's satchel round the neck of unfortunate, torn Austria, and out of irony, with devilish cunning, send her to take her share with her own predatory enemies, in the plunder of Hungary. They compensate her with Western Hungary, with a piece of land that promises endless revolts and is meant to act as a living wedge to prevent for ever an understanding between the two despoiled peoples. It is a devilish plan, the most perfidious part of the terrible Peace Treaty. It pretends to be a present, but it is a curse and a disgrace.

A single candle was burning on the table, and by its light we could see a map on the wall—the map of Hungary! That unit of a thousand years which was not created by man but was made into one country by nature. The thing I could never believe, which was always deemed a threat meant only for the Revolutionary Bolshevist Government, the frontier of Hungary as delineated by Clemenceau, has disclosed itself in the Austrian treaty as the real aim of their vengeance. In the name of peoples and nations the men at the Peace Conference are preparing a crime which is only paralleled by the partition of Poland.

Suddenly I see, like a train of misty ghosts, a shackled procession pass before my eyes: the granite walls of the Carpathians; the mysterious rushes of Lake Fertö; the sea under the Carso; the Danube rushing through the Iron gate; the summits of Transylvania; the forests of Mármaros—all of them under a foreign yoke! I did not own an inch of that ground, and yet it was all my own. They take it from me, and equally from everyone who is Hungarian. Aladár Huszár has drawn upon the map the frontiers fixed by the Paris Peace Conference. It is as if a knife were passing through our flesh, leaving a line of blood wherever it passes. The ancient frontiers are all left far beyond the line and deep in the country there is an awful gash. The red line proceeds on the map, staggers now and then as though in horror, stumbles, recoils and then goes on, leaving ancient Hungarian cities without, cutting pure Hungarian regions in two, leaving a miserable, truncated body—the Hungary of the Peace Conference!

Those who have never leant over the map of their own country, those who have never drawn with weeping eyes new frontiers within the old historical boundaries at the bidding and according to the predatory desires of enemy peoples, those are ignorant of the meaning of torture, of lust for vengeance, of revolt, of hatred, of patriotism.

"We shall take it back!..."

Which of us said it? It matters not. It is not the saying of one person, it is the word of a whole nation. Even in our misery and destruction we had the strength to say it. "We will take it back!" That is the phrase which all our coming generations will breathe. That is the phrase mothers will teach to their infants. Bride and bridegroom will pledge each other's troth with that phrase before the altar. Those who go will leave this phrase as an inheritance, those who remain will take their oath upon it. We will take it back! The last clod, the meanest tree, every spring, every blade of grass, every stone.

Nothing moved in the silence of the night. Only the flame of the burnt-out candle flickered.

"Let us go... we must sleep. This is the last candle in the house."

*   *   *

July 24th-29th.

THERE is one piece of news today that gives us some hope. Even if the ship seems still afloat, it is sinking, for the first rats are leaving it. Michael Károlyi, who proclaimed he would hold out to the last breath, who has betrayed Hungary and has driven her into Bolshevism, has been arrested with his wife and secretary at a Czech frontier post and sent to Prague. Retribution must be near, for he was afraid and fled. It is reported that since the banks refuse to pay more than two thousand crowns to any one individual, he provided himself with several millions of Austro-Hungarian Banknotes and a false passport. He wanted to go through Vienna to Milan, but Italy did not desire his presence. Bavaria refused to admit him, but Prague offered him an asylum. They owed it to him. Without Michael Károlyi the Hungarian Highlands would never have passed into Czech captivity.

He has gone, fled from the nation's just vengeance, but he cannot escape the long arm of God's justice. Millions of Hungarians driven into slavery and homelessness, seas of spilt Hungarian blood, miles of Hungarian land, cry out to heaven against him.

A mean man, a debased politician, and one of the greatest traitors in the world's history.

Iscariot has passed.

*   *   *

July 29th-31st.

SOMETIMES one can learn a town's news by watching its street corners. Today some soldiers gathered opposite the house. One of them said something, gesticulating, while the others stood and stared at the pavement. There were no red flowers in their caps, though I saw some in the gutter. Shortly afterwards I saw them leave the village with their bundles on their backs and disappear through the corn-fields.

Everybody is talking about the tremendous losses of the Red army. The official papers try to screen them: "Our victorious armies... The whole of Rumania's forces opposing them... We withdrew our troops behind the Tisza, in perfect order, without any losses in men or material."

"Twenty-eight thousand dead," says rumor, and ten thousand men are reported drowned in the Tisza. Soma Vass need not plant his nurseries for gallows, the wholesale murder of Hungarians has been successfully accomplished on the banks of the Tisza. And while they died, Comrade Landler, the Commander-in-Chief of the Red army, and other comrades watched them from a safe place through field-glasses. The Rumanian victory and the defeat of the Reds are both paid for in Hungarian blood. Never have Hungarians died a more tragic death.

If this sort of thing lasts much longer there will be no one but lunatics left when the end comes. Every hour brings new tales of terror. In Budapest, Tibor Számuelly is gaining more and more power. He wants to become Dictator. Hitherto the Dictatorship has been too lenient, so the terrorists are going over to his side. And their one idea, before they lose their power, is to be revenged on the nation. Already the Directorates have received secret instructions and are drawing up lists. Számuelly is preparing for a massacre of the citizens. None shall be spared, neither artisans nor peasants.

News comes from the other bank that the Czechs are returning. They say they have orders to occupy Vácz on the 3rd. More and more soldiers are disappearing from the village, and Terror Boys are continually flowing in from Budapest to take their place. There are already eighty here.

After the arrival of the evening train people steal in the dark towards the Ipoly. Hitherto it has been Hungarians who were escaping, now it is mostly Jews who slink along the walls carrying parcels. In the town hall they are feverishly packing up the archives of the Directorate; the Jewish comrades have again withdrawn into the background.

Szijgyártó has now become the absolute master of the town. Among other things he issued an order today that every individual who is not registered and whose stay is not considered justified by the Directorate must leave Balassagyarmat within twenty-four hours, on pain of being summoned before a Revolutionary Tribunal. Those who come from Budapest will be sent back there under police escort. Once more there is talk of searching houses; the terrible hand groping for me has returned. It will be bad luck if it catches me now when its days are already numbered.

We discussed the matter and the old plan of escape was revived— across the Ipoly, somehow to Vienna, to Szeged; but again the horror of asking hospitality from the Czechs in my own country, my poverty, my illness, interfered.

"Let's wait and see how things develop," said my friends.

How often have they said that!

Suddenly I thought of the house in Szügy: I could not leave without bidding it farewell; so I walked over to it and saw the garden and its mistress once more.

When I was the re last the crops were still standing; now the wheat was in sheaves and summer walked between their gold over the fields. Then I came to the garden and found that the clean-swept courtyard was no longer a soldiers' right of way. Crimson ramblers were blooming on the walls of the house, and round about the pump the down-trodden grass had sprung up again. On the terrace, green plants and garden furniture had taken the place of ammunition boxes. How rapidly the ruts of ammunition carts and service wagons and dirt and garbage disappear. Will it be like this elsewhere too?

Before I left, Mrs. Beniczky walked through the garden with me and we stopped for a moment near the trees between which I had caught a glimpse of the hussar bugler among the Red soldiers, near the bushes whence I had watched Pogány's car. How much had happened since then! The trees had become dark green and grave; the garden had passed its nuptial glory. Its wreath had faded, its most beautiful flowers had gone.

When I reached the small railway station of Balassagyarmat I saw that soldiers were running about, throwing their arms into wagons. "They are evacuating the town," said a railway man, laughing scornfully. On the open track, amidst piles of boxes and bags, carriages, bedding, machine-guns, and pianos were standing near the wagons, ready to be loaded. The streets were quiet, but carts were standing at the doors of some of the houses and people were hurriedly packing things at random into them. They are running away! Yet Comrade Landler reported in 'The People's Voice' of the 29th that: "There is no change in the situation at the front."

The Red press is indulging in paroxysms of fury against the Szeged Government. "Cheats, scoundrels, Jingoes," are the epithets bestowed by Béla Kun's newspapers; and all the time little handbills are being secretly passed from hand to hand. They were dropped by an aeroplane from Szeged: "The hour of delivery is at hand! Prepare to support the National Government!"

The village listens, tense under the Red posters which disfigure its walls. It listens abstractedly, as though trying to hide its thoughts, and behind closed doors and windows people put their heads together. Stories born of desire are spreading, but the insufferable thought that we are in need of help from the Rumanians dominates our imagination and hopes:

> The national army has already left Szeged!... Whole Red regiments have passed over and have laid down their arms. White Hungarian troops will come with the Rumanians. Perhaps tomorrow... In Budapest the commander of the garrison has prepared the population for a general alarm should the Dictatorship of the Proletariat be in danger. The whole town is covered with posters... An hour after the alarm has been sounded nobody must be in the streets. Soldiers must hurry to their barracks, workmen to their respective headquarters. Within an hour from the alarm all electric trams must be withdrawn... All shops and public offices must be closed at once, as well as the doors and windows of houses. Simultaneously with the alarm martial law will be declared.

Such preparations have never been made before, either in May when the Rumanians attacked, or in June during the Counter-revolution. Those who come from Budapest speak of the disruption of the Red army as it retires, of its anarchy, of mutinies of Terror detachments, of Számuelly's autocracy. It is impossible to get a clear picture of what is happening: "The White army is approaching! The Rumanians are advancing from the Tisza!"

One can hear the crackling and collapsing of the Dictatorship. The powers of the Entente have sent a note, and the Cabinet has felt obliged to publish it in its press. This note is no longer addressed to the Soviet or the Dictatorship of the Proletariat. At last, then, the Allied and Associated Powers are going to address themselves to the Hungarian people! Under the title: 'Declaration of the Entente on the Blockade!' the Red press screens the Note of the Powers in which they declare: "We sincerely desire to make peace with the Hungarian people..." But peace can only be concluded if the Hungarian people is represented by a Government which "represents really the will of the people, and not by one whose power rests on terror."

It has taken the Entente Powers four and a half months to come to this decision! No wonder they have been slow to discredit Béla Kun, for, after Károlyi, he has rendered them invaluable service. He has ruined and robbed Hungary of her last sources of strength. Now they can take possession of the booty which is no longer capable of offering resistance and can pay with our thousand years' old possessions the war bills presented to them by their little allies.

*　*　*

August 1st.

THE news reached the village last night. The Red army has gone to pieces. Comrade Landler reports that after "the unchanged situation at the front, we are attacking the Rumanians who have crossed the Tisza... The Red army is in perfect order and has gained a victory over the Rumanians... We have retired, unbeaten, of our own accord."

The members of the Balassagyarmat Directorate are unable to disguise their nervousness, the comrades are rushing about the shops clamoring to buy no matter what so long as they can get rid of their white Soviet banknotes. But however much they pester and threaten, the shopkeepers refuse to sell. The shop windows are empty, only the propaganda shop of the Commissariat of Education still offers its wares—pamphlets, portraits of the Commissaries, Red stars, badges with the 'Red man' and plaster busts of Lenin and Marx. But these are at a discount today. The town is practically without traffic and the telegraph wires bring incessant orders from Budapest: "Let everyone remain at his post. Let none dare to run away..."

Steps halted outside and I heard a Semitic voice say: "Let us lead it into other channels..." What did that mean? While I was pondering the front door-bell rang. The Sub-prefect has come with a wire from Budapest. Béla Kun's rule is over!

Something snatched at my heart and I felt that I wanted to shout.

"It's certain to be true," the Sub-prefect said. "A purely Socialist

Government is being formed." And he folded his hands carefully as if he were afraid of committing himself.

A purely Socialist Government! That was not what we had expected! Now I remembered the rumors that the delegates of the Entente had not been negotiating with the Viennese committee of Count Stephen Bethlen, nor with the Government of Szeged, but had been exchanging pourparlers for days, not with Hungarians, but with William Böhm, Kunfi and with Károlyi's henchman, Garami.

I thought at once of what I had heard outside my window: "Let us lead it into other channels."

So the Jews are still to be our leaders: the Red hangmen of yesterday are resuming their old garb of moderate Socialism and are preparing to pass the power from one hand into the other. The world-revolution has not come off, and there have been other mistakes in their calculations; they reckoned every item as they thought—the threats of the Entente, the attacks of the Rumanians—but they forgot to take into account that dying Hungary might have energy enough to cross its arms over its torn breast and undermine Bolshevism from within with its old weapon, passive resistance, despite the failure of the Entente and Rumanian arms.

There were shouts in the guard-room opposite:

"Who said that? Arrest him!" And Red Guards and Terrorists rushed towards the post-office. If the postmaster said so, he must be arrested. But instead of answering them the postmaster called up Budapest, a Terrorist meanwhile holding one of the receivers. And along the wires the question rang to Budapest. The answer came at once: "The Government has resigned, the Soviet exists no longer. Budapest is mad with happiness."

The Terrorists glared at each other terror-stricken, but they did not arrest the postmaster; instead they went to the Directorate for instructions. But the Red offices in the town hall were empty and the comrades had disappeared. Some of them had been suddenly taken ill and had been obliged to go home. The news rushed along the darkening streets and in a few seconds it had spread all over the town.

Peace on earth and goodwill among men!

The house became too narrow for me. So did the garden. A violin was being played next door, sobbing to the accompaniment of a piano. Then, in spite of ourselves, we all burst into the forbidden, outlawed, Hungarian hymn. We just stood and sang, and the National Anthem went up in that summer night, to the starlit firmament.

Below, in the dark, on the other side of the street, noiseless dark figures slunk away. In the light streaming from open windows the neighbors stood bare-headed. They were praying too.

XV

August 2nd.

THE shepherd's flute sounded slowly through the breaking morning. I felt disappointed; my elation had passed; my mind was still racked with anxiety. Everything seemed the same in the streets: the red flag was still floating over the county hall, the Red soldiers were leaning out of the guard-room window just as they had done during the victories of the Dictatorship of the Proletariat over the Czechs. A schoolmaster who lived near by was walking in his shabby Sunday coat towards the teachers' Communist school. What has happened? The gates of the prison are open; are the captives afraid to leave it?

A little boy took his red, white and green toy flag from above his bed and waved it out of the window. A man in the street shouted at him threateningly.

About noon the wife of a neighbor came, bearing alarming news: they want to arrest Aladár Huszár. He went to the teachers' Communist school and distributed ribbons with the national colors and made a speech to the teachers. When Comrade Weiss, the examining Commissary, arrived, the National Anthem was filling the place. In his fury Comrade Weiss tore up all the teachers' certificates. The Jewish teachers stood by him, while the Hungarians left the place with Huszár, singing the National Anthem. Outside Red guards met them and tore the national colors off all of them.

So when Aladár Huszár came home we hoisted a huge red, white and green flag on the house.

The drum! What has the Town Crier to say now?...

"It is forbidden to wear or exhibit any emblems..." Presently two hooligans invaded us and tore down our flag, but we don't care. The whole village is in a ferment. Patrol followed patrol. A man feverishly pasted pink posters on the walls, displaying the telegram of the Secretariat of the Socialist-Communist Party:

As the result of an agreement with the Entente, a
WORKMEN'S GOVERNMENT
formed by the trade unions has assumed power. The officials of the
existing workmen's organizations will continue to act without
interference... The strictest martial law is to be proclaimed.

Green posters were then stuck up beside the pink ones all along the street, containing the text of the new Government's telegram. They called themselves a Workmen's Government instead of a Revolutionary Cabinet, Ministers instead of Commissaries. President: Peidl; Interior: Peyer; Justice: Garami-Grünfeld; then followed three of Béla Kun's Commissaries: Agoston-Augenstein for Foreign Affairs, Haubrich for War and Dovcsák for Commerce; at the end of the list the former President of the Soviet, Garbai, Minister for Education.

I remembered the conversation I had overheard yesterday: "Let us lead it into other channels..."

Moritz Kohn has arranged his fraudulent bankruptcy and suddenly Mrs. Moritz Kohn's name appears above the shop. But what is the National Army doing?

The Dictatorship of the Soviet collapsed with the Red army; its position became hopeless on the 31st of July when it became known that the Rumanians would not stop a second time at the Tisza. Béla Kun had hurriedly convoked the Workers' and Soldiers' Council of Five Hundred yesterday afternoon. And in the great hall of the new town hall, where on the 21st of March a handful of men had proclaimed the Dictatorship of the Proletariat, Béla Kun resigned in a halting, tearful voice. During the night he fled with the other Commissaries and their families to Austria, finding protection under the wings of their Co-religionist Chancellor Renner. With the help of the Peidl Government they made their way to the frontier, *protected by an escort supplied by the Italian military mission in Budapest!* It is said that Számuelly has disappeared. But among those who fled with Béla Kun was the blood-thirsty Weiss—and so were Schwarz, Vágó and Pogány, and the twenty-stone lawyer, Comrade Landler, the Red Commander-in-Chief. They absconded from their army between the Danube and the Tisza, after having driven it into death and destruction, though they had sworn to stand by it to the last drop of blood.

Without wounds received on the field of Bolshevik glory, but with many millions of Austro-Hungarian banknotes, they disappeared into the obscurity from which they had emerged to Hungary's misfortune a few months before. They have gone, as Michael Károlyi did before them. So the country hoisted its tricolor flag once more. But the Government of

Peidl, which not only tolerated but abetted and organized the flight of the criminals, would not tolerate such a resurrection; so it forbade the flag and proclaimed martial law.

Aladár Huszár has been arrested in the street and is in prison. The commander of the Red garrison wants to have him executed for the National Anthem incident, and for wearing ribbons of the national colors, but the chief of the police telephoned to Budapest, asking that he be reprieved. The answer came: "Keep him in custody and let the Terrorists take him to Budapest." The Terrorists openly declare that they are going to settle with him on the way. Mrs. Huszár wanted to see her husband, but the Terrorists would not let her. "Comrade Szijgyártó is interrogating him now." The news spread like wildfire. Machine-guns were mounted in front of the county hall.

Then the whole town began to simmer and even the inhabitants of the red-postered houses came forth—officials, teachers, the whole educated class, the people of no importance coming to protect the unimportant folk's friend. The railway men, the postmen, all of them, clamored that Huszár should be set free. And suddenly the Red garrison went over to their side.

The drum again:

"Anybody found in the streets after 9 p.m. will be arrested by the Red patrols."

But just then the Red guards sent a message to Comrade Szijgyártó that if the prisoner was not released by nine they would lay down their arms and refuse to serve any longer.

People were talking excitedly in the streets, saying that the Rumanians were already in Aszód and were coming in our direction. Comrade Szijgyártó shook his fist with rage: "I ought to have had him hanged at once." The crowd became more and more threatening and at nine o'clock Aladár Huszár was at home. He was quite calm. Comrade Szijgyártó had ran at him with raised fists, had pointed a revolver at him, and threatened to shoot him...

Suddenly we heard sobs from the end of the table. It was only then that we noticed the children. With wide open eyes, deadly pale, they were standing there and they had heard everything. When we were as small as they my mother would not allow anyone to tell us gruesome stories; but in spite of their parents the children of this age live through things which we were not even allowed to be told in fairy tales.

*   *   *

August 3rd.

THE town is in the hands of the Terrorists and no news comes from Budapest. The last message came this morning. The delegates of the Entente are negotiating with the new Government and are inclined to recognize it. The Rumanian advance has ceased.

In the streets of Balassagyarmat the Communists, who were trembling yesterday, are again assuming a provocative attitude; the comrades who were ill recovered suddenly. The propaganda shop has been opened again and the window is full of Communist Declarations. More than two people are not allowed to meet in the street.

The Terrorists wanted to arrest Aladár Huszár again, but he had fled. The door-bell is ringing all day—detectives and red guards inquiring for him. And in the village the inhabitants and the railwaymen are arming secretly.

* * *

August 4th.

A SHOT was fired close to the house and this was followed by a regular fusillade. People came running out of the houses and for some minutes there was confusion. The wife of Gregory, the coachman, tumbled in breathlessly: "What goings on!—the soldiers have barred our street. They are driving the people into the houses at the point of the bayonet."

I thought, at once of Aladár Huszár and hoped they had not arrested him. His wife received many messages not to show herself in the street and naturally we wanted to know what had happened; so by the irony of fate, it was I who crept out of the house.

The people I met spoke excitedly; everybody was coming from the direction of the county hall and nobody was going that way. A man said: "Turn back, you cannot go there. A new detachment of Terrorists has arrived and there is a corpse in the street."

So the trouble was not about Huszár. I thanked him for the warning, but went on. Another running crowd was coming towards me. A servant girl leant against the wall and began to tie her boot laces.

"What's happening there?"

The girl answered, panting:

"They have red caps, goodness only knows what they are, perhaps French, but they are firing furiously."

191

The shooting had stopped now. Two schoolboys were peeping out from behind a door: "The Jews have taken up arms," they said mysteriously. The street leading to the station was absolutely empty and nothing was audible but my steps. Men in leather coats were standing in groups in front of the county hall and round the machine-guns bayonets were glittering in the sun. I looked round rather alarmed, this was the first time I had seen the place and I had pictured it differently. There was no tower on the town hall and not a trace of my imaginary arcades or old pump. It was a pity, but the disillusionment of a dream is always so.

As if I had suddenly been perceived the bayonets turned towards me and the men in the leather coats shouted furiously: "Back!" Someone looked out of a ground floor window. The soldiers promptly stuck their bayonets into it. "Bloody bourgeois, in with your head, or I'll knock it off!" I saw that the Terrorists were coming in my direction, so I thought it was time to turn back.

In the afternoon a detective called. He was one of those whom we call 'radishes,'—Red outside and White within. He inquired after Aladár Huszár and told his wife that the red-caps who had been mistaken for Frenchmen were hussars back from the Tisza front and that the firing was caused by an attempt of the town guards to disarm Comrade Szijgyártó. He was saved by the Terrorists, who were now masters of the town. Then he looked carefully round: "The Lenin Boys have decided to hold out to the last. They want to revenge the fall of the Dictatorship and intend to plunder tonight. There are a hundred of them. They are out to kill and have marked this house. Be careful!" He looked round again. "And please don't forget to tell Mr. Huszár when he gets back into office, that I am not a Communist."

Hours passed. The news passed like a shudder through the streets. Many locked their front doors. I buried my papers again and we also hid the money that was in the house. We all packed up our most necessary things. As evening fell, we could bear our isolation no longer. I must try... I will go towards the station; perhaps I shall hear something by chance. But the streets echoed with emptiness and the station was deserted. Only a workman was sitting on the weighing machine filling his pipe.

"When is the next train for Budapest?"

"There won't be any train," the man answered and lit his pipe. Then he closed his eyes.

I went homewards. New posters were showing on the walls: –

"Strict martial law. All gatherings are prohibited and those who do not obey the injunctions of the Red guards will be shot on the spot... Szijgyártó. County Commander."

Near a paling a short elderly Jew was standing and talking to a woman. Quite coolly, obviously so that I should hear it, he said: "At half-past five the Rumanians entered Budapest."

I stumbled, though my foot had not hit an obstacle, and the blood rushed to my face. The Rumanians! I could hardly grasp it. The Rumanians! That is the reason, then, why our people could not come! That is the reason why the Entente stopped them! That is why so many of us had to die during the long months of waiting! The occupation of Budapest was reserved by the Great Powers for the Rumanians so that the city might become their prey and they might still act the role of deliverers.

I felt giddy as I walked home. The blow and the humiliation were so great that everything else became indifferent.

Budapest is in the hands of the Rumanians!

The clock struck nine; suddenly I heard a violent knocking and furious cursing at the end of the corridor, and a fat, angry man rolled into the room. He had forgotten to take his hat off, and his pipe was in his mouth. It was old Schlegel, a stout old German market gardener from the banks of the Ipoly, a fiery Hungarian patriot, who within the last few months had helped innumerable refugees across the river.

"Donnerwetter! The devil, why don't you open your door? I knock—the curfew—they shoot people down out there."

Now that he was in safety, he calmed down and put his fat hand on Mrs. Huszár's shoulder: "I just came to tell you, you need not be anxious. Your husband is in my house. We have plenty of arms. If the Communists try their slaughtering trick here, I'll come too and shoot them like dogs." He produced from his pocket a huge rusty revolver and waved it like a mace threateningly above his head. "That is all I had to say."

I stole to the front door to see if all was clear. The new moon had already set and there was not a soul in the street. I made a sign to the old man and in his gouty way, his right leg always foremost, he passed me into the street. Without a word he touched his hat and with shaky, baby-like steps disappeared at the end of the street between the high stalks of the Indian corn. The electric light went out. The town moved no longer.

Our vigil was illuminated by a single candle, and we kept looking at the clock. It was said that the Terrorists were guarding the streets leading out of town so that nobody should be able to escape. Looting was to begin at midnight. Even if they did their work quickly it would take them half an hour before they came here. This house was said to be marked as their third point of attack.

Somehow I remembered a horror of my childhood. I was quite small. My grandmother Tormay was telling us stories about her Huguenot ancestors. She told us how, before the massacre of Saint Bartholomew, the men of Catherine de Medici had locked all the gates of Paris so that none should be able to escape and then marked with chalk the houses inhabited by Huguenots. "But that happened more than three hundred years ago," my grandmother said, "when people were still wild and cruel."

The clock struck midnight.

I asked Mrs. Huszár to escape at once with her children into the fields of Indian corn as soon as the shooting started. We listened. Nothing... only the clock struck again. Half-past twelve. My friend was standing near the window listening, and I thought how often we had sat up through the nights like this during the last few months.

"Do you remember? That night when we kept saying. 'Now the Czechs have fired!' 'Now the Reds?'"?

Our fate has not altered. The Dictatorship of the Proletariat is still alive and continues to torture us.

One o'clock!

A hen fluttered up the roof of the house opposite. Under the stars silence pervaded the summer night.

Half-past one!

A dog barked, and all round other dogs responded.

"They are coming!"

The anxious moments passed. The dogs were silent again and in the cool dawn the first cock crowed, followed at intervals by others. It reminded us of clocks striking the hour in succession.

The sun rose. The Terrorists have not come. Who can say why? The St. Bartholomew's night of Balassagyarmat has not come off.

*   *   *

August 5th.

THIS morning we learnt that before starting on their plundering expedition the Terrorists found a supply of champagne in the cellars of one of the hotels. They got so drunk that they could not even stand. So a few hundred bottles of champagne saved the town. Comrade Szijgyártó was the only man who remained sober. It appears that he received an ambiguous message from the Budapest Workmen's Government and in the course of the night he sent his detectives out to find whither he could escape. When his men returned they reported that the roads to the villages were guarded by armed men, so he was obliged to wait till the Lenin Boys had slept off their drunkenness. But meanwhile the old police of Balassagyarmat had assembled. Now people are talking of the Terrorists' intention to escape by train, but the police will disarm them at the station.

Everybody was out of doors. Here and there a young man in a leather coat, with a brand new hat on his head, appeared, looking innocently at the crows.

Mrs. Huszár noticed it too and we looked at each other. "They have changed their garb..."

Suddenly policemen, railwaymen, guards with white flowers, officials, women and boys began rushing towards the station. The whole street was running and its rush was watched from both sides by the posted horrors of the Dictatorship of the Proletariat. The Red soldiers, wild sailors, half-naked workmen wading in blood, shapeless female monsters. Yesterday they were all alive; now, as I passed them quickly they receded on the walls beside me as the phantoms of a terrible past.

A youth came running from the direction of the county hall shouting at the top of his voice.

"The Lenin Boys have escaped!" While people were waiting for them at the station they fled with their booty from the other end of the town. People swore and angry voices shouted: "Scoundrels! But they will be caught!" In that moment, as if a chain round the town's chest had broken, Balassagyarmat breathed freely again. Men raised their heads, spoke loud and freely, many careworn faces made an attempt to smile. There was talk and laughter under the trees lining the streets. Then a boy started to work and others took it up—arms were raised, sticks and pocket-knives worked feverishly, and in a few minutes, all through the town, the posters of the Dictatorship were hanging in shreds from the walls. Thick layers of paper fell on the pavement, bright colored scraps covered the cobbles, and were trodden in the dust.

The grape harvest has come in the land of hunchbacks.

*　　*　　*

August 6th.

DAYS have passed since the murderers of the country have fallen and fate has not yet done justice to them. Reality has achieved nothing, so it remains for imagination to sit in trial over the criminals.

People tell each other that Michael Károlyi and Béla Kun have been given up by the Czechs and Austrians and that both have been hanged.

Between the Danube and the Tisza and in Western Hungary the peasants are arresting the hiding butchers of the Dictatorship and delivering them up to the justice of the crowd, who make them eat the posters scratched from the walls. Then they are executed by those whose father, mother, husband or child they have murdered.

Then comes one authentic piece of news: Tibor Számuelly has committed suicide. He was the first who tried to escape. The Cabinet had not yet resigned when he rushed in his car to the aerodrome, hoping to fly to Russia. But not one of the pilots would undertake the job. Then he started with some of his hangmen on a lorry towards Austria but was arrested on the way, and while unwatched shot himself dead.

"That is not fair," said a farmer, "he ought to have been strung up on a dung-heap."

"He deserved the torture chamber, not a bullet!" And the people curse the scoundrel furiously for having escaped human justice.

But once again our elation is stifled by sorrow, for we are receiving more and more unexpected names of the victims of the Dictatorship of the Proletariat. In the last hours, during its agony, the reign of terror has snatched the lives of Oscar Fery and his faithful companions, Menkina and Borhy.

Oscar Fery, the organizer of the Hungarian county police, was the heroic soul of the Counter-revolution. He was a brave soldier, who, notwithstanding that he was a Lieutenant-General, stayed in Budapest during the Commune so that in case of need he might be on the spot to lead his police. The Dictators were afraid of him—he did not run away! A few days ago, he was dragged from his home at night and with two faithful officers was taken to the Terrorists' barracks. When the fall of the Dictatorship was unavoidable, the prisoners were killed in the cellars one after the other. Oscar Fery was the last, and as he was being taken to the cellar he fell over the mutilated bodies of his companions. There was an awful storm that night, the roaring of the wind dominated every sound. Yet for hours one could hear the screams of the victims in the cellar of the barracks.

The murderers have escaped, but their saviors continue to rule over Hungary while the Entente negotiates with them. And the Rumanians are in Budapest.

"One can't go on living like this. We would much rather be killed." I have seen weeping men today.

* * *

August 7th.

THERE are no trains yet from Budapest and the town is surrounded by a ring. Nobody can get out of it; no passengers, no newspapers come to us. The Workmen's Government has cancelled all the orders of the Dictatorship, and no fresh orders have come through yet. Only a part of the troops from the Tisza front could be disarmed. The soldiers have overrun the country and many are robbing and plundering.

A doubtful rumor spread yesterday evening. It was said that an opposition Government had been formed in the capital. Is it true? Or, as so often before, is it only an invention arising from our hope? Yet hope *is* rising.

"You sit down and write an article in remembrance of Balassagyarmat," said Aladár Huszár. "The old patriotic newspaper has reappeared."

For months I have been writing only for my own self and the idea of publicity came disturbingly to me, as if someone, were watching my pen over my shoulder. "Resurrection..." I chose that title for my article and I signed my name—the first time since the events of March.

As I wrote it many thoughts passed through my mind. The name of Elisabeth Földváry, my companion and protector during the sad days, has fallen off me as a cloak. I return it to those who have a right to it and I hope they will forgive me for using it. I give it back—but not with a light heart. The cloak, worn for so many months, has practically grown on me, and refuses to part from me.

I must seek a road that leads me back to my own self. And while seeking it, two individualities collided within me: my own, which has to fight and work, and the other, the poor, tired, shy, retiring one, which has realized the pleasures of obscurity and the peace of quiet irresponsibility. Suddenly I feel frightened. Will that which life has left me be enough for what life expects from me?

The door flew open as if torn by a hurricane:

"Come, come, all of you!" shouted Aladár Huszár, holding a paper in his hand. "Great news. A proclamation..."

"Why? What? Whence?" He read, deeply moved:

To the Hungarian people! Inspired by the everlasting love with which I cling to the Hungarian people, looking back on the sufferings we have gone through together in the last five years, I give way to the request addressed to me from all quarters and will attempt to solve the present impossible situation!

We no longer asked any questions, we knew who it was who for five years had suffered in common with us, he who loves the Hungarian people with everlasting devotion, the people forsaken by everybody, whom nobody loves. The Archduke Joseph!

After all the hatred—everlasting love! A tear ran down my cheek; I did not wipe it away but left it there to wash off the traces of so many sufferings.

A Government has been formed and its members are Hungarians, not foreigners. Stephen Friedrich is Prime Minister.

There was a time when Friedrich had been misled by Michael Károlyi. He took his part in the October Revolution though in the course of the winter he had opened negotiations with the Counter-revolution. He too is responsible for those events, but he is the only one who has shown contrition and has redeemed his fault. After the closing of the darkest and most humiliating pages of Hungary's history he has written his name on the first clean page.

The sun was shining and on the roof of the county hall the red, white and green flag was being hoisted. The eyes of a whole town filled with tears.

On October 31st the hands of traitors drew the flag into the Revolution as a snare. Then, in tragical disgrace, it was made to float over the country which its enemies occupied and tore to pieces. The sight of it became a torture, my soul revolted against it, and I turned away from it that I might not see it; it became unclean and was besmirched. And when everything that it stood for had been crushed and dissipated, they tore it down with derision. From that moment it became ours again; it was persecuted like ourselves. It was sentenced to death, stood before the Revolutionary Tribunals; prison and the gallows were in store for those who harbored it. The flag became a martyr. Because innocent Hungarian blood has been shed for it, because it has been consecrated with blood, and blood has brought it back to us and raised it above us—God have mercy on him who dares to touch it! Its tricolored folds are now unfurled under the sky. And beneath it, on the walls of Balassagyarmat, there stand the letters of the Palatine's message: "...with ever-lasting love..."

Peasants, gentlemen, workmen, and Red soldiers of yesterday gathered in front of the proclamation and read it, deeply moved. I stood there too. The sun had set and yet it seemed that some mysterious afterglow lit up the faces...

*　*　*

August 8th.

THE day has come. The terrible spell is broken. Hungary again takes her fate in her own hands. And today I am to see my mother again...

Life returns to the groove whence it was torn some months ago. Through the breach in the walls which have encircled us the horizon is widening, the first train to the capital is starting. And I take leave of the house which has given me home, I take leave of the people, the children, of my little corner near the window and of the shady palings of the back garden, of everything that has been kind to me in my misfortune, of all the unforgettable things...

Through the windows of the train the station buildings were already receding. Then the last little houses dis- appeared, the waters of the Ipoly, the poplars on its banks, the glittering heights of the distant Fátra. Then everything became small and distant. The green trees gathered close together, the roofs sank in the distance, and the flag above the county hall seemed to rise higher and higher. Its staff had become invisible, only its folds were floating like a huge, tricolored bird which had stopped in its flight above the town. And winding like a thread of silver between its swampy meadows the Ipoly kept me company for a time. Then parched fields came towards me, a sad, dry country. In the fields of Indian corn the empty, straggling stalks rustled in the wind raised by the train. And this rattling noise is heard everywhere in Hungary today, for everything has been burnt.

Somebody in our compartment whispered: "It was for today that Számuelly had fixed the massacre of the bourgeoisie... It was to have begun in Budapest. Then all over the country... Lenin and Trotsky had ordered a stricter Dictatorship."

'Lenin speaking!' The awful words dissolved like rotten things in the air. He speaks no longer here! Nor does Számuelly; but there are voices from gallows-pits, from the graves and from the unburied dead.

The track curved, and from the direction of the old castle of Nográd we could see a storm racing towards us. In a few moments the sky was black. The train threw itself against the hurricane, then was compelled to stop. The heavy carriages trembled; the trees slanted and the dust rose in dark clouds. The wind moaned like a monster organ. Such a wind preceded the world-war. To prevent premonitions I said quickly: "If we stick to each other and do not forget... In one year, in two, or ten or even a hundred years, Hungary will arise again, for there is a little speck of earth which belongs to us. Six foot of ground at the foot of Golgotha was enough to bring the Resurrection..."

The storm passed to the west and the spires and cupolas of chastened Budapest appeared again in sunshine above the plain and the hills.

I took leave of my companions at the station and then a carriage carried me off. I was alone. Flags were floating above me on all the houses—curious flags, that had been cut in half when the terror was requisitioning them for an *auto-da-fé*. On the walls the orders of Rumanian generals were posted-on white paper. Like ambulant ruins, the electric trams with smashed windows crawled along their rails. The shops were still closed and between the blinds one could see that the windows were empty. The dusty glass showed traces of removed posters. After the robberies of Communism, life had not yet returned to the beggared town.

With steel helmets and fixed bayonets a Rumanian patrol came round a corner. The blood rushed to my face, and then I noticed something else: in ramshackle cabs Rumanian officers with painted cheeks and rouged lips were sitting with young Jewesses. How quickly they have made friends! And how happy they seem!

A motor lorry was standing in front of a house from which Rumanian soldiers were removing typewriters. War contribution—everything is war contribution. With mighty swings they threw the delicate machines one on top of the other. A thud, a crash—that was the end of them! Rumania is acquiring the tools of Western culture. But instead of broken typewriters it might have acquired capital in the shape of hundreds of years of Hungarian gratitude, if it had been content to leave the little that was left to a ransacked people.

Over the bridge flags were playing in the breeze. Suddenly I saw them no more. There, above the hill, sadly, stood the royal castle. Opposite, on the shore of Pest, the House of Parliament was standing with its darkened stones. The building seemed quite young a year ago. How suddenly it has aged, how tragic have become its bloodstained cellars, its bullet-marked walls, the square where the rabble watched the executions, the stairs leading to the river!

On the side of Buda the flags were floating too, on the bridgehead, on the houses. Towards the end of the town the palings showed now and then the traces of torn-off red posters.

Then I came in sight of our hills. But since I had last been here the forest has disappeared. The Dictatorship of the Proletariat has exterminated that too.

Now I was going up the hill; nobody was waiting for me, nobody knew I was coming. All the way along I was smiling to myself.

The high, double roof of our house showed up bright against the blue sky. The gate was open, the pebbles crunched under my feet, I opened the front door.

A white wall, an oaken staircase, flowers on my mother's table. And I stood there, irresolute. Steps were approaching, peculiar steps, as if one foot were slightly dragged behind the other. Blessed steps, beloved steps, I ran to meet them! My mother stood in the door.

I felt that I turned pale. Already the flame was dying within her and she was preparing for the long journey. But I will keep her back, she must stay with me. She opened her arms and I felt her, who had always been taller than I, so small, so elusive, against my heart. I will keep her back, will make her stay.

And in her arms my outlawry died. I was home again.

APPENDIX

The Criminals of the Dictatorship of the Proletariat

By OSCAR SZOLLOSY, LL.D.,

Councilor in the Royal Hungarian Ministry of Justice

LENIN'S well-known axiom to the effect that in revolutions for every honest-minded man (unfortunately) are to be found hundreds of criminals, can scarcely be applied to Hungarian Bolshevism, for among the notorious exponents of the same even the lamp of Diogenes would hardly have enabled us to detect one honest-minded man. Criminalists of long standing who lived through the horrors of the Red Regime in Hungary, which lasted from March 21 to the end of July, 1919, could testify, even without the decisions of the court of laws, that the leading spirits of the 'Soviet Republic' (with the exception of a few fanatics) consisted of common criminals, to the greater part of whom might be applied with perfect aptness the definition of Anatole France, *'encore bête et déjà un homme.'*

Every revolution has its idealistic champions, its enthusiasts who inflame the masses with a fiery passion and are themselves ready to endure all the suffering of Calvary in the service of the creed which they profess. Fanatic apostles of high aims may be sympathetic even in their fatal errors; and there is always something sublimely tragical in their fall. Who would doubt the unselfish enthusiasm of Camille Desmoulins, of Jourde, or of Louise Michel for their ideals, for which they were content to suffer and die?

In our moral judgment we distinguish between political and other criminals; a similar sharp distinction is made by the general conceptions of criminal law, for political agitators are liable to confinement as first-class misdemeanants, while thieves are imprisoned in common jails and murderers are condemned to the gallows.

Revolution, as a movement of the masses aiming at the violent overthrow of the existing system of law, from the standpoint of criminal law is a single cumulative criminal act; committed against the community as a whole, a movement called into being by the cooperation of individuals grouped into a mass in which individual actions are merely insignificant episodes. The masses, however, cannot be called to account under the criminal law; the judgment on them is pronounced by the nation and by history. The work of the judge is to investigate the individual guilt of the persons taking part; in this manner he finds himself dealing with numberless varieties of revolutionary acts from agitation, riot, through destruction of movable property and numerous other offences, to murder; a series comprising practically all the acts known to the criminal code. But of all these offences the only ones which may be classified as political crimes are those unlawful attacks against the aims of the State and the realization of the same which are of a political character by virtue alike of their objects and their nature (e.g., incitement against the constitution or against the binding force of the law); in cases where only the tendency or motive is of such character, while the means employed are base, as is true of most revolutionary offences, for without violence and dangerous threats there can be no revolution; we are confronted, not with political, but with common crimes. The incendiaries of Paris who set fire to the Tuilleries were common criminals, though they acted from a political motive.

And those who, clothing themselves in the red cloak of revolution, with Phrygian caps on their heads, 'work for their own enrichment,' are not revolutionists at all—merely criminals.

Bolshevism, the wildest form of Marxian Communism, which annihilates capital under the pretext of making property public, destroys or distributes among its own votaries the private possessions of others, abolishes the right of choice of labour, subverts the thousand-years old system of production and, in order to effect all these things, ruins all the institutions of an historic State, concentrates the proletarians in the 'council' system with the object of exercising dictatorial power over the bourgeois classes, persecutes religion and national sentiment, places physical labour above intellectual work, transforms the common seaman into an admiral, employing the real admiral as a scavenger; this suppression of the common liberties, more tyrannical in character than the despotism of any Caesar; could not have maintained itself for even the briefest space of time without resorting to the means of extreme terrorism. Therefore, having disarmed the bourgeois classes, and rendering them defenseless, it placed King Mob on the throne and used the same to keep the other members of the community in constant fear and trembling.

In our country the Dictatorship of the Proletariat was nothing more or less than an organized rule of the mob, under the demoniacal direction of

Belial, the spirit of destruction of Jewish mythology.

But what were the elements composing this mob?

So long as the State power is the expression of the common will of the people and has at its command disciplined physical force, the authority of the State and the moral constraint involved suffice to hold in check those criminal propensities and hidden instincts which are latent in the masses. Under such circumstances the expression 'mob' is restricted to vagabonds, professional criminals, the denizens of the common haunts of crime who are a public danger. But, the moment the rule of law is overthrown and the respect for authority vanishes, the lid of the box of Pandora flies open, and the criminal or unhealthy instincts hitherto kept in check rush unimpeded from their secret hiding-places, and the mob is recruited by men who have so far been peaceful and industrious day-laborers, factory hands, students, tradesmen or officials. And those degenerate individuals who are criminally inclined are only too eager to join any movement which enables them to give free vent to their inclinations. During the opening weeks of the Bolshevik regime Budapest became the gathering place of international adventurers flocking thither from all quarters of the globe; 'Spartacus' Germans, Russian Jews, Austrian, Rumanian, Bulgarian, and Italian communists hastened thither in the hope of finding rich booty under the aegis of the Soviet Government. At a mass meeting held in the suburbs, speeches were delivered by demagogues in six different languages.

But more foreign still to this country than the rabble of strangers were the leading People's Commissioners themselves, though all were born on Hungarian soil. They hated, not merely the bourgeoisie, but the whole Hungarian people, with whom they never had anything in common. Their hatred was most violent against the agricultural peasant class, which forms the bulk of the nation, whereas the industrial laborers represent barely more than five percent of the whole population. While at Petrograd, in the service of Lenin, Béla Kun had had Hungarian prisoners of war, officers and privates alike, shot *en masse* with machine-guns, for refusing to join the Russian Red Army.

When the future People's Commissioners, laden with Russian gold, emerged from obscurity, they pushed into the background the former leaders of the working classes. In their incendiary speeches and newspaper articles could be heard the hissing of the vipers of hatred. The terrible trials of the four and a half years' war, its demoralizing effect, the exorbitant demands advanced after the defeat by soldiers embittered by battle and grown accustomed to a distaste for a life of work, the unemployment caused by the shortage of raw materials, and the discontent of the industrial laborers that had long been lurking beneath the surface; all these circumstances in a few months ripened the seeds sown by the wicked and unscrupulous agitation of the adventurers. Their adherents consisted, besides a few educated persons of disordered intellect or greedy of profit, of a small fraction of socialist laborers (who terrorized the rest of their fellows) and the mob described above.

Were these men really capable of believing in the incredible; of believing that the results of a social evolution of a thousand years could be changed in a single night by the help of bands of terrorists? Did they believe that they could violate human nature by means of their peremptory 'orders' (edicts), or that the world-revolution with which, as an inevitable certainty, they constantly sought to cajole their partisans would really hasten to their assistance? Did they honestly desire to 'redeem' the working classes—which, in fact, they ruined—with their devilish system? And is the bestiality of their instruments the only charge that can be laid at their doors? There were evidently some men among them who cherished such a belief and such a desire; but it would be extremely difficult to draw such a conclusion from the nature of their deeds. On the contrary, it is certain that almost all of them were actuated by the hope of personal aggrandizement, by a morbid and unbridled desire of omnipotence; they desired to seize for themselves everything that seemed of any value to them in the country and to destroy everything that stood in their way. An exceptionally favorable opportunity for the realization of their aims was afforded them by the desperate situation of the country and the lethargy of the exhausted bourgeois classes; and to this end they hastened to exploit the infatuation of the masses.

Pre-eminent among them, alike for ability and for skill in the application of Bolshevik ideology, was the People's Commissioner for Foreign Affairs, the keen-witted, astute and extraordinarily active Béla Kun, who remained to the end the soul and leading spirit of the Red regime. Already during his activity as a provincial journalist, this lizard-faced, well-fed agitator had shown the greatest contempt for the morals in general acceptance among the middle classes and had consequently been only too ready to sell his pen as a means to hush up delinquencies committed by the bourgeoisie. He had been compelled, in consequence of petty embezzlements committed at the expense of the proletariat, to resign his post in the office of the Kolozsvar Workmen's Insurance Institute. Earlier in life he had been a votary of night orgies; and during the "lean" days of the Soviet regime he did not abstain from sumptuous banqueting, while everywhere the masses intoned the refrain of the Internationale, "Rise, starving proletarians, rise!" As People's

Commissioner, he took up his quarters in a fashionable hotel on the Danube Embankment, under the protection of a body-guard armed with hand grenades. His inflammatory speeches, in which he employed all the hackneyed casuistry of the demagogue, at first exercised a suggestive influence even on the more sober-minded section of the working classes. He preached the necessity of an inexorable application of the dictatorship; and he himself—ignoring his own revolutionary tribunals—gave orders for the perpetration of secret murders committed in the dark. It was in this way that he got terrorists to kill two Ukrainian officers who had come here to repatriate Russian prisoners of war and whom he suspected of implication in a plot against his person. In a similarly secret manner he provided for the murder, among others, of Francis Mildner, captain in the Artillery, for having (as he, Béla Kun, declared) encouraged the pupils of the Ludovica Military Academy to "stick to their guns" during the Counter-revolution in the month of June. Moreover, he gave Joseph Cserny, the formidable 'commander' of the' terror-troops,' a general authorization for the perpetration, by means of his underlings, of similar murders.

The only one of his associates who surpassed him in bloodthirsty cruelty was Tiberius Számuelly, a horrible figure who was the object of universal abhorrence, even among the working classes—a man who experienced a perverse enjoyment in the destruction of human life. This degenerate successor of Marat and Hébert was a sharp-featured, narrow-chested Jewish youth of low stature; according to medical men who knew him, his blood was tainted, and he was consumptive. Prior to the war, he acted as reporter—without talent indeed, but never without a monocle—to a clerical news agency; during the war he was an officer in the reserve; and, at the age of twenty-eight, his hatred of mankind and his experiences in Russia qualified him for appointment as a People's Commissioner. He was a type of humanity of the lowest kind, degenerate alike physically and mentally. In the Governing Council he came into conflict even with Béla Kun, because the latter declined to comply with his delightful suggestion that the mob should be allowed at least three days' free pillage immediately after the proclamation of the Dictatorship of the Proletariat. It was he who, at the meeting of the Budapest Workers' Council, raised the cry of 'Death to the Bourgeoisie!' and the following day the seething crowd swarming along the boulevards echoed his cry: "Death to the Bourgeoisie!" In April he was authorized to exercise in person, in the rear of the Red Army and in places where there was any counter-revolutionary movement, the rights of the revolutionary courts-martial. And, indeed, he accomplished his task thoroughly; those whom the members of the local Workers' Councils branded as White he had hanged, without even the formality of a trial, on the nearest pear or apple tree. As a rule, his manner of sentencing to death the victims brought before him, was by a motion of the hand or by secret "cue"; though sometimes he pronounced formal sentence in the words: "Step under the tree!" These words were enough for his hangmen. He condemned to death persons "taken up" at random against whom there was not even the shadow of a suspicion—mostly for the simple reason that they belonged to the detested peasant class. At Duna-pataj he ordered his underlings to bury a wounded peasant, whom he saw being treated by a surgeon, alive in a grave together with the dead. At Sopron-Kövesd he had an old railway booking-clerk of the name of Schmidt hanged, and compelled his son to watch the dying father's convulsions for twenty-five minutes, and then hanged the son on the same tree by the side of the father. A short time previous to the overthrow of the Commune, he endeavored to establish a military dictatorship; and his particular adherents had drafted a list of the State officials, police officers and aristocrats who had been selected as doomed to be slaughtered within three short hours.

A dwarf in comparison with this monster was the red-handed, black-souled Joseph Pogány, one of Count Stephen Tisza's murderers and the demon of demoralization of our former army. From being a socialist journalist, he became President of the Soldiers' Council, later People's Commissioner for Public Education, and finally Commander of an Army Corps. He was the son of a Jewish "corpse-washer" of the name of Schwarz; and, though endowed with but mediocre ability, was incredibly ambitious. In his maniacal endeavor for self-assertion, the comic elements were overshadowed only by the depravity of the means he employed. Grotesquely adipose in figure, he loved to ape the poses and gestures of Napoleon, and reveled greedily in the delights of power. He travelled without exception in a Pullman car or in an automobile; and at one of the health resorts on the shores of Lake Balaton—when the misery of the country was at its height—he arranged horse-races in which his Red Hussars took part, for his own distraction and in his own honor. At the first news of the approach of the Rumanian army, he warned the entire population of Budapest that they must consider themselves as the hostages of the Soviet Republic. (It was at the same juncture that 'Comrade' Surek, inspired with noble zeal, proposed at the Central Soviet meeting that all hostages should be butchered at once and mountains raised of bourgeois corpses!)

Hardly had the men of the Soviet seized the reins of government, when the *homo delinquens* commenced his revels; every base and filthy impulse was let loose, greed and bloodthirstiness held a bacchanalian feast. When the old order was restored it was found necessary, as a result of the denunciations received, to institute proceedings in no less than 15,000 criminal cases; and the number of persons kept in detention by the Public Prosecutor in the metropolis alone exceeded three thousand: on the occasion of their arrest, almost all of the latter were found to be in the possession of stolen money or other stolen valuables.

Typical criminals were placed in possession of all our public institutions—with the exception of the jails and convict prisons, from which, indeed, individuals apparently harmless to the proletariat State were released *en masse* (those discharged from the convict prison at Sopron, for instance, included a gypsy condemned for robbery and murder) to make room for respectable men, hostages and political prisoners. The former convicts were wanted to recruit the ranks of the 'political terror-troops' and the Red Guard, as well as to furnish functionaries to do the more important work of the administration of justice.[4]

Hitherto it had been the sole ambition of journeymen in general to be able to set up for themselves as independent masters of their respective trades: now, they were informed by the *Voros Ujsag* (Red Journal) that masters were without exception dishonest extortioners, since they employed workmen for wages: so they came to despise, not only their masters, but their handicrafts, too, and ended by joining the Red Guards or some other band of pillagers.

During four months and a half all Budapest wore the appearance of one vast condemned cell. The night visits of savage Red Guards and drunken terrorists, domiciliary visits (the most convenient pretexts for the 'official organs' to plunder flats), the 'commandeering' of food and dwellings, compulsory recruiting, the taking of hostages, the arrest and torture of innocent persons, and the glaring posters with their gruesome threats—kept the inhabitants, stripped of everything and nearly all suffering the pangs of hunger, in a state of nervous tension, while suicides of embittered fathers were every-day occurrences. Those who had hitherto been held in check by the authorities, had now become the authorities themselves; and, to the citizen accustomed to a disciplined mode of life, nothing can be more disheartening than the knowledge that the

[4] A story which is far from improbable, though it certainly sounds like a popular anecdote, runs to the effect that, at a trial of one of the proletarian tribunals, in answer to the 'Public-Prosecutor's' question: 'Where did you take the stolen articles?' one of the persons accused of theft said, 'To the woman in Budafok to whom you and I took that bicycle last year!'

'authorities' are the greatest enemies to the security of life and property.

When, under the pretext of 'nationalization,' the Soviet authorities proceeded vigorously to confiscate property, thirty-four banks were occupied by armed forces and placed under Communist management. The entire stock of money and securities was seized, as well as the jewelry, gold coins and foreign currency deposited in the safes. From the Austro-Hungarian Bank (Budapest branch) two hundred million crowns were taken and conveyed to Vienna for propaganda purposes; while foreign currency of the value of at least forty to fifty million crowns was distributed among the immediate adherents (male and female alike) of the new masters of the country. Of the foreign securities seized several millions' worth were sold; while the Sacred Crown, the most jealously guarded of all the nation's treasures, was offered for sale. (The crown adorning the dome of the royal palace was covered with a red cap.)

The salaries of the persons employed by the new bureaucracy and the wages of the workmen were raised so enormously that there could be no doubt as to the probability of a speedy bankruptcy of the State. A prison warder was paid wages amounting to about 30,000 crowns a year. The Exchequer was soon empty; and there was a shortage of the means of payment. At this juncture Julius Lengyel, People's Commissioner for Finance, declared to a meeting of the 'trustees' (*Vertrauensmänner*) of the officials of the bank of issue that 'there are excellent foreign and native forgers able to make perfect counterfeits of the Austro-Hungarian banknotes.' The services of these 'excellent forgers' were actually requisitioned; and they made an enormous number of forged Austro-Hungarian banknotes, of 200, 25 and 2 crowns respectively. Thus the workers' delight at the rise of wages became converted into bitter disappointment, for they were paid in forged notes which possessed a very trifling purchasing value. The country folk refused to have anything to do with money forged under the aegis of 'authorities' whose term of power was so problematical, and in consequence ceased to supply the capital with food.

Meanwhile Terror was working at high pressure, not sparing even the better-disposed among the working classes. Its appointed instruments—the Detective Department of the Ministry of the Interior, with the blood-thirsty Otto Korvin-Klein at its head, the Revolutionary Tribunals, and the Political 'Terror Troops'—never for a single moment lapsed from the level of their respective callings.

Otto Korvin (Klein), a hunch-backed, clean-shaven gnome of twenty-five years, was a well-paid official of a joint-stock company when he was called upon to join the ranks of the red, blood-stained knights of hate. It was he who issued orders for the seizure as hostages of the notabilities of our public life: politicians, judges, bishops, writers, manufacturers, generals; he who was known as *ornamentum civitatis*—the former Prime Minister, Alexander Wekerle, a man of seventy years—the former Ministers of War (Home Defense), Hazay and Szurmay, the Speaker (President of the House of Deputies), Charles Szasz, the most distinguished of Hungarian publicists, Eugéne Rakosi, Bishop Mikes, etc.—all these men now became the inmates of a common jail. But in many cases, the instruments of Korvin's vindictiveness—the terrorists and detectives—did not even trouble to convey the hostages to prison; dragging the victims out of bed and away from their homes in the dead of night, they simply murdered them and robbed their corpses. Alexander Hollán, Secretary of State, and his aged father were shot on the Chain Bridge, their bodies, bound together, being thrown into the Danube. Louis Naváy, a former speaker of the Lower House, together with his younger brother and a local magistrate, while being conveyed from Makó to Budapest, were dragged from the train at Félegyhaza, placed on the brink of a grave dug in the neighborhood of the railway-station, and then shot and stabbed with bayonets until they were dead; on the same occasion, the Soviet mercenaries, as they proceeded on their journey, shot three more hostages in the train and seven at the railway-station of Hódmezövásárhely.

Maybe these unfortunate men had a happier fate than was that of some of the political prisoners whom Korvin subjected to his diabolical inquisition in the cellars beneath the Houses of Parliament. What was enacted there, in defiance of all human feeling, surpasses the utmost limits of bestiality. Some had the soles of their feet beaten with rubber sticks or their bare backs belabored with belts or straps; others had their ribs or arms broken, or tacks driven in under their nails; some were compelled to drink three liters of water at a draught, or had rulers stuck down their throats, to force them to make disclosures. By the side of a certain lieutenant-colonel Korvin placed a guard with a hand grenade, ordering the latter to kill the unfortunate officer, if he dared to open his mouth; another prisoner he threatened to shoot unless he spoke immediately. A lieutenant was found wearing on his breast an image of the Blessed Virgin: 'hang the thing up as an ornament for his gallows,' shrieked the inquisitor in a paroxysm of fury. A prisoner named Balogh, who refused to confess, was dragged by the terrorists—his hands tied behind his back—up to the scaffold erected in the cellar and left hanging there with the blood running from his mouth and nose. For intimidation, the inquisitors showed the accused persons a heap of noses, tongues, and ears that had been cut off corpses. One of Korvin's hangmen, a Russian Jew, with a limp, and curly hair, named Gerson Itzkovitch, laughingly vaunted that he was in the habit of gouging out a bourgeois' eye with a single turn of his Cossack knife, 'like the stone from a peach.' Those who were tortured to death in the course of the inquisition were generally thrown from the stairs of the Houses of Parliament into the Danube; the actor Andrew Szocs was thrown down from the third floor into the courtyard, where his body was left to decompose for several days.

In order to prevent the wailings and death-cries of the victims being heard by outsiders, a grinning chauffeur was told off to keep the motor of his automobile incessantly whirring in front of the ventilation holes of the cellars.

These frenzied blood-orgies betray all the symptoms characteristic of that perversion which manifests itself in a perverse and fiendish delight in the shedding of blood, in shrieks of pain, and in maddening tortures.

Korvin's female typist, Manci Hollos, endeavored to comfort an imprisoned lawyer in these terms: 'You will make a handsome corpse; it will be a pleasure to gouge out your eyes and kick your broken ribs.'

Hysterical women, too, were given a plentiful scope of activity by Bolshevism, which induced women to wear short hair, in order to be more like men, whereas the men wore long, flowing hair, after the Russian fashion. Elizabeth Sipos, the notorious agitator with whom Korvin contracted a marriage during the Dictatorship, devoted her energy to spying out the counter-revolutionary plans of army officers. Margaret Romanyi agitated in favor of Bolshevism among the telephone operators; while Gizella Adler, in her capacity as political commissary, armed with a revolver, herself delivered to the custody of the Red Guards such persons as seemed to her to be suspicious. Mrs. John Peczkai, a woman doctor, took pleasure in assisting at executions; her hobby was to be allowed to determine whether death had ensued, and she showed a particular eagerness in making inquiries as to when and where the next execution was to take place, Ethel Sari (a notorious pickpocket, who later on became Secretary to the People's Commissioner, Vago) took part, with her husband, the gorilla-headed terrorist, Andrew Annocskay, in the butchery at Maká, in the meantime methodically pursuing her usual occupation of professional pickpocket.

Those whom Korvin's accomplices or the Red Guards brought direct to the revolutionary tribunals, might have congratulated themselves on at least escaping the cellars of torture of the Houses of Parliament; but mutilation, starvation and intimidation were the order of the day in the prisons. In the prison attached to the Budapest Central Court of Justice alone 1,461 persons were held in custody, persons arrested as politicians, and not charged with any criminal act. The tribunals, composed of untrained individuals (industrial laborers and persons 'with a past'), were not bound by any regular rules of procedure and passed sentence with a rapidity of courts-martial under military law. The Budapest Revolutionary Tribunal sentenced to 'confinement in an asylum' an accused person who evinced symptoms of dull-wittedness; and against this sentence there was no appeal.

The Governing Council appointed the lawyer Dr. Eugéne László political commissary for all the revolutionary tribunals. This man was the offspring of a marriage between cousins, and his mother died insane; his fellow- lawyers and journalists (for previously he had been law reporter to a daily with a wide circulation) spoke of him among themselves as 'mad László'; yet he was one of the most fanatical of Communists and in his degeneracy was quite the equal of the more calculating Korvin and the more ignorant Számuelly. These qualities were amply sufficient to fit him to act as super-reviser of all judgments passed by the revolutionary tribunals; and his legal training enabled him to do his work by simply ordering the members of the tribunals to pass the sentences dictated by him. In the case of Dr. John Stenczel and his associates, who were charged with being counter-revolutionists, acting in touching agreement with Otto Korvin, László conferred the dignity of judge on Joseph Cserny, directing him to sentence all the accused but one to death. As President of the Tribunal, after ten minutes' hearing of the case, which was a mere parody of the administration of justice, Cserny pronounced sentence of death on eight men and then, by way of motive for the sentence, whistled between his fingers; of the men condemned in this manner, three were shot, while the others were graciously reprieved and sentenced to imprisonment for life. (One member of this tribunal was Francis Gombos, a worker in the cartridge factory, who was known to be ever ready to agree to a sentence of death; he 'despised human life,' though, it would appear only in the case of others, for, when at a later date the Court of Law sentenced him to death, he broke into sobs and implored mercy.)

This same Eugéne László, who, during the Dictatorship of the Proletariat, had no fewer than four flats in Budapest, was far less severe in respect of the standard of morality applied to his own actions, for—as appears from the evidence of his own officials—he stole from the Budapest mansion of Baron Ulmann clothes, silver cigarette-cases and other portable articles, which he then sold at a high price, Joseph Cserny having bought from him, among other things, caps for 100 crowns. These individuals also made a practice of arresting as hostages rich merchants, whom they then released from prison—as a proof of their magnanimity—

in return for money and rice!

A quite different type—one might almost say a true type of Apache—was 'Comrade' Joseph Cserny, the broad-shouldered and big-limbed sailor whom Béla Kun himself entrusted with the organization of the 'terror troops.' He was of a very powerful physique and possessed remarkable muscular strength; and he was possessed with the conviction that in the general upheaval he was called upon to play a pre-eminent part and must to that end be a ruthless murderer. Not even Béla Kun himself was suffered to contradict him on this point; and when, under the pressure of the Entente Missions and of the workers, it was proposed to disband his troops, he forthwith conceived the idea of offering his services to the counter-revolutionists. From among the volunteers who applied to him for 'a job'—these persons were the very scum of society—he selected men of the lowest repute, dare-devils 'with a past' ready to perpetrate any crime: the criminals known as 'Lenin Boys,' more than 400 in number, whose special vocation was to stifle any counter- revolutionary movement. What they really had to do, however, was not to take part in any open fighting or in regular military operations, but to inspire terror in districts where any counter-revolutionary movement had already been suppressed by the Red Army—by murder, torture and pillaging. We know now, from the sentences of the courts of law, that this 'institution' was 'a gang organized for common wholesale murder' and robbery, re-assured in advance by Ernest Seidler, People's Commissioner for Police, who said: 'You may put out of the way as many "bourgeois" as you like; I will see that everything is hushed up!'

The 'Lenin Boys' took possession of Count Batthyanyi's mansion in the Theresa Boulevard, which was transformed into a veritable fortress; in the cellars were amassed enormous quantities of ammunition, while the 'garrison' had at their disposal field guns, *minenwerfers*, and twenty- four machine guns. The pavement in front of the house was barricaded, while before the gate heavy motor-lorries armed with machine-guns were kept constantly in readiness. Each 'Lenin Boy' was armed to the teeth with revolvers, a bowie knife and hand grenades. The whole town knew the 'Lenin Boys' by their leather coats and flat caps with bag-like flaps at the back. (Cserny himself carried a long, sharp hunting knife stuck in one of his yellow top-boots.) To their fortress-mansion the 'Boys' conveyed by motor-lorries enormous quantities of 'commandeered' clothes, food, wine, jewelry and ladies, who, after being forced to take part in their wild orgies, were boxed on the ears and 'chucked out.'

These bandits had a peculiar slang of their own to express their methods of assassination—viz., 'to send to Gades,' 'to refrigerate,' 'to send floating,' 'to send home'; their torture and flogging might be 'under-done' or 'well-done' (slang phrases adopted from the kitchen jargon). Whenever Korvin or Gabriel Schon (the political commissary attached to the District Commander of the Red Guard) telephoned to Cserny, saying: 'I am sending you a man; send him to Gades,' the person in question was dead by the following morning, and his corpse 'sent floating' on the Danube.

From among these ruffians were selected the Soviet House Guards, as well as the Számuelly Detachment, which was quartered in the leaders' special train, and was always kept in readiness to travel away.[5]

Cserny's spy, a boy of fourteen years from Nagyvarad, of the name of Nicholas Gelbert, was able to obtain an entrance everywhere—as an unsuspected child, and indeed carried on his trade with astonishing zeal; on one occasion he himself shot a captain, for which act he is said to have received from Béla Kun a reward of 10,000 crowns.

When the 'terrorists' were temporarily disbanded, forty of the 'most trustworthy' were transferred to the detective section operating in the Parliament building; later on, however, the gang was again organized and took up its quarters in Buda, in the Mozdony-utca school.

These brigands 'dispatched' a host of persons without the formality of a trial, either by the orders of their superiors or on their own initiative, in the latter case either to humour their cynical lust of blood or with intent to rob. One day an ensign of hussars, Nicholas Dobsa, having lost his certificate of identity, went to the Soviet House to procure a new one; in consequence he was brought before Gabriel Schán, the Political Commissary, twenty-three years old, who had formerly been a law student and had become one of the most blackguardly desperadoes of the Red regime. The ensign smiled when speaking to his inquisitor; this was reason enough for Gabriel Schán to have him dispatched as a 'saucy youth' to Cserny in the Batthyanyi mansion. Two 'terrorists' (Géza Groo and John Nyakas) seized the unfortunate young man, dragged him to the cellar, and beat him unmercifully, fracturing his lower jaw and one of his arms; then they dug a grave for him and shot him. Merely because he had smiled when speaking to Gabriel Schán!

Dr. Nicholas Berend, a University professor, on the day of the counter-revolution in June waved a white handkerchief at the gunboats which bombarded the Soviet House; he was shot and his body robbed by terrorists, who took his money, watch, clothes and shoes (in a word,

---

[5] There were similar detachments outside of Budapest, the same being delegated to hold the provincial towns in mortal terror, e.g., the 'Fabik Detachment' in Szekesfehervar, the 'Gombos Terror Gang' in Gyor, etc.

everything), and then threw his corpse into the Danube. This was how this notorious 'political institution' showed its respect for the medical profession. In the evening of the same day, a medical student named Béla Madarasz, who, preparing for an examination, remained absorbed in his books in his garret room, and kept a light burning beyond the prescribed hour, was dragged by the terrorists into the street, where one of them gave him a blow on the head, while another stabbed him in the abdomen; after his gold watch had been taken from him, he was thrown into a dust-cart and 'sent floating' in the Danube.

Gustavus Szigeti, a merchant who had been arrested in Veszprém on suspicion of having harbored Count Festetich in his house, was, at the instance of the Political Commissary for Veszprem, who offered a reward of 5,000 crowns, taken bound by the terrorist Gabriel Csomor to a sandbank in Lake Balaton and there stabbed to death by that ruffian, who fastened a piece of a broken grave-stone to the corpse, cut off the tip of the left ear, and sank the body in the lake, afterwards sending the ear-tip to the Commissary as authentic proof that he had killed the victim.

The Soviet rulers indulged a special hatred towards the rigorous chiefs of the former gendarmerie too. A few days prior to the fall of the Soviet Government, Edward Chlepko, Commander-in-Chief of the Red Guard, on the basis of a pre-arranged anonymous denunciation, had Lieutenant-General Oscar Ferry arrested, together with two lieutenant-colonels of the gendarmerie. The political detectives Bonyhati (formerly a lieutenant in the reserve) and Radvanyi—two men whom even Cserny dubbed 'blood-hounds'—conveyed the unfortunate officers to the Terrorists' barracks in Mozdony-utca, where, after three days' fruitless inquisition, all three were hanged by the 'Lenin Boys' on a water-pipe in the cellar. These victims, too, were buried in the Danube.

During the reign of horror in Budapest, Számuelly's 'death-train' rushed from one end of the country to the other, landing its hellish passengers at the scene of every counter-revolutionary movement. So far as we have hitherto been able to ascertain, the official assassin of the Dictatorship executed thirty persons in Szolnok, twenty in Kalocsa, sixty-one in the small village of Duna-pataj, in addition killing a host of other innocent people in twenty-five different towns and parishes. The most 'eminent' of the hangmen of this Hungarian Jefferys were Louis Kovacs, Arpad Kerekes (Kohn), and Charles Sturcz, who, at a mere sign of the hand from Számuelly, hanged or shot seventeen, forty-six, and forty-nine persons respectively.

The usual custom of these human brutes was to place the victim on a chair beneath the tree selected for the purpose, then to throw a rope round his neck and order him to kick away the chair; whenever the victim was unable, owing to his terror of death, to do so, he was beaten with rifle-butts and prodded with knives, until the instinct of escape from this sanguinary torture compelled the writhing victim to comply with the command. These beasts beat gray-haired old men to death; in some cases they gouged out the victims' eyes before killing them with all the refinement of Bolshevik cruelty. In one case, after hanging a parish notary, they forced his wife, who was approaching confinement, to watch her husband's death agony. They even slapped the faces of the dead and kicked them, using obscene language in their abusive mockery of their victims.

'I could not continue to watch these scenes' an army surgeon confessed; 'I broke into a convulsive fit of sobbing—a thing that never once happened to me during four years of service at the front.'

In comparison with these monsters, the jackal is a mere lamb, the rattlesnake an innocent gold-fish. They walked in human guise; but the bestial instinct for plunder and butchery latent within them was not restrained by any human feeling or kept within bounds (was, indeed, rather enhanced) by human intelligence.

Yet, undoubtedly, the awful responsibility involved must be borne by those who either directly enjoined or at least watched, tolerated, and approved the perpetration of the crimes committed by them.

Each of the responsible leaders knew that by 'Commune' the criminal means liberty to steal, and by 'terror' blind butchery.

These leaders were the conscious promoters of a fearful material and moral devastation, and must have known that the very existence of a whole generation of working men was at stake. 'Thus crimes are born, and curses—but not new worlds!'

With their souls full of hatred, they made boastful promises of earthly bliss to those whom they swept to perdition.

'No greater catastrophe than Bolshevism could have befallen the working classes,' says—in one of its manifestoes—the council of the newly-revived Social Democrat Party. Is it worth our while to inquire whether, amid all this horror and terror, there is to be found anywhere even a spark of that 'holy madness' which makes the apostle ready to die the death of a martyr for his creed?

Rigault, the Chief of Police in the French Commune, and one of its blackest figures, waited in Paris for the coming of the troops from Versailles; when the soldiers thronging into his suburban hotel mistook the proprietor for him and were about to seize him, Rigault hastened towards them with the words: 'I am Rigault! I am neither a brute nor a coward!' Ten minutes later, Rigault was dead.

And the Budapest People's Commissioners—the men who had so often emphasized 'the unparalleled cowardice of the bourgeoisie' and abused our heroes and our martyrs—when the assassin's dagger slipped from their grasp, packed in feverish haste the foreign currency which they had 'sequestered' for their own private use from the Austro-Hungarian Bank, and, boarding their special train, fled in a panic to a milder climate, away from this plundered, devastated and unhappy country.[6]

---

[6] Béla Kun and a large number of his fellow-Commissioners escaped to Vienna. Our efforts to obtain their extradition by Austria were fruitless; under the pressure of the Socialists the Austrian Government refused, and subsequently handed them over to the Russian Soviet authorities.

After the re-establishment of law and order, of the revolutionary criminals arrested ninety-six were condemned to death, the rest being sentenced to various terms of imprisonment. Of the persons condemned to death fourteen were reprieved, eighteen (together with 400 other condemned persons) handed over - in exchange for Hungarian prisoners of war—to the Russian Soviet, while sixty-four were hanged, the latter number including Korvin, László, Schán, and Cserny.